THE ALASKAN ALIBI

THE ALASKAN ALIBI

Mystery, Murder & Frontier Justice

STEPHEN F. FROST

Copyright 2020 by Stephen F. Frost
Owner: FrostMysteryBooks, LLC, an Arizona Limited Liability Company

All rights reserved. Published in the United States by IngramSpark.

Front jacket photographs by Adobe
Back jacket photograph by Alamy

ISBN-13: 9780578884172 (*ebook*)
ISBN-13: 9780578884165 (*paperback*)
ISBN-13: 9780578910154 (*hardcover*)

Map of Alaska—National Geographic Society

MANUFACTURED IN THE UNITED STATES OF AMERICA

First Edition: May 2021

DEDICATION

FOR TWENTY YEARS my wonderful wife, Coral, has enjoyed hearing of my experiences in Alaska. She encouraged me from day one to capture those stories in this novel. In addition, she is an excellent writer and editor in her own right after working twenty-five years as a court reporter. There isn't a page in the book where her input can't be found. She is my continuing inspiration.

ACKNOWLEDGEMENTS

I MUST THANK my editors, starting with New Yorker Brian Gresko, who provided some initial editing and encouragement and gave us Chapel Hill's Lindsey Alexander, who provided developmental editing. Next aboard was journalism major and family friend Rebecca Wilson, who relentlessly toiled over the manuscript, resulting in improvements to every page. From there, fellow Alaskan and current Los Angeles editor extraordinaire Ryan Quinn copyedited the manuscript. With the manuscript completed, it needed to be dressed up for public consumption, and that became the task of interior graphics designer Phil Gessert from Amarillo, Texas, who formatted the novel. Finally, an enticing book cover was needed and David Prendergast, the best of Dublin, Ireland, provided the invaluable design you see *on the shelf*. It takes a dedicated crew to edit and market a novel, and we had a great one. Of course, without the incredible support of family and friends, the book would not exist. My Sincere Appreciation to Everyone.

–STEVE FROST

PREFACE

S EWARD'S FOLLY? THINK again. Alaska is over twice the size of Texas and could stretch from Atlanta to San Diego. It cost just thirty-seven cents per acre and is enriched with an abundance of minerals, oil, and fisheries. Our forty-ninth state contributed greatly to the defense of the country during World War II and to our oil reserves in the 1980s.

I lived in and practiced law in Anchorage from 1975 to 1990, and this book reflects my observations and the people I met during those years. It was an exciting time, with the construction of the Trans-Alaska Pipeline System beginning when I arrived. The project pumped billions of dollars into the Alaskan economy, and Anchorage's marine climate made the city the premier place for the oil field people to live during the construction. But with the massive influx of people from the Lower 48 came violent crime. This is one story of how crime affected the lives of one family.

Writing and editing a full-length novel is not for the timid. I am grateful that I was able to write this story over the last three years and relive some of the unique experiences I had with clients and the courts in what is, truly, America's Last Frontier.

PROLOGUE

S CREAMS PIERCED THE NORTHERN WILDERNESS. Cries of pain and horror echoed under a full October moon that illuminated a foggy mist and covered the remote tundra. On an isolated Alaskan sandbar, a man stood silhouetted against a Piper Super Cub, his left hand intertwined in long, blond hair. With merciless force, he yanked back the head of a terrified young woman. While being rhythmically slammed against the plane, Emma felt her bare skin stick to the frigid metal fuselage.

Her mind, numbed by exposure to the subzero temperatures, frantically searched for a way to extricate herself from this horror. She was puzzled by the smell of freshly baked bread drifting incongruently amidst the ghostly scene. After what felt like forever, the man's labored breathing and vicious frenzy stopped abruptly with a final guttural curse. *Please make it end*, she prayed.

"Run!" he ordered. His eyes reflected a dark intense madness. "You heard me; run for your fucking life!"

Dazed, her survival instincts flooded her body with adrenaline. She staggered backward and fell against the plane before she recovered her footing and began to run. Her crystal-blue eyes had been pummeled into swollen slits from the beatings she'd endured since her abduction hours earlier. She fled on bloodied, frostbitten feet across the icy shards of lava rock and gritty sand toward the dark wooded unknown. *Think about bears later*, she thought.

As she stumbled over the uneven landscape, she paused and looked over her shoulder to see her attacker retrieve a rifle from the plane. Every fiber in her body surged to red alert. In her flight, she never saw the killer's determined gait as he stalked her down the beach and across the vast, shadowy terrain.

An explosive round blasted through her back with the force of a freight train and spun her around as she fell under a treed canopy. Her life began to seep away, and the beautiful girl knew she would not be going home. Ever. A calm hush of acceptance enveloped her as she gazed through snow-laden tree branches at the twinkling stars above.

The killer knelt next to his prey, bringing his pockmarked face near hers. His eyes glistened from the thrill of the hunt as he pressed a pistol against her forehead. She lived long enough to whisper "Mama" before closing her eyes against the kill shot.

Grabbing a shovel from behind the seats, he dug a shallow grave. One final stomp on the tundra covered her body, and he flew his Piper Super Cub back to his "normal" life in Anchorage.

The Alaskan wilderness inexorably erased every trace of seventeen-year-old Emma Foster and the unimaginable horrors she'd endured that fateful night.

CHAPTER

1

FOUR MONTHS EARLIER—JUNE 7, 1983—ANCHORAGE, ALASKA. Thirty-seven-year-old Donnie Baker tossed his denim jacket and black cowboy hat into the back of his 1978 midnight-blue Silverado pickup.

He'd just dropped off his date as Dolly Parton's "Islands in the Stream" blared through custom speakers, filling his pickup with a carefree ambiance. Tilting his head back, hands drumming the steering wheel to the beat, he bawled out Kenny Rogers's lines, "Baby, when I met you...we've got somethin' goin' on..."

It was a beautiful summer night in Anchorage and he and his girlfriend danced most of it away at the Pine's Club, swaying to the romantic country songs they loved. Dolly sweetly warbled, "Everything is nothin' if you got no one, and you just walk in the night..."

Donnie was turning onto 6th Avenue in front of Merrill Field, the municipal airport, when he swerved to avoid hitting a naked girl running toward the pickup. Crazy, but the first thing that ran through his head was what his buddies would say: *In your dreams, Donnie.*

Dark hair obscured the girl's face, and she was sobbing as she banged her fists against the passenger-side window. Abruptly sober, he turned off the radio, leaned across the seat, and opened the door. She was handcuffed and couldn't climb the step to get up into the pickup.

He reached for the blanket in the back seat where Roy, his black Lab, usually slept and shook it out as he ran behind his vehicle to wrap it around the petite girl. She collapsed in his arms as he boosted her up into the passenger seat.

"Take me to the Merrill Field Motel." She looked behind the pickup in terror. "Hurry! Please, please hurry!"

"Jesus, shouldn't we get you to a hospital first?"

Bruised and battered as she was, she adamantly insisted he take her to the motel. "Go!"

"No way. You need to see a doctor right now."

"I'm all right. I can do this myself." She began to exit the pickup.

"Okay, okay, I'm taking you."

As much for himself as for her, he kept talking. Softly, he reassured her, "My name's Donnie...just take a deep breath and try to calm down, okay? I'll get you there. You're safe now, don't worry, everything's okay."

He took a right turn onto Orca Street and into the motel parking lot. She elbowed the passenger's door handle open and wiped her face with Roy's blanket before she looked at him, her eyes wide and frightened. Appearing barely older than a child, mascara-stained tears flowing down her face, she stammered thanks and jumped down from the pickup's running board. "Just keep the blanket," Donnie hollered when she turned and waved back at him from the motel room door.

Her name was Colleen Preston. Her pimp went by DeeTroit in homage to the new Dan Ackroyd movie, *Doctor Detroit*. They lived together in the shabby motel room.

Two Anchorage police officers arrived at the motel following DeeTroit's anonymous call at 1:20 a.m. DeeTroit had wisely disappeared before they arrived. "Oh my God," Officer Collins gasped as she looked over the beaten little figure that stood traumatized before them.

Still shivering, Colleen gripped the dog's blanket around her nude frame. Overweight and cynical, Collins unlocked the cuffs before plunking down on the wooden chair against the blackout curtains. Her partner, Officer Stone, glanced around the sparsely furnished room. The only place left to sit was the toilet, so he leaned against the door.

"Can you talk to us for a minute before we get you to the hospital?" Stone asked.

Nodding, Colleen began. "I was working at the Wild Cherry last night, and this guy was sitting at the end of the bar."

Collins prodded, ticking off the routine questions. "Was he white, black, old, young?"

"He's an old guy. White. Umm, ugly. He's sorta bald. And he stutters and, umm...he has these black-framed glasses that wouldn't stay up on his nose." She began to cry. "He offered me $200 for a...you know, a blow job. I said, 'Sure.' You know, 'No problem.' So, we went out to his pickup. I got in and put my purse on the floor, and he..." She stopped to blow her nose. "And he...he held a gun to my head and..."

Sobbing, she told them she screamed when he handcuffed her, trapping her in the pickup. "But he told me that if I didn't shut the fuck up, he...he'd shoot me. He was going to kill meeee..." she wailed.

"And then?" Collins quizzically glanced at her partner.

"He drove me to his house. We went through a back door into a kitchen and then down these narrow stairs to a basement. There were dead animal heads all over the place. Then he, umm...he chained me to a post, and then he..." She took a series of shuddered breaths.

"Then, he raped me. He kept raping me over and over. It was, like, hours before he finally stopped and fell asleep on this old couch with a huge animal head above it that stared down at me. I was still chained to that post and couldn't leave."

Stone interrupted. "So, how'd you get out by the airport?"

"When he woke up, he made me get back in his pickup, and he drove to Merrill Field. He said he wanted to take me to his cabin. He wouldn't take the handcuffs off me, and I just had my boots on, so I was freezing. But he said, 'Get used to it.' When we got to his plane, he started loading a bunch of stuff. So, when his back was turned, I jumped out of the pickup and ran to the road. Some guy picked me up and brought me here so I could call my boyfriend."

"Could you identify this man if you saw him again?" asked Officer Collins.

"I'll never forget what he looks like. I can even show you where he lives."

"You sure you're up for that? Why don't we get you to the hospital first? You're in pretty bad shape."

"No. You guys have to get him. Then I'll go to the hospital."

Jack Jansen was furious with himself. His hands shook as he brooded over the night's events that ended when the girl climbed out of his pickup.

"Trouble, trouble, trouble," the small man mumbled during the drive home. "Goddamn it, Jack," he berated himself, pounding the steering wheel in frustration.

When he got home, he made a frantic call to his minister who, in the past, answered many of his late-night phone calls. His stutter was more pronounced in his desperation. "Th-th-this is Jack."

"I'm listening. You just take a deep breath there, Jack."

"I spent way too much time with the girl. So, now I think, th-th-the whore's trying to fra-fra-frame me. She said she'd call the cops if I didn't pay her a lot more money. She even threatened to tell my wife everything. I duh-duh-dunno what to do. You gotta help me."

"Calm down, Jack, we'll figure this out. I'll get right back to you."

Jansen paced the floor until the phone rang.

"Okay, Jack, here's what happened: You were playing cards tonight at Bill and Barbara Hamlin's house. You left their house about three hours ago and stopped by the strip club for a drink. You took a young lady to the parking lot, and when you finished with her, she said she wanted more money than you had agreed to give her. She threatened to call the cops and say you raped her. You refused to be blackmailed and pushed her out of your pickup and drove home."

"I'm so sorry to trouble you."

"No, no, don't worry about a thing. I know how sorry you are. We'll see you on Sunday, okay? God bless y'now, Jack, and your family."

Jansen heaved a sigh of relief and hung up as two police cars crunched over his icy driveway. Walking to the front door, Officer Beeson paused briefly to remove the glove on his right hand and touch the hood of Jansen's pickup. "Warm."

His partner, Officer Pope, rang the bell. Jansen opened the door and looked past the two officers and squinted toward a police car backing out of his driveway. It was too dark for him to identify the tiny figure hunched down in the back seat. Colleen Preston was finally on her way to the hospital.

"Evening, Officers. Was I driving a little fast on my way home?" Jansen mentally compartmentalized the night's earlier events and adopted a relaxed, cavalier demeanor. He was neither afraid nor angry. In his mind, he had done nothing wrong.

Ignoring his question, Beeson was all business.

"Can you give us your name?"

"Jack Jansen. What can I do for you guys?"

"I'm Officer Beeson." Gesturing to his right side, he said, "My partner, Officer Pope. We'd like to ask you a couple of questions."

Jansen peered earnestly at them through the thick-lensed, black-framed glasses he'd shoved back over his nose. "Sure, but it's a little late to be making house calls, isn't it?" Jansen gamely chided.

The officers exchanged brief eye contact and played along. Beeson looked over Jansen's shoulder into the house and said, "We saw the lights on, figured we wouldn't be imposing too much. You mentioned you just got home. Mind telling us where you were tonight?"

Jansen kept to the minister's script. "Just playing cards over at my friends' house most the evening. I stopped by the Wild Cherry on my way home and had a couple drinks."

Pope took over. "Who're your friends?"

"Bill and Barbara Hamlin."

"What's the address?" Beeson asked.

Jack blinked warily and adjusted his glasses again before answering.

"I don't know their address, but they live across town, umm...you know, just off Tudor Road and Lake Otis. They own Hamlins' Cabinets."

"We'll find them. For now, you mind coming down to the station and answering some questions?" Pope asked.

Jansen's hands were in his pockets. He shrugged amicably and smiled. "I have to be at my bakery in about two hours. Can I come in after work today, around five or so? I'll bring you guys some donuts."

Pope stared at Jansen. "A young woman has made some serious allegations against you." He paused, allowing Jansen to absorb that newsflash. "So, we need to clear parts of her story."

Jansen remained amazingly cool given the circumstances. "Yeah, just talk to the Hamlins. After you do, let me know if you still want me to come to the station."

"We can do that," Pope said as he backstepped down the sidewalk.

The officers now had serious doubts about Preston's story. Walking to their car, Pope said, "We'll have a couple officers check out his story, and if it's all good, we'll close this investigation before we head down a prostitute's rabbit hole."

Beeson added, "She might be trying to blackmail him or something."

Later that morning, two officers pulled up in front of a two-story home on the outskirts of Anchorage. They knocked and heard the occupants arguing about who would answer the door. A tall, slender woman opened the door a crack and with a gravelly whisper uttered, "Hello."

"Good morning, ma'am. I'm Officer Sorensen, this is Officer Jewell. Mind if we ask you a couple of questions?"

Mrs. Hamlin didn't answer but turned and yelled over her shoulder. "Bill, there's a couple cops here wanna talk t'ya."

Sorensen was a five-foot-five blond rookie on the force, tipping the scales at one hundred pounds. "Ma'am, if you're Barbara Hamlin, we'd like to talk to both of you."

Apprehension wrinkled Barbara's face as she responded nervously, "Okay," and hollered once again. "Bill, come out here!" William Hamlin appeared, and Mrs. Hamlin slid behind him. "Morning," the large, middle-aged man said, opening the door wide. "What can I do for you?" Sorensen was taken aback at his sheer girth as he stepped toward her at an angle and ducked slightly to wedge his body into the doorway. She instinctively straightened into a ramrod military stance.

"Can you tell us what you were doing last night?"

"Yeah, we played cards here at home. A friend joined us. His family's out of town."

Jewell took over. "All right. Who's the *friend*, and what time did he or she leave last night?"

"Jack Jansen's his name. I guess it had to be around midnight or so when he left." Hamlin turned to his wife for confirmation. "Wouldn't you say so, honey?"

Nodding diffidently, she confirmed, "Yeah, it was about one."

CHAPTER
2

TWENTY-ONE YEARS LATER—HOMER, ALASKA. Logan Finch gazed down at the distinctive four-and-a-half-mile Homer Spit as his plane descended. The spit extended into Kachemak Bay and was surrounded by a vast array of volcanic mountains and rivers. It also contained many hearty and ridiculously independent Alaskans.

It was a beautiful two-minute drive from the airport to the Homer Small Boat Harbor, down the leeward side of the spit along Kachemak Bay. Nestled in the harbor were the sturdy workhorses of the commercial fishing fleet: long-liners, purse seiners, and gillnetters. It was also home to charter and tour boat operators providing fishing trips and sightseeing tours. Logan owned one of the few pleasure boats in the harbor.

After the long flight, he was relieved to escape running into his dock neighbors as he slid the main cabin's glass door open, filled the water tanks, and turned on the heat.

Logan was born and raised in Anchorage and knew every town from Nome to Juneau and Barrow to Attu. It was Friday, May 13, 2004, when he returned to his favorite town.

Coming of age in Alaska, Logan came to understand the dichotomy of the Last Frontier. Geographic beauty is starkly juxtaposed against harsh, pitch-black winters and icy streets that are strewn with fatal auto accidents and snowplow remains. There are airplane crashes, deadly earthquakes, active volcanoes, and ferocious seas that kill the most experienced fishermen. And there are murders.

In the 1970s and '80s, Logan witnessed the incredible influx of people to Alaska, eager to cash in on its natural resources of fish and oil. The twentieth-century carpetbaggers from the Lower 48 risked all in pursuit of wealth and, in some cases, fame. He observed the high-stakes poker game of Life in the Wilds bolstered by sex, drugs, gambling, and death. He watched Alaska, the ultimate intimidator, exact its form of justice on anyone who dared to over-imbibe in its natural beauty and resources.

Flying into Homer is one of the most beautiful sights in the world—an arctic version of a flight over Rio de Janeiro. The general perception among the sourdoughs is that the worst part about Alaska is having to go through Anchorage to get there. People visit or move to Alaska wanting to live in the wilderness with moose, elk, and mountain goats grazing in the front yards of their log cabin homes. The reality is that Anchorage is a hip city with modern houses, McDonald's restaurants, movie theaters, churches, Costco, and Nordstrom.

Homer, long considered the crown jewel of Alaska, is located at the end of the road, 222 road miles south of Anchorage. It is one of those places you wanted to get to. It is quaint, isolated with bountiful scenery and majestic animals grazing outside your cabin door.

Having finished teaching at the University of Arizona's law school for the spring semester, Logan locked up his winter home in Tubac. He looked forward to boarding his summer accommodations, a thirty-nine-foot Carver 356, *The Coral Dawn*. He'd purchased the boat the previous year after selling a twenty-four-foot Bayliner that he and his former partner, Pete Foster, shared since 1979. It was a luxurious upgrade—faster, safer, and much larger than its predecessor.

Logan, rugged and athletic, was a baby boomer with fond memories of the 1960s. That free-love lifestyle followed him throughout his life. He never married, and once he'd established his law practice, he did his very best to date every eligible female in Anchorage. The mustached fifty-one-year-old lawyer shifted his computer bag to his left shoulder. He surveyed the airport's dirt parking lot and spotted his 2001 periwinkle-blue Volkswagen. It was right where his former girlfriend, Lacey, left it the previous fall. He opened the door, laid the computer on the passenger seat, and grabbed the keys from under the floormat. Nobody ever stole a car in Homer. No place to go. Even if someone did take it for a joyride, Logan wouldn't care so long as it was back at the airport each spring.

He heated a can of chili in the microwave and gobbled it down before falling asleep in the aft cabin. He awoke the next morning to the sun blasting into the stateroom. *Damn, forgot to close the shades!* The aroma of coffee drifting throughout the cabin confirmed that he'd set the timer correctly the night before and, despite the Alaskan chill, verified that the boat still had electric power. Keeping his clothes on from the day before, he pulled on his Eddie Bauer jacket. Shivering, he swirled a dollop of Hershey's chocolate into his steaming coffee and warmed his hands around the mug as he used his elbow to nudge the door open to the aft deck. He grabbed the morning newspaper off the dock and climbed to the upper helm's captain's chair.

Bright and sunny, the outdoor temperature was a brisk forty-nine degrees and felt colder with the morning dew. It would be seventy degrees by midafternoon. Logan exhaled with a palpable sense of freedom as he surveyed the harbor, spit, glaciers, and surrounding mountains from his perch twelve feet above the water. *An exhilarating slice of heaven.* Arizona's desert heat seemed light-years away. Alaska was home. Always would be. Returning was the highlight of Logan's year. He slept better in the cold, and just breathing the fresh, crisp morning air was energizing.

But this year, it wasn't the weather and the fishing that brought him back to Alaska a month earlier than usual. It was the call from Lacey Carpenter. For the past four summers, Logan maintained Lacey's law practice while she commercially fished in Bristol Bay for five or six weeks. The weeks of fishing brought in more income than her year-round law practice. If the fishing was good, most fishermen and fisherwomen made enough money in six weeks to raise a family of four for the entire year. You must know the right people, and Lacey did.

The past winter, Lacey had defended two criminal clients in Anchorage. Although she skillfully swayed the juries from the second-degree murder charges to manslaughter, each trial was extremely stressful. She told Logan she was simply exhausted because she hadn't been able to break up the dark winter months with her usual treks to Hawaii.

While waiting for the cabin to warm, Logan read the *Homer Tribune*, which unfailingly reflected Alaskans' stance on government, taxes, and the laws of the country's forty-ninth state. For most Alaskans, that visceral feeling of being vehemently against all forms of government intrusion continued to be a compelling reason to migrate to or stay in Alaska. Logan read the paper and smiled; not much had changed since 1995 when he'd resigned from representing the City of Homer after having endured sixteen years of city council meetings.

He looked up from the paper and gazed west to the Alaska Range where jagged pinnacles extended majestically to Denali. The peak, formerly Mount McKinley, is the third highest and third most isolated peak on Earth. Geologists have speculated that Denali is part of the volcanic system that includes the towering glacier-covered Iliamna, Redoubt, and Augustine volcanoes. Iliamna last erupted in 1876. Mount Saint Augustine formed an island in Cook Inlet, and its eruptions have been recorded from 1883, 1935, 1963, 1964, and 1976. Mount Redoubt's last eruption in 1989 spewed volcanic ash to a height of forty-five thousand feet. Logan had observed it in full swing with gray clouds emanating from its inner furnace. Alaska was still forming, much like Hawaii, only on a vastly more gargantuan scale.

Suddenly Logan's entire body shook. He thought back to 1964 when the second largest earthquake in the recorded history of the world hit his home in Anchorage. The quake destroyed seventy-four homes in and around Turnagain Heights, and four of the Finches' neighbors lost their lives. Incredibly, Anchorage recorded only five deaths, one of whom was the sole traffic controller on duty that afternoon when the airport tower collapsed. Although news reports claimed 139 people died in the earthquake, only fifteen were the direct result of the quake itself. The tsunami that hit Alaska killed 106 people. Five more perished from the tsunami on the Oregon coast, and an additional thirteen died when the tsunami hit California.

It was a defining event for the Finch family. Their lives would be forever measured in terms of Before and After. The fear entering an elevator or staircase was debilitating for the Finch family, as was their relentless vigilance over one another's every move, ailment, and whereabouts. The almost daily earthquake tremors that Alaskans experienced always brought back anxieties for Logan and his parents. They were not alone in this.

Many years later, when his folks moved to Arizona, Logan followed them with the conditioned response of Pavlov's dogs. He bought a house in nearby Tubac and visited or called them daily. Their family bond distilled into an obsessive joined-at-the-hip existence they were powerless to change.

Anxious to ignore this past, Logan flipped back to the second page of the paper and read the tide chart. The best fishing took place during slack tide, and that would begin at 12:15 p.m. He needed to fuel the boat before motoring twenty miles west across Cook Inlet. It would take an hour to reach *his* halibut fishing ground. Even though halibut lurk on most shoals surrounding Alaska's shorelines, locals aggressively protected *their* fishing grounds with tongue-in-cheek secrecy: *If I told you, I'd have to kill you.*

He shrugged aside the fleeting concern that his fishing plans would conflict with his morning appointment with Lacey. She knew he loved nothing more than fishing on a sunny day and she'd keep their meeting short.

Ah, Lacey. Holding his empty mug, Logan sighed and leaned back. He propped his sneakers on the flybridge and closed his eyes to the warming sun. He looked forward to seeing her. Like Alaska, Lacey was...enigmatic.

CHAPTER

3

LOGAN WAS APPREHENSIVE AS HE sauntered into the Cosmic Kitchen. He hadn't spoken to Lacey since the previous summer except for her brief telephone message begging for a break and when they agreed to meet for breakfast.

He met Lacey when she was forty-four. She'd just passed the 2000 Alaska Bar Exam and rented his and Pete's Homer branch office. He remembered driving over to deliver the keys and being greeted by her husband, Ben, a smiling six-foot guy with a mop of sandy-blond hair, who was raising the back doors of a U-Haul. In her faded overalls, Lacey was happily directing her moving draftees—their twenty-year-old daughter, Blakeley, and seventeen-year-old son, Greysen. *Now, that's a beautiful family.* Logan felt a sense of awe.

His musings were interrupted when Lacey arrived. She brushed her shining auburn hair to the left side of her face and smiled at Logan. Her dark emerald eyes sparkled. Lacey was attractive. Real attractive, even with a briefcase in hand. He stood for the warm hug. She tilted her face upward, her petite frame on tiptoes, and greeted him with a quick kiss on the cheek.

"Hey, stranger."

Lacey appeared much younger and healthier than the previous fall. She remained slender, but the deep sadness that had lined her eyes and face after losing her husband had mostly disappeared.

Three months after opening her law office, Ben Carpenter's ninety-foot trawler sank off Attu Island during a storm in the spring of 2000. None of the nine-member crew were recovered. Taking a seat, Lacey smiled as Logan pointed to the Big Bang Breakfast Burrito on the menu and said, "No way we'll eat all that. It's the size of a small planet. But we can give it a try."

"Let's do it. So, how was your flight back home, Mr. Finch?"

"I don't mind admitting that I always worry when I take the commuter plane from Anchorage to Homer, given Ryan Air's safety record. But since those crashes happened in bad weather, I figure I'm safe if I fly up in the summer and leave in the fall."

"I hear ya. That's why I never fly in the winter or bad weather conditions."

"You know, Lace, you should sell that Cessna of yours and take commercial flights to Anchorage, Kodiak, and Bristol Bay. Despite your cautious approach as a pilot, no one knows when the weather will change. It can happen in just minutes."

"Yeah, but they're not nearly as much fun and they never work with my schedule. Besides, just five pending NTSB investigations, and there's only been twenty-three deaths in the twenty-nine accidents that occurred over the last twenty years. So...pretty good record for commuter flights in Alaska. Before I forget, how are Pete and Erika these days? It's been a few years since I've heard from either of them."

"They're great. They live on Lake Washington just north of Seattle. I talk to the old buzzard every week but still can't get him to come back to Alaska with me. He says he's still scared to fly. Whenever I go through Seattle from Tucson, I stay with them, like I did a couple nights ago. But I think other than my sporadic visits, they're practically hermits; they never go out. Much different than the old days."

"Afraid to fly, is that why they never came back to Alaska?"

"Oh, partly...after their daughter Emma disappeared, they couldn't even think about Alaska."

Lacey hesitated to discuss Emma's disappearance and was grateful their server, Leslie, interrupted with a breakfast burrito draped over a Thanksgiving turkey–sized platter. "Well, look who's back home. You bail out of here every fall, leaving us youngsters to endure the freezing winters."

Leslie appeared youthful, but she was probably pushing fifty. She was beloved by the locals and the seasonal guests, and as much a mainstay of the Cosmic Kitchen as its legendary brunches. Warm, dark brown eyes under a feathered fringe of soft blond hair and a perpetual smile emanated a kindness that welcomed everyone.

"So, how are your folks doing?"

"Oh, as well as can be expected, I guess, considering their ongoing battle with senility."

Logan's forced optimism was tinged with bittersweet resignation. No matter how hard they tried, no doctor on Earth could put the brakes on their mental deterioration.

Concerned, Leslie prodded, "Where are they living?"

"They share a room in a nice assisted-living facility in Green Valley, a little north of my place in Tubac, near the Mexican border town of Nogales. Memory loss is the facility's focus, and they have around-the-clock care. I hated like hell to move them there, but they seem surprisingly happy. So, I run over to see them several times a week."

Logan smiled. "Sometimes they think I'm just another caretaker, and that's tough, but we get through it."

Lacey added thoughtfully, "As an only child, you're all they've got."

Unable to add cheery platitudes to the parents-with-dementia topic, Logan shrugged and stirred his coffee. Leslie took the hint and retreated to the kitchen.

"So, Lace, let's talk about something happier. How are those great kids of yours doing?"

Lacey's face lit up. "After Blakeley graduated from the University of Washington—yeah, I remember you're a Husky too—she moved to Dillingham as the store manager for Northern Commercial. Greysen's still grinding it out at an LA Starbucks; my handsome G's a wannabe scriptwriter.

Logan winked. "Takes after his English lit–major mom."

"I know!" Lacey laughed. "And I love that. Just wish they lived closer to home. Fortunately, I wind up with cases in Dillingham occasionally, so I see Blake a few times a year. And she comes here when she gets time off."

Turning their attention to business, Lacey opened her briefcase and handed Logan a long list of clients and case status reports. She reviewed everything in a matter of minutes. Logan looked concerned. "I'm not leaving for Hawaii for another ten days. There will be plenty of time to get you squared away at the office."

That first summer in 2000 when Logan first oversaw Lacey's practice, they became friends. The following summer, their friendship evolved from a flirtatious kiss into a knock-your-socks-off, head-over-heels romance. Unfortunately, there were geographical complications. Logan had lived in Arizona since he retired in 1996, staying close to his aging parents and teaching law. Lacey's life was tied to Homer. She had become a beloved attorney in the small town and its frontier surroundings. Caring for those in need had always been her focus, in stark contrast to the big-city law firms' emphasis on revenue and billable hours.

For three years, the lovers coped with the bittersweet frustrations of a long-distance relationship by spending passionate summers in one another's constant presence. Then Lacey reluctantly faced reality and told Logan when he left last fall, "I can't do this any longer." Logan understood; he'd known that that day might come, yet he left hoping Lacey would have a change of heart over the winter and call. She didn't.

As they shuffled through the paperwork, Logan searched her face for some indication the next ten days would include some personal time together. However, she made it clear that a tête-à-tête wasn't in her day timer as she animatedly launched into a description of the Maili Cove condo she'd rented for her two-week vacation. Like Secretariat snorting at the starting gate, Lacey was anxious to bask in the Hawaiian sunshine. Logan knew the coming days would seem like an eternity to her. Alaskan winters are a grueling marathon of parkas, snow shovels, and freezing weather. Pushing aside his disappointment at her pending departure, he managed a weak smile.

They finished breakfast at ten o'clock, giving Logan time to fuel up and hit the bait shop before motoring out to his halibut grounds. He paid the tab and agreed to come by Lacey's office about the same time Friday morning for a meet and greet.

"My old executive chair still in the attic?"

"Of course." Lacey smirked. "Nobody ever opens that door except to deposit another box of closed files. I think you guys still own the place because neither of you is willing to clean out the attic."

Pete and Logan purchased the old two-story home on Pioneer Avenue in 1978 when they were retained to represent the city. The house was centrally located with parking; minimal remodeling converted it into a law office. The first year they stayed in Homer for the city council meetings and camped out on the sparsely furnished second floor. During the summer, they traded weekends so each could partake in Homer's legendary fishing season. The following year, they purchased a twenty-four-foot Bayliner, which became their living quarters and freed up the entire second floor of the house for storage. Documents and relics loomed precariously on both sides of a nebulous trail that meandered through the attic's dusty interior.

Following their quick goodbye hug, Logan returned to his blue Bug and Lacey walked the block and a half back to her office. Smiling to himself, Logan watched her cross the street. *Would she wave?* And...she did. She was magical to him. Still.

Logan's next stop was the Sport Shed Fishing Tackle Store. He needed a fishing license, bait, and a Homer Jackpot Halibut Derby ticket. Then, das boat.

His dock neighbors, Mike and Sasha, took care of *The Coral Dawn* over the winter months and kept him posted on any problems. Potential problems in Alaska weren't necessarily just weather-related. There were mechanical issues as well as damage caused by drunken fishermen on the docks. Today, the dock was quiet except for shrieking seagulls and the soft splash of inlet waves against the breakwater. He gave the engines a five-minute warm-up, untied the lines, and proceeded to the gas dock.

"Morning, Lars," Logan hollered at the craggy old gas jockey ambling down the dock.

"Morning, stranger. Where ya been?"

"Where I go every winter...sunny Arizona. Anything happen while I was gone?"

"Nah. No earthquakes other than the usual weekly rumbles. Volcanoes haven't erupted either, but sure looks like Redoubt's ready to blow."

They gazed at the venting volcano. "I noticed smoke earlier today. I don't want to deal with any fallout from that volcano erupting again, so try to keep it under control, okay, Lars?"

"You got it, boss. Are you going for halibut today?"

"Would I be doing anything else?"

"Where ya going?"

Smiling, Logan defaulted to the well-worn refrain. "Lars, I'd tell ya, but then I'd have to kill ya."

While Lars nodded and obligingly grinned at the colloquialism, he grabbed a post as the dock began to sway for about fifteen seconds. Logan saw what was happening and although he could feel the motion, he broke out into a cold sweat and closed his eyes. It wasn't until Lars asked, "You all right?" that he opened his eyes.

"I'm good. How are you, Lars?"

"Okay, but ever since the '64 quake, I think every shake will turn into another big one."

"You and me both."

The gas bill was over $400. *Hell*, Logan thought. *Halibut sure ain't cheap.* He waved a salute to Lars and turned the bow out to sea.

Catching halibut was akin to snagging a tire. The large, white bottom fish moseyed along the ocean floor looking for anything to eat that tasted bad and smelled worse. Halibut smell like very few creatures on Earth. However, halibut fishing wasn't the only reason Logan kept a boat in Homer. On the waters of Kachemak Bay, he never had to talk to anyone. He didn't have to answer the phone, attend a meeting, or be a good son. *The Coral Dawn* was a zero-obligation and earthquake-free zone where tensions melted away and his constant lower back pain receded. He could just be.

The sun beat down from a cloudless sky and glaciers glistened on the surrounding mountains. Twin Volvo engines cruised at twenty-four mph, comfortably hitting twenty-eight hundred rpm. Logan set course and an hour later began checking the depth meter. When it displayed a hundred feet, he'd arrived in halibut heaven.

CHAPTER
4

H E WAS TWENTY MILES OFFSHORE by early afternoon and the temperature was approaching seventy degrees. It was a day that could convince an atheist to believe there might be a god after all. The Washington Husky purple-and-gold flag on the stern stiffened in the breeze while the skull and crossbones flag fluttered from the bow. Logan removed his shirt for a little more sun and, glancing down at his tanned torso, it occurred to him that he might be one of the few guys in Alaska without a tan line that ended at his shirt collar.

Logan baited his hook and dropped his line overboard.

Lulled by the flat waters slapping gently against the hull, he was nearly asleep when an explosion of water propelled him to his feet. A blue whale surfaced spectacularly to look him over. Neither the whale nor Logan blinked as time stood still. Logan found himself instinctively holding his breath as he realized his life lay at the whim of this mythically proportioned leviathan.

At sixty-plus feet, a casual flip of his tail would swamp the boat. The creature determined neither the captain nor his vessel were amusing, edible, or a threat and rolled nonchalantly beneath the waterline, leaving the boat to rock in its wake for the next five minutes. *Thrilling. Invigorating. And, yes, scary.*

As Logan reeled in the fishing line, it was apparent from the weight that either a flat tire or halibut would greet him. As the fish broke the surface, it exploded to life. That always startled Logan even though it always happened. A hook in a halibut's mouth triggered no reaction, yet breathing air snapped these monsters from their contented lethargy.

From the swim step, he reached for the .22-caliber revolver holstered on his belt. He didn't want a full-blown physical fight with a large—dangerously large—critter. Often a bullet or two to the head would stun the halibut. Sometimes it just made the beast angrier. A bullet was seldom fatal. Once in a boat, however, a thrashing halibut could easily break a man's leg. Logan always used an abundance of caution in landing these big guys.

Logan fired two shots to the halibut's head, between the eyes, difficult to do with eyes on the same side of the head. The stunned fish settled down after the second shot. He caught it under the right cheek with the gaff hook and lifted. He guessed the fish weighed about fifty pounds, but as it emerged from the cold sea, the weight seemed to double. "Damn," he muttered. Big...probably 110 pounds, but no Jackpot Derby tags.

Logan dragged it up the swim step, tied its tail to the rail cleat, and let it bleed out for about fifteen minutes. The strong fishy odor grew more pungent in the sun as Logan washed and scrubbed the fish.

Homer advertised itself as the Halibut Fishing Capital of the World. Every year from mid-May to mid-September, thousands of anglers from around the world came to fish in the Homer Jackpot Halibut Derby. It was Alaska's longest-running halibut fishing competition and boasted the largest total payout. This year's seventeenth-annual Jackpot Derby included the $50,000 City Prize for biggest fish and, if you caught a special tagged fish, you'd win the Stanley Ford F-150. To celebrate the anniversary, in addition to the hundred tagged fish, the city tagged an additional thirty fish worth fifty bucks each. A fish with a previous year's tag won an additional $100. Logan glumly analyzed the math: *Catch four of those babies and I'd cover my gas costs! Whoopee!*

Previous derby winners brought in fish exceeding three hundred pounds. In 2003, someone caught the $50,000 fish but failed to buy the ticket. The poor doofus wound up with nothing except a colossal halibut! An unforgettable cautionary tale that compelled Logan to buy a ticket every season.

Pete was a winner when the derby was in its infancy. His prize was a meager $5,000 for a 305-pounder and the derby ran from Memorial Day to Labor Day. *No celebration today, though,* Logan thought. *But the season's just starting.*

He laid down a plastic tarp to lay the fish on and noticed a movement out of the left corner of his eye. Seals and whales often ventured near the boat, but this was different. It was smaller and it submerged more quickly than either a seal or a whale. Looking again, he spotted a sea otter floating on its back, presumably waiting for a handout. Logan obligingly threw out some chips before dragging the halibut up the two steps to the aft deck. The otter observed Logan's generosity and gave him an appreciative nod while remaining on its back, adroitly gathering the chips as they floated by. Once all the chips were on its chest, the otter radiated sheer contentment as he munched away at the unexpected windfall.

"Why did you come out here for chips, little one?" Logan laughed. "There's an entire buffet at the dock!"

Catlike, the inquisitive little mammal carefully groomed its furry face while maintaining eye contact with Logan. These friendly creatures were seen almost daily in the boat harbor. They often played chest ping-pong with rocks for hours, presumably practicing for when real food arrived.

Logan again baited the hook and let out the line until the weights hit bottom. Lying back on the upper deck, thoughts of Lacey surfaced, reigniting an emptiness he tried to ignore. His thoughts then drifted to Pete and Erika and their deceased daughter. He couldn't imagine the depth of Pete's and Erika's loss.

Years earlier, however, Logan was drafted into coaching the girls' fifth and sixth grade basketball teams at Anchorage's Huffman Elementary School. Coach Logan was surprised at their entertaining charm and the fountain of energy they exuded. He fondly recalled giggly little girls that were as adorable and precocious as puppies.

Closing his eyes to the warm sun, he chuckled at the memory of his challenges coaching little blond Emma to guard her "man" when playing defense. "Listen, Emma, it's important for you to stay between the girl you're guarding and the basket," he instructed. "Do. Not. Ever. Leave. Her. Remember to keep both hands up in the air so she can't shoot the ball and stay about three feet away." He stared into her bright blue eyes to see if she was listening and if she understood what he was telling her before adding a final warning: "Make sure their basket is always at your back."

The first half ended, and Logan noticed that Emma hadn't returned to the huddle. Annoyed, he scanned the court. There was Emma, hands in the air and standing exactly three feet behind an opposing player leisurely drinking from the water fountain. Emma may not have had a glowing future in basketball, but she was a star at following directions.

Her disappearance when she was barely seventeen years old on a frigid Friday night in October 1983 shocked everyone and was an utter tragedy for Pete and Erika.

"Damn." Logan brushed away the sudden tears. His reverie of those carefree bygone days was always eclipsed by the loss of that shining, effervescent spirit.

CHAPTER
5

A s Logan relaxed, hoping for a prize-winning halibut, fifteen hundred miles away Pete and Erika Foster were oblivious to a caravan of vehicles, led by two state patrol cars, approaching their Arrowhead Point home on Lake Washington. Their piece of heaven, as they referred to their fortresslike granite and stone home at the end of a cul-de-sac on an isolated peninsula jutting into the north end of Lake Washington, which is the twenty-mile lake buffering exclusive neighborhoods from Seattle.

Pete was relaxing in a worn cotton Seahawks T-shirt when the doorbell rang. Logs smoldered in the massive river rock fireplace while the afternoon sun streamed through two-story glass windows framing the lake view. It was almost too warm for the sweatpants, although he'd appreciate them a lot later. Shoving his feet into an old pair of moccasins with broken-down heels, he reluctantly rose from his overstuffed wingback chair and shuffled to the door. No guests were expected, and visitors were rare. Pete was bewildered when he opened the front door to see a uniformed Washington State Trooper.

"Are you Peter Foster?"

Pete nodded and, looking past the trooper, saw several unmarked patrol cars occupying the enclave's parking area. Turning back to the officer's steady gaze, Pete asked, "Can I help you?"

The officer responded bluntly, "Mr. Foster, you're under arrest for the murder of William Hamlin." Pete was read his rights while being aggressively handcuffed. The officers firmly escorted him from the house as Erika rushed to the front door. "Pete," she yelled, "what's going on?"

As he was shoved into the trooper's vehicle, a tense, grim expression replaced his previously relaxed demeanor. Just before the car door slammed shut, Pete hollered, "Call Logan!"

Erika ran to the phone on the antique armoire in the entryway before a detective barked, "No phone calls, ma'am, until we've secured and searched the premises." He handed her paperwork, then stepped aside for the SWAT team of leather-jacketed officers bedecked in full tactical gear. Erika stared uncomprehendingly at the herd of black-booted strangers invading her home.

As they swarmed the house, the detective tersely asked, "Any guns in the house?"

Erika gestured mutely down the hall, and the detective accompanied her to the guest bedroom where she pointed to the bed. There's a key under the mattress. The guns are upstairs, in the office...in a locked cabinet."

The detective handed off the key and two officers bolted up the stairs. In a well-rehearsed move, they unlocked the cabinet and snatched two rifles and a pistol. The desktop computer in the office was confiscated, along with a laptop sitting in the kitchen. Then they were gone, leaving an eerie silence in their wake.

The detective was replaced by an Alaskan State Trooper. She handed Erika a search warrant. It cited "all guns and computers in the house." Nothing else. A dazed Erika asked about her husband.

"Well, ma'am," she explained, "he's on his way to the King County Jail and will be charged with murdering William Hamlin. Guess you know all about him, huh?"

"Hamlin?" Erika repeated. "No, never heard of him."

The detective gave a curious, searching look, pursed her lips as if to speak, but appeared to think better of it. She nodded goodbye and left. The entire incident was over in minutes. Erika's hands shook as she stood in the doorway holding the search warrant.

CHAPTER
6

LOGAN WAS WEIGHING THE PROS AND CONS of boating back to the harbor before the tide receded when his phone buzzed. "Thank God I got you!" Erika frantically exclaimed. "We need your help. Pete said to call you, and I'm scared to death."

"Erika, I'm listening," Logan soothed. "What's happened?"

"Pete's been arrested! They've charged him with murder! They rushed into our house and..."

"Whoa, slow down. Where's Pete?"

"The detective said he's going to the King County Jail."

While trying to wrap his mind around Erika's words, Logan squinted at the blue horizon. "Who do they think he murdered?"

"Bill Hamlin. They think he murdered that guy who gave Jansen his alibi."

Logan hadn't heard Jansen's name in years, not since the guy confessed to murdering nineteen young women. The actual number of murders, Logan recalled, was thought to be closer to forty-seven. Pete and Erika's daughter, Emma, was believed to be one of Jansen's last victims. Logan flashed back to the present and assured Erika that he'd catch the next flight to Seattle.

"Thanks, Logan. I'll get word to Pete."

Logan quickly retrieved the halibut and methodically washed down the boat and swim step, corralled his fishing gear, and fired up the engines from the flybridge. The engines turned over with some hesitation. *Gotta check those batteries*, Logan thought. These routines usually ended a pleasant outing, but not today. Logan's world was abruptly out of alignment.

Erika sipped her glass of merlot as she sat in her living room. The fireplace embers were a vestige of a quiet afternoon turned nightmare. *Logan will be with us tomorrow.*

Leaning back in Pete's armchair, she closed her eyes to the day's nightmare and her old memories of Alaska.

Shortly after Erika graduated from high school, she'd married Yuri Rostykus, her childhood sweetheart. Eight years later, Yuri was working as a petrochemical engineer for Alyeska Pipeline Service Company when he was diagnosed with brain cancer. Pete drafted their wills. A month later, May 1976, Yuri died, and Pete probated Yuri's estate. They were among Pete's first clients in Anchorage.

Pete assisted Erika through the probate process. Their friendship grew, then evolved into dating in 1977. In 1978, they exchanged wedding vows in the backyard of their new home on the hillside south of Anchorage. After the "I dos" and traditional kiss, Pete took their flower girl's hand and Judge Ripley performed the adoption ceremony of twelve-year-old Emma, officially making them a family of three. Toasting commenced amid happy tears at the promise of a joyous future.

Their lives were irrevocably shattered when Emma vanished five years later. She'd completed her evening shift at the Flying-In restaurant across the street from a strip club known as the Great Alaskan Bush Company. She was last seen at about 10 p.m. walking to her car, which she'd parked near Merrill Field.

The city rallied around the distraught parents. Friends and neighbors shared Pete's and Erika's tears as they grappled with paralyzing grief. There were search parties and candlelight vigils, anything and everything to keep Emma's picture and story alive.

Eventually, details of a serial killer emerged in newspaper and television reports. Anchorage baker Jack Jansen confessed to abducting seventeen young women and flying them to a remote area in the Alaska wilderness where he tortured and raped them. He released them before hunting them down as prey. He buried his victims in shallow graves. There was coverage about the Anchorage PD ignoring Colleen Preston's kidnapping, accepting false alibis, and failing to investigate Jansen, thereby allowing him to murder at least ten more innocent young women. Investigators, including Pete and Erika, believed that Emma was one of those ten victims, but an imprisoned Jansen always denied committing her murder because she was not a prostitute. It was an unending nightmare as the days became weeks. Then months. The first anniversary of Emma's disappearance produced a flurry of media attention. Sadly, it brought no new tips nor hope for answers. The local media moved on to the renomination of President Ronald Reagan, coverage of an underground nuclear test by the USSR, and a suicide car-bombing attack on the US embassy in Beirut. Pete and Erika felt abandoned and profoundly alone.

Immediately following Emma's disappearance, Pete and Erika remained staunchly optimistic that Emma would be found alive. Friends, uncertain how to help or what to say and do, eventually returned to the everydayness of their lives. Pete and Erika became members of a ghastly club bonded through the heartache of losing a child. Through the shroud of their new reality, they perceived the finality of their loss that effectively isolated them in a painful adjustment to life without her.

Erika lived on antidepressants, haunted by nightmares in which Emma plaintively cried, "Mama."

Pete's commitment to his law practice diminished to rote rituals. He drove to the office, turned on lights, checked mail, and returned phone messages. Their lives became as bleak as a dying coral reef, a bleached and fragile exoskeleton of their once vibrantly beautiful young family. These grieving parents eventually fled Anchorage to distance themselves from the horror of what happened to their darling girl.

CHAPTER
7

L OGAN'S MIND RACED WHILE CRUISING BACK to the boat harbor. *Murder? When? Why? How?*

Pete had been the life of every party—a nonjudgmental guy, a good listener, and a friendly jokester who didn't define life in terms of black and white. His warm, outgoing personality reflected a belief that people mattered and deserved respect and dignity regardless of their occupation, age, or family origins. His banter was irresistible.

Pete's cluttered office and credenza—files stacked precariously, unintelligible phone messages on Post-it notes, and a heap of dated mail—evidenced his firm belief that organization was highly overrated. He swore he knew where everything was, and if anyone moved anything, he knew it. When confronted, he paraphrased Albert Einstein: "If a cluttered desk is a sign of a cluttered mind, of what, then, is an empty desk a sign?"

Pete and Logan met in 1973. Both were first-year law students at the University of Puget Sound in Tacoma, Washington. Logan, while strolling to classes on the first day, noticed the guy with the wild blond mane. He discovered that they'd rented an apartment in the same building. Pete proved to be larger than life, with an effortless charisma that attracted the few female law students.

By contrast, Logan was inconspicuous. He ignored fashion and wore clothes from J. C. Penney. Upon graduation, he was Alaska-bound, where plaid flannel shirts and Levi jeans were standard. He was cautious and quiet. In the late sixties, he calculated the war in Vietnam was not ending, so he enlisted to avoid being drafted. His strategy kept him out of the jungles of Southeast Asia and stationed in Germany for two years.

Next door to Pete and Logan's apartment complex was the Creekwater

Tavern. It was new and catered to the area's technical school students. It was a haven for the baby boomers, where the law students dovetailed with the clientele. Logan got a closer look at Pete's subtle MO at the Creekwater. The servers emulated a Barbie doll image and catered to Pete's every whim. He seemed oblivious to their charms until it was a Friday night and he'd downed his fourth beer. Then he'd leave the Creekwater with one, sometimes two, on his arm. Back then, everyone assumed Pete would be at least sixty before he got married.

Pete formed a coed softball team for his fellow students. He and Logan were friendly but not close. One fateful day after the first inning of a game, Monta, the team's best pitcher, who was rarely flustered on the field or in the classroom, approached Logan and was uncharacteristically abrupt. "Hey! Say something to Pete about his jeans!"

Pete was the catcher and was wearing his customary jean cutoffs. As he crouched behind home plate, a tear in the crotch revealed a noteworthy set of balls dangling to the ground. Logan contained his laughter and explained the problem to Pete, who wasn't a bit chagrined but did *stand* behind the plate for the rest of the game. After the game, Logan and Pete had a few beers with the team, and each retelling magnified the hilarity of the moment.

In their third year of law school, Pete found a volunteer job at the Pierce County Legal Aid. "Hey, Logan, they need another volunteer!" They wound up sharing a cubbyhole and were elated that they each had their own desk. It was legalized slavery for wannabe attorneys, but welcome on-the-job training where they practiced limited law in the county's superior courthouse.

McNeil Island Federal Penitentiary became a Washington State corrections facility in 1981 in West Pierce County. It was the last prison in the United States accessible only by air or sea. Law students provided prisoners with free legal counsel. Pete and Logan's new partnership now included volunteering at McNeil Island.

On Saturday mornings, they caught a Washington State ferry and crossed south Puget Sound to the prison. Journeying along were nearly twenty working women scheduled to visit the inmates. On view were smoldering eyes lavishly layered in mascara and thick, false eyelashes, lots of legs ending in flamboyant platform heels, and bolstered cleavage seductively displayed in sheer, low-cut blouses. The women sashayed like rock stars as they perp-walked from the dock to the prison amid enthusiastic cheers from the inmates.

Pete and Logan spent Saturday mornings in the prison's law library. They met with two to three prisoners per hour and tried to provide answers to the inmates' legal questions. As it turned out, the aspiring partners learned much more about the law and the appellate process from the prisoners than the prisoners ever learned from them. The prisoners were sharp and savvy, had years of experience reading cases in the prison's law library, and were not impressed with the two law students.

But a revisitation of their decades-long friendship did not resolve the current problem. Pete, Logan surmised, must have been in a self-defense situation where he had no choice, or, more likely, they arrested the wrong guy. The longer he thought about it, the more improbable it was that Pete hurt anyone. *Murder is out of the question.* As *The Coral Dawn* approached the harbor, Logan decided against calling Erika. He reminded himself that defense attorneys never talk to a criminal client or key witness before seeing what the prosecutors have in their files and evidence lockers. *Put on the brakes, old boy. Why am I even assuming Pete wants me to represent him? I haven't tried a felony case in years.*

Logan docked the boat and booked the earliest flight to Seattle for the following day. He called Lacey and she expressed concern for Pete and Erika but longed to languish on the warm beaches of Hawaii while Logan took care of her Homer law practice. She clung to that hope when Logan said, optimistically, "Don't cancel your plans yet, Lace."

CHAPTER
8

L OGAN GUTTED, CLEANED, and sliced the head and tail off his catch. He tossed the scraps to the crab ten feet below, providing them with a gourmet dinner. He decided to filet the halibut later. He cut the fish in half and stowed it in a large black garbage bag. He anchored the bag to a cleat before dropping it into the water where the fish would keep until morning. He showered before falling asleep and into a recurring dream...saving people in an earthquake. Or being rescued. His mother was always present. She was young, like when he was a kid. Most of these memories were nightmares; some were not. He dreamed of flying over the Alaskan coast, Superman style, saving people the way he wished his family could have been rescued.

A familiar, soft *woof* woke Logan the next morning. There was a pause followed by another courteously low but insistent bark. Toby, an irrepressible Australian shepherd, had discovered Logan was home. Doggy blue eyes shined with unconstrained enthusiasm. Toby positioned himself, his tail waving madly as his forelegs braced for the leap from his sailboat to Logan's gas guzzler's swim step. Logan hustled up to the deck, and Toby's elation hit full throttle with an exuberant body wag.

Toby's shipmates, Mike and Sasha, ignored the commotion as Logan walked to the swim step and opened his arms. Toby jumped the three-foot divide and Logan caught him. This ritual began four years earlier when Toby was a puppy. He had total confidence in Logan's ability to catch him midair every time. As Logan got older and Toby got bigger, Logan was less confident of snagging Toby mid-leap.

Mike and Sasha lived year-round on their sailboat. Mike fished commercially in the summer. They left Alaska every winter for about six weeks, during which time Lacey watched both Logan's and their boats. Mike was close to fifty, a husky Scandinavian guy originally from Sequim, Washington. He came to Alaska in the late seventies to work on the oil pipeline. Sasha was a forty-two-year-old native Athabascan, born just outside Fairbanks.

Sasha was stunning: Tall, slender, big brown eyes, shiny long black hair, and high cheekbones. The Alaskan Inuit and Yupik peoples, known as Eskimos by non-natives, tended not to have those features. Logan heard tales of beautiful Athabascan women while growing up in Anchorage. Sasha exceeded all the tales.

In the land of the midnight sun, it was bright and sunny at six in the morning as Logan started packing, uncertain how long he'd be gone. He decided to travel light and buy as needed should he stay in Seattle for an extended time. Just as he zipped his duffle bag, he heard Toby bark the signal that Mike or Sasha was awake.

"Morning, Logan," Sasha hollered. "Who stole my dog?"

Coming to the aft deck, Logan was again struck by Sasha's natural beauty. "Hey there, gorgeous! Where's your old man?"

"In bed, waiting for coffee. Why are you up so early?"

Mike should be waiting for more than coffee. "Oh, a couple of last-minute things popped up and need my attention in Seattle. I'm flying out this morning on the 7:25 back to Anchorage."

"Geez, you just got here." She bent forward over the rail, and when she looked up, she intercepted Logan's admiring glance. *Awkward moment*, Logan thought.

"I know. Listen, Sasha, I caught a big halibut yesterday. I cleaned it last night but haven't filleted it. If you wanna fillet it, I'll divide the fish with you."

Sasha pointed to the rope dangling from the aft portside cleat. "That it?"

"That's it...want me to throw it over to you?"

"No, I'll get it after breakfast. You hungry?"

Logan sat down in the aft-deck chair.

"Starving, but I have to leave in forty-five minutes."

"No problem. I'll holler at you when the food is on the table. Want coffee now?"

"No, thanks, I have some perking. How about I treat you and Mike to my coffee?"

"Gosh, I never get offers like that around here. You're on."

Logan ate on Sasha and Mike's sailboat while sitting in the captain's chair. Sasha sat portside by the railing as Toby's head swiveled back and forth tracking their conversation.

"Good coffee. Maybe we keep you around." Sasha's accent reflected her native heritage.

"Hey, countin' on it."

"If we gonna take care of things here, least you can tell us why you go away so soon."

Logan winced, but it wouldn't be a secret for long. He'd have to talk about it eventually, whether he wanted to or not. "Ah, it's upsetting. You guys remember my buddy, Pete?"

Sasha nodded.

"Well, sounds like he's in trouble."

"What kinda trouble?" Mike asked as he opened the cabin door and came up the short stairwell.

"He's been charged with murder."

"Wow, what happened?"

Logan wished he could vent about the worry he felt for his friend and the challenges ahead. "I can say the accusations relate to the serial killer Jack Jansen. And they're just accusations. Pete didn't kill anyone." He glanced at his watch.

"Ah, guys, sorry, it's time to go. Thanks for the delicious breakfast."

Sasha assured him they would watch over *The Coral Dawn* and freeze his half of the halibut. By six forty-five, Logan was walking down the dock as Toby barked his goodbyes.

CHAPTER
9

WHILE DRIVING THE SPIT ROAD, LOGAN CALLED an old law school buddy, Jim Carter, the one guy in Anchorage with the lowdown on Bill Hamlin. Logan's red-bearded Irish buddy worked at the *Anchorage Daily News* before and after attending law school. They hadn't spoken in years. Carter knew where the bones were buried and could quickly retrieve all written information about Hamlin.

Carter won a Pulitzer Prize for an investigative piece on the power of the Teamsters Union before and during the pipeline construction, back in the late seventies and early eighties. It was whispered among his friends that Carter chose a law school in Tacoma, Washington, to avoid the discovery of his dead body in a melting berm during spring thaw. That was not an unusual event back then, especially when the Teamsters were involved.

It was Saturday, but Carter answered his law office phone on the third ring. Logan got to the point quickly. "Jim, I have a big favor to ask."

The Irishman was implacable. "What kinda favor?"

"I'm in Homer and jumping a flight to Anchorage, then on to Seattle. I need you to find out everything you can about a guy named William Hamlin."

"That won't be hard...don't think anyone around here's ever going to forget the guy and his wife who lied to the police."

"That's him. Think you can dig up anything more?"

"No problem. I'll make some calls, then meet you in the Crown Room."

"See you there."

As the Beechcraft flew over Turnagain Arm, then descended to Anchorage International Airport, Logan recalled the events surrounding the Hamlins and wondered why, inexplicably, they were never charged, even when the police and prosecutor's office knew their lie led directly to many more murders.

Planes jostled for position at the gates of Anchorage International Airport, one of the busiest cargo airports in the world. The small plane was dwarfed by cargo jets with logos—UPS, FedEx, and others—stenciled on their tails. Anchorage's international air traffic ranked up there with Hong Kong, Memphis, and Shanghai due to the great circle routes from Europe to Asia.

Logan's plane rolled cautiously to the arrival gates and, in minutes, he spotted his Irish friend seated at the bar of the Crown Room, nursing a whiskey and soda. *Breakfast of Champions*. After a firm handshake greeting, Logan was sipping ginger ale while leaning forward to hear what Carter had to say.

"I'm going to start chronologically, give ya a little background history about Jansen," Carter began.

"Geez, Jim, we haven't talked in years." Logan laughed. "But, sure, go for it."

Carter tilted his head to the side, shrugging away the obvious with a smile. He was a guy who thoroughly enjoyed sharing his vast knowledge of Anchorage history. "Years before his arrest for killing young women and girls, Anchorage police continuously dismissed dancers' reports about disappearances."

Logan knew the testosterone-stoked guys swarming the shadowy Tenderloin District on their few days off from working the pipeline. It would have been unthinkable to seriously suspect that the diminutive baker quietly hunched over in a church pew on Sunday mornings with his wife and kids was a deranged serial killer.

Carter snorted in disgust. "Turns out, the Hamlins and Jansens rubbed elbows at the same Evangelical Baptist church. The Hamlins saw no biblical dichotomy in providing Jansen with an alibi, after which he was free to rid their fair city of at least another ten girls."

Pausing to nod thanks to the bartender for refreshing his drink, Carter continued. "Jansen maintained that it was his righteous destiny to destroy them. Of course, it's uncertain whether he truly believed God applauded his clean-up efforts, but he was deadly accurate that no one worried about a few dancers not showing up for work. His killing spree began to unravel in June of 1983. A young dancer and prostitute, Colleen Preston, escaped and was picked up across from Merrill Field. She described Jansen to a T and directed detectives to his house. But after the Hamlins' false alibi, the Anchorage prosecutor's office didn't follow up with the girl that got away."

Carter emptied his glass in one long gulp and set it gently on the table while glancing at the bartender with a raised eyebrow and a nod. "In the fall of that year, for some reason, it was the Fairbanks prosecutor's office that obtained search warrants. Jansen's home and vehicles, including the plane he wasn't licensed to fly, were finally searched and he was arrested. They found women's jewelry, maps marking the locations of the bodies in the wilderness, the murder weapons, and remnants of Preston's clothing in a burn barrel. "

The details were familiar to Logan and he frowned. "Yeah...ever find out why Fairbanks?"

"Nope." Carter looked sideways at Logan. "But it's mighty unusual. At his sentencing, your buddy Pete delivered a violent right hook to Hamlin's chin just before Jansen was sentenced to 461 years and transported to prison at the Palmer Correctional Center where he was placed in solitary confinement for his own protection."

"Yeah." Logan chuckled. "I saw that."

"In 1988, I wrote a blurb when Hamlin disappeared. Tracing Barbara Hamlin's movements this morning, I read that she'd sold their South Anchorage home a few years after Jansen's sentencing. Then she changed her name and moved to Arizona. Bill Hamlin's remains were found a few months ago on Pete's old property."

Logan glanced at his watch. "Thanks a million, Carter. Really appreciate all this."

"Don't mention it, glad to help."

"I gotta run to make that plane to Seattle. Your drinks are on my tab and I wanna buy you another before I leave. I can't thank you enough."

"Oh, you'll return the favor someday. That's how it works," Carter observed. "And, yeah, I'll take another drink. After all, if you're in Alaska, it's always noon somewhere. Right?"

CHAPTER
10

Erika pulled into the passenger arrival zone at Seattle-Tacoma International Airport where Logan approached the curb. He tossed his duffel bag into the back seat, climbed in, buckled up, and then kissed Erika's cheek. "Hey, how are you doing?"

Logan saw the swollen eyelids and red eyes of a woman in her early fifties. Erika mustered a wan smile and asked, "Okay if we go directly to the jail? Pete's anxious to see you as soon as possible?"

"You bet."

Neither were up for chitchat on the drive, so they silently stared through windshield wipers at the weather mirroring their mood: light winds, overcast gray skies with drizzling rain. Erika delivered Logan outside the King County Jail while she went in search of a parking garage. Inside the jail, Logan flashed his Alaska State Bar license, then lit up the metal detector like a Las Vegas slot machine, courtesy of his titanium knees. After clearing security, he approached a Plexiglas window where he requested an attorney-client room to meet his client. His mind raced.

How was Pete doing? When could Pete get out of jail? Could he help if there was a trial, and would any of this affect Lacey's plans?

A jailer ushered Logan through a clanging elevator door that stopped abruptly on the fifth floor. As they waited for the heavy metal bars to part, the sick feeling of being trapped in lockup was palpable. Throughout his career, Logan had endured it with each jail visit. The heavyset, blond jailer's keys ricocheted loudly with each step. They stopped at a door with a reinforced glass-and-wire window. She unlocked the door, stood back, and impassively gestured Logan forward. Inside was a small table, two metal chairs, and Logan knew, a hidden camera and microphone. A primary reason Logan wanted Pete out on bail was the zero privacy inside the jail and the lying snitch possibilities. Logan was also painfully aware that bail was usually impossible to get for capital offenses.

He pulled out a chair and sat as the door banged open. There stood his friend and former partner, an unshaven ghost of himself, dressed in jail-issue orange. There were dark bags under his bloodshot eyes and a two-day beard. Logan gave an Academy Award–winning performance at acting natural. He hugged Pete, not easy given the cuffed wrists and ankles.

Pete's muffled, defeated voice was heartbreaking. "Hey, friend."

"Jesus, what the hell's going on?"

The jailer removed the cuffs from his wrists and ankles and stepped out of the room. Pete half-smiled as he sank into a chair. "Just doing my time. I was arraigned this morning. Bail's a cool five million bucks. The public defender let me read the formal complaint and the governor has already signed the request for my extradition to Alaska next week. They move fast down here. I could probably fight it and delay things a bit, but we both know that'd be futile."

"Yeah. What can I do to help?"

"Represent me, of course. I might even pay you."

"C'mon, Pete, you know that's not necessary."

"Okay, thanks, we'll work that out. I'll stick with the public defender on Monday and waive my right to any extradition challenges. They'll put me on a plane with an Alaska State Trooper, which gets me out of these four-star accommodations."

"Uh-huh...and ya think Anchorage's Sixth Avenue Jail is better?"

"I've seen both. At least in Anchorage the toilet is enclosed. Jesus, here the damn toilet's in the middle of the room and shared with fifteen of my new best friends. And, adding another dose of humiliation for the inno-cent-until-proven-guilty, it's also visible from the women's holding cell. Damned fucking embarrassing! Small wonder innocent guys plead guilty. It's the quickest way out. Anyway, enough about me and the joys of incar-ceration. How's Erika doing?"

"I'll know more after I talk to her tonight. She was in shock yesterday, but she looks as good as ever."

Pete nodded and adjusted his chair. "Always does. I just hope she can handle the pressure. When and if I get out on bail, it'd be great to have her with me in Alaska for a few months."

"We'll look at that tonight. By the way, remember Jim Carter? I called him this morning and he gave me quite the refresher course on the Hamlins, including police insider info. Seems the prosecutor matched Hamlin's dental records to an old skull found on your Huffman Road property."

"I know...it's in the probable cause statement. No surprise the judge found probable cause to hold me."

Logan attempted to put a positive spin on the picture. "Case seems thin at this stage, but let's discuss it once you're in Anchorage. Our priority is getting you out on bail."

"It would make things easier if you can do it...but that seems like a long shot."

"Hey, buddy, you have a one-man dream team."

Pete grinned. "Yeah, I do, don't I? Soon as we get to Anchorage and see the prosecutor's files, we'll know if there's a defense, and if not, we can deal with that too."

"What are you talking about? Of course there's a defense. A damned good defense and we'll find it. You're innocent, for Chrissake."

Pete shrugged and sighed. "I hear you. This place is depressing, but having you here helps...more than you know." His voice trailed off.

Time had passed, yet their old friendship remained the same. Once again, they had work to do—together.

The jailer reentered the room. It was time for Logan to go. Logan gave Pete a quick hug before the shackles went on. "Pete, you hang in there. We'll talk tomorrow."

In the elevator, Logan worried. *Am I too old to participate in this fight? Trial work demands massive energy, commitment, and a steel-trap memory and is doubly difficult when representing an innocent friend. Maybe easy in my thirties and forties, but I'm mid-fifties now and rusty. It's been years since I've defended an alleged felon. Representing Pete will be a significant departure from teaching a few law advocacy school classes.*

CHAPTER
11

ERIKA CAME DOWN THE STAIRS the following morning and found that Logan had an itinerary mapped out on the kitchen table. "Pete's going to be extradited to Alaska by the end of the week. I'll arrange for a bail review hearing in Anchorage, and it's best if you remain in Seattle, Erika. We may need you to get funds expedited to a bail bondsman."

"And there may be other things that I can do to help him. I feel so bad about the situation he's in."

"He's fine, Erika. He's innocent. He knows the drill. He'll get stronger, especially if we convince the judge to set a reasonable bail."

"Do you think there's a chance of that?"

Logan fibbed, knowing it was a long shot. "Of course."

Erika's eyes glistened with unshed tears. "Logan, no explanation necessary."

They discussed the available collateral and their financial discussions determined that Erika might be able to raise a million and a half in a week if the bonding company would take cash and a lien against their Lake Washington waterfront home. Understandably, Erika was more comfortable and optimistic discussing finances than the case against her husband. "Once Pete's out of jail, I'll come to Alaska."

"Pete will be happy to hear that. The case will probably go to trial within the next three months. We'll stay in Homer so we can use Lacey's office and fly to Anchorage for hearings and the trial. That will allow me to take care of Lacey's clients and meet with Pete to prepare his defense. I'll arrange housing for you and Pete."

"Do you need seed money?"

"Nah . . . let's get Pete out of jail before we worry about that."

"I like Homer," Erika said. "When will you leave?"

"Today, if possible, assuming Pete's extradited next week. Unfortunately, it's Sunday, but I'll try to contact the prosecutor's office anyway."

Logan ate breakfast waiting for a response to the email he'd sent to the prosecutor. He was watching CNN's election news. Bush and Kerry would be debating their respective positions for the next six months. An hour later, an email arrived and confirmed the extradition hearing was scheduled for tomorrow morning and that Pete would most likely be transported to Alaska by late Friday or early Saturday.

"We want him out of here, and Anchorage wants him."

Logan exhaled. This ought to move fast. His flight would put him in Homer by early evening, so he'd invite Lacey to meet him for dinner. He called Lacey but avoided divulging details since Erika was in the room. His evasiveness also assured him Lacey would meet him for dinner. *A welcome light at the end of this dark day.* Erika drove him back to the airport.

"I feel like I'm abandoning you and Pete, but right now I can do more for you in Homer than in Seattle," Logan said.

Erika pulled in front of the departure gate. "We appreciate everything you're doing for us. Just focus on getting Pete out on bail and taking care of Lacey's office. We're good. I'm going to go see Pete now."

Walking into the airport, Logan found a quiet area and called his folks. He usually checked on them every three or four days, but amid all the chaos, he suddenly realized it had been a week since he last called. An orderly answered.

"Your folks are napping, but when they wake up, I'll try to help them understand you called."

Help them understand, echoed in Logan's mind. It was undeniable. He was losing his folks . . . at least mentally. And as for their physical demise . . . he couldn't think about it. During the flight to Anchorage, Logan leaned back, and almost immediately the drone of Alaska's Airlines' 737 lulled him to sleep.

While he slept, he dreamed about his childhood. His parents, Sarah and Scott, were hard-working people who delighted in doting upon their only child. Sarah had been the city's leading planner throughout Logan's life. Her clients were the movers and shakers in the construction industry. Although her skills were legendary in obtaining zoning changes and exceptions for projects that propelled Anchorage's rapid growth, volunteering for the Anchorage Audubon Society was Sarah's true passion. Until she and Scott moved to Arizona, Sarah was an ardent participant in conducting the annual Anchorage Christmas Bird Count, and she was especially proud to be among the top thirteen Anchorage Listers in 1979. Scott's creativity was reflected in his home building construction company. His frugal land purchases avoided the ice lenses which drove many home builders into bankruptcy. Lenses were simply large blocks of ice beneath the tundra that melted when heated by a house or building that was built over it. That melting caused the structure to sink and led to many lawsuits. Scott always spent the additional money to drill on every property he acquired before closing the purchase. The 1964 earthquake changed their emotional lives but not their economic successes. Like the original settlers arriving in New England so many years ago, they were slavish adherents to the American work ethic in a land of opportunity.

Once Logan returned to Anchorage and began practicing law, his parents' subtle suggestions to settle down and raise a family became a featured course at every family dinner when they retired. Logan would always respond simply, "I'm looking for that but just haven't found the right woman."

"I've heard your chances of finding the right woman are increased," his mother said pointedly, "if your dates aren't snagged on your way out of the bars on your way home."

He arrived at Café Cups thirty minutes early and sat at the bar. The place was eclectic with a diverse menu that included the best seafood in Homer. As Lacey entered, he was surprised to see her in a short emerald-green silk skirt, sleeveless black sweater, black sheer nylons, and heels. He couldn't remember the last time he'd seen Lacey in makeup. He was flattered and pleased by her efforts, but self-conscious in his jeans and flannel shirt.

Wow! He told Lacey how beautiful she looked and awkwardly admitted feeling like a pair of dirty brown shoes. She shyly ducked her head, so Logan missed her smile. *Mission accomplished.* They both froze for a moment before Logan plunged in.

"Gotta say, it's gonna be hard to give bad news to such a stunning beauty."

"Uh-oh, you're buttering me up. The news must be really bad."

"It is, actually. I hardly know where to start."

The hostess took them to a quiet table in the corner. A candle set the mood—whether for romance or a funeral, it was too soon to predict. They ordered seafood and Logan chose a bottle of wine. The server filled their glasses and Logan hesitated; just like at the jail, he found it suddenly hard to breathe. *How best to say this?*

Lacey observed his uneasiness and raised her glass with a smile. "How about you start with Pete, and finish with how this will *not* affect my vacation."

They clinked glasses and Logan fortified himself with a long sip. With her calm, cheerful attitude, clearly Lacey knew how Logan felt and was doing her damnedest to lift his spirits. It was sweet. And effective. *Nothing to do now but tell her the hard truth.*

"Pete's been charged with the first-degree murder of Bill Hamlin in Anchorage."

"Oh m'God! Who's Bill Hamlin?"

She leaned forward attentively as Logan summarized the facts, charges, and history of the case.

"So, where's Pete now? What's next? What are you guys gonna do?"

"Pete's still in the Seattle jail. They'll probably extradite him to Anchorage this coming weekend. He asked me to represent him, and we're going to try to get him out on bail as soon as possible. What do you think his chances are?"

"Not good. Don't often see bail in a capital murder case. Since Pete has money, he could disappear to a country that doesn't have an extradition treaty with the US. It would be virtually impossible to find and return him to Alaska," Lacey concluded.

Logan anticipated that response. "We have to try."

"*We?* You gotta frog in your pocket? Are you forgetting about my vacation plans, my law office, my fishing, and *my* time constraints?"

Logan smiled benignly and trotted out the upside. "This is a golden opportunity for you. In exchange for your help, you may never have to pay rent again."

"I'd have to get that in writing."

They sat back in their chairs, thoughtfully sipped wine, and carefully avoided one another's eyes. The uneasy silence ended with the arrival of their food. Logan's wild Alaska king salmon was grilled to perfection, as were Lacey's seared halibut cheeks. They toasted the sumptuous seafood, but their candlelit, romantic dinner dissolved into a business mediation.

"I need this vacation," Lacey implored. "I don't mean to whine, but I'll be better rested and refreshed, not fatigued and falling asleep at trial."

Logan acquiesced. "All right. Go to Hawaii, get tan, swill mimosas. I'll even deliver you to the airport. But before you leave, we'll drive to Anchorage and do the bail review hearing. If we get Pete outta jail, he and I will work the case, and I'll watch over your practice until you get back. Then we'll unleash three rested legal minds with the support of your office staff."

Lacey stalled, swirling the wine in her glass, before she nodded. "Okay, I'm in . . . however, it takes more than free rent to pay my staff and personal bills."

"I understand."

Logan thumbed through his calendar. "Okay . . . this is Sunday. You fly out a week from tomorrow. With any luck, Pete's hearing will be that morning and he'll be out the same day. Then I can be at your office taking care of business before you're smearing on suntan lotion at the beach."

"Perfect. Let's go up to Anchorage on Saturday and see Pete when he gets in."

They strolled back toward Lacey's office and his parked car. Logan shook his head in awe by a surge of confusing emotions. *God, she's beautiful*, he thought. Maybe it was the wine, or perhaps the turmoil surrounding Pete. He didn't know or care to parse his feelings. Instead, he moved forward to kiss Lacey.

Ah, damn . . . nothing worse than a "just friends" kiss on the cheek.

"Hey, I wanted to thank you for helping with the case. No romance intended."

"Right . . . and I have some waterfront property on the Bering Sea to sell ya."

CHAPTER

12

A FTER A SHARED BREAKFAST aboard the sailboat with Mike, Sasha, and Toby, Logan went fishing, but after three hours, there were no derby tags nor jumbo halibut in sight. Lacey's paralegal, Pam, had prepared documents for the Anchorage Superior Court for the bail review hearing and scheduled the hearing for the following Monday, June 7, at 9 a.m.

Daily check-ins with Erika and the Seattle prosecutor assured Logan the schedules were on track. Logan struggled maintaining a strictly professional relationship with Lacey. Working closely together made it impossible to ignore their chemistry. He invited her to dinner for Friday night.

Logan decided to pull out all the stops and reserved a table at the west end of the Chart Room, a restaurant set on one of the most breathtaking waterfront locations in Alaska. It's part of the renowned Land's End Resort located at the tip of the Homer Spit and has the enchantment of a faraway island surrounded by water reflecting blazing sunsets. Weatherworn as a beached shipwreck, the restaurant boasts a panoramic view of nearly two hundred degrees, encompassing the Mt. St. Augustine volcano, the ever-spewing Mt. Iliamna, and the Mt. Redoubt. These three massive sentinels, all very much alive, are an imposing foreground to the majestic Alaska Mountain Range.

Once again, Lacey dressed to kill. And nailed it. Her charcoal cashmere sweater was tucked into a high-waisted black pencil skirt. Sheer black stockings peeked seductively from the thigh-high slit—and the boots she wore to combat the cold night air. Logan chuckled. *Only Lacey could make her tiny, size 6, fur-lined Doc Martens an alluring fashion statement.* Shoes, boots, it didn't matter. Lacey had great legs and tonight, they were more was on display than he'd ever seen outside the bedroom.

Conversation began with the timing for their drive to Anchorage the next morning. With the itinerary settled, they silently absorbed the view, keenly aware of their smoldering attraction for each other. The evening sun performed its magic—a brilliant spectrum of red and tangerine-orange flames over Kachemak Bay. They watched as the sun began to glisten against the snowcapped peaks. Logan's hand reached across the table and Lacey smiled, taking his hand into hers.

"Lace, I have a confession to make," Logan admitted. "I'm having the damnedest time keeping my distance and maintaining a professional relationship with you."

"Why?"

He wanted a response, not another question. "Umm...I don't know, I just am."

"So...what do you want to do about it?"

"Honestly? I want to grab you, hug you, squeeze you and kiss you, and return to a professional relationship only when absolutely necessary."

"And you think we can do that...again?"

"That's the question."

"As I recall, the last time we tried, you vanished. Almost in the middle of the night. Are you thinking this summer will be different?"

He knew he was listening to her heart speak. She had his full attention.

"You know, Logan...for me, sex and intimacy are two sides of the same coin. When you left, I felt blindsided." She shook her head emphatically. "I won't relive that. So, let's not pretend we're going to be together. I used to dream of that, us married and happy. I imagined a life waking up every day with you here in Homer. I loved you so much...all winter long."

Logan considered four possible responses. He could whine and beg. He could assure her it would be different this time without giving specifics. He could ply her with alcohol...or he could respect her feelings. For the first time in his life, he made the *good guy* decision, but disappointment tinged his response.

"I hear you. And I respect that. I won't make promises I can't keep, but most importantly, Lace, I don't want to hurt you again."

Logan surprised himself; he meant every word. As he vividly recalled their passionate intimacy, his faced flushed. Lacey stared at him in disbelief, temporarily speechless. As so often happens, timing is everything, and the waiter chose that moment to approach their table. Logan ordered two more glasses of wine.

Lacey accidentally gulped her wine, nearly choking. "So...Logan." She smiled. "I wasn't expecting such a sensitive reply. We do have magic. But reality eventually creeps in." Wistfully, Lacey toyed with the stem of her wine glass. "The magic of what-ifs create a wondrous carpet ride, but I no longer believe that happily ever after will happen for us."

"Nothing good can happen unless you first believe in it," Logan suggested hopefully.

Potential responses swirled in Lacey's head, and then distilled: "Yeah, yeah, yeah."

They ate and drank while enjoying the glowing aftermath of the sunset until it was suddenly closing time. They left the restaurant and walked to Lacey's car. She paused. "So...see you in the morning."

"Sure." Logan smiled. *Not the ending he'd hoped for.*

CHAPTER
13

L OGAN HOPED LACEY WOULD SUGGEST sharing the suite on the first floor as they checked into the Captain Cook hotel in downtown Anchorage. No deal. So, he walked her to the elevator where she kissed him on the cheek. He retreated to his suite overlooking the street. Lacey understood Logan's need for first-floor lodgings. In Logan's mind, an earthquake was always just minutes away. Just thinking about being off the ground in Anchorage made him shake with fear.

An hour later, they met in the lobby before driving to the jail. Pete appeared unshackled and still sporting an orange jumpsuit as he walked through a steel security door. He was clean-shaven and his hair was combed. *He looks better than at our last meeting*, Logan observed. Pete sat down on a cold metal chair at the table.

"Great to see you, Pete," Logan greeted.

Lacey deceptively appeared unfazed by Pete's appearance. "You look really good," Lacey volunteered. "Haven't seen you in a few years, but Logan's definitely gonna get you outta here."

Logan took her cue and lightly responded, "Thanks, Lacey. All I need is a little more pressure." He handed Pete a memo and affidavit requiring his signature. Pete smiled and his face brightened as he read through the documents. "Reading this, I'm beginning to believe I have a realistic hope of getting out of jail."

The conversation digressed into familiar, safer talk. They reminisced about the softball and football teams they played for during their early years in Alaska. Pete was animated. Lacey enjoyed the comradery. At times she covered her ears while yelling, "T-M-I." Pete's face fell when the guard announced their time was up. "We'll see you bright and early Monday morning, then," Logan offered.

"Unless you want us to come back tomorrow?" Lacey added.

"No. No, I'll be fine. I feel better than I have in quite a while. Getting out of here would be incredible, though."

As they left the jail, Lacey cheerfully told Logan that she'd made reservations at the Crow's Nest Restaurant on the fourteenth floor of their hotel. Logan confessed, "Visiting jail is stressful, but, Lace, going up to that restaurant scares me to death."

"I worried about that," she said while patting his arm. "Let's cancel if it's just too much." Then she teased, "But really, what are the chances of an earthquake happening in the next hour?"

"Oh, about the same as Good Friday in 1964," Logan groaned.

Logan recalled that the Finch home didn't shake or lurch. It roiled. The earth beneath their home fractured into bottomless fissures as landslides triggered a liquefaction process that converted the ground into a fluidlike mass. In less than four minutes, their beautiful neighborhood became a treacherous field of quicksand that was later renamed Earthquake Park.

His mother instinctively pushed him out the front door and they ran toward the city. They fled for their lives over the buckling landscape until they reached solid ground a hundred yards away. They turned and looked back to see their three-bedroom rambler disappear into a crevasse of mud. Everything they owned was gone.

Logan and Lacey shared their first free day since Logan's return to Alaska. They drove along Turnagain Arm to the ski resort in Girdwood. The relatively new Alyeska Resort included a four-star hotel. They rode the tram to the top of the mountain and to the Seven Glaciers Restaurant. Logan wasn't afraid of heights so long as he was not enclosed in a building. The restaurant was perched twenty-three hundred feet above sea level on Mount Alyeska. After the tram ride, they strolled along the restaurant's gold carpet, past a glass-and-steel wine-tower wall, and into the dining room that radiated an optical phenomenon called alpenglow. They looked down at a brown bear with her cubs and a Dall sheep perched precariously on the upper hillside—the term *hillside* being relative. A hillside in Alaska would be a mountain anywhere else but in Tibet.

Glaciers surrounded the restaurant and Turnagain Arm. The body of water and mudflats below were beautiful and unique, foreboding, and dangerous, yet deceivingly tranquil. When the tide returned to the inlet, inexperienced or inebriated hooligan fishermen were sometimes stuck in the mud and then gone forever. Family dogs rode the small icebergs out to sea in the spring.

Lacey took in the view. "This is the reason I stay in Alaska...days like these and scenery like this. The serenity of it all brings tears to my eyes. It's truly an existential experience." Then she repeated the adage, smiling at Logan, "If you can just get here from Anchorage."

Logan was swept away by Lacey's spirit. They ordered crab cocktails and a bottle of wine. While savoring the view, Logan fidgeted uncomfortably before he finally spit it out. "Can we talk about us again?"

"You know, I love you to death, but you'll sprint back to Arizona when fishing's over or the gavel ends the trial. Then I'll be left with a huge hole in my heart. Again. You get that, right?"

"I love you too. More than ever. But, yeah, I get it. So," he lightheartedly inquired, "how about I order us another bottle of wine?"

Lacey mustered a forced half laugh. They toasted yet again, but Logan knew there would be no second bottle of wine. He'd give anything if they had a future together. But she was spot on. He would return to Arizona at the end of the summer to care for and attend to his parents' needs, to teach at the law school, and to avoid earthquakes, and she would remain in Homer.

Lacey stared at the table as she started to speak. "I once thought there was *us*. But you really set me straight." She looked directly at Logan; her resolve on that subject was clearly nonnegotiable. "It's much safer—and better for me—if we don't think or talk in terms of *us* anymore. I don't want to go from *us* to you in Arizona and me in Homer. I thought you understood."

"No, you're right. I get it. I do."

"It doesn't seem like you do." Their eyes met. "There won't be a *seasonal us* ever again." It was a silent drive back to Anchorage.

CHAPTER
14

T HE PAINFULLY YOUNG PROSECUTOR Beth Brummett asked if the judge would recuse himself, given his preexisting familiarity with Pete and his counsel. An animated Judge John Sumner harrumphed, "If I recused myself from every case where I knew a litigant or an attorney, I would hear precious few cases. No social relationships exist, now or ever, with either of these attorneys. So, Counselor, I will *not* consider recusing myself. Should you file a formal motion to recuse me, I'll deny the request." Peering down at her over his glasses, he declared, "Then you may take it up on appeal."

Judges were randomly assigned cases, and Pete and Logan could not have hoped for a more thorough and experienced judicial umpire than Judge Sumner. The judge's comment was a dare the prosecutor best not take. Filing such a motion had many risks. If Brummett lost on appeal, Sumner would remain the trial judge with his professional ire potentially influencing the outcome of the game. *Nope,* Logan thought and smiled, *there would be no formal appeal from the prosecutor's office.* Logan sent a slight nod in Pete's direction.

Logan stood and approached the bench. His dark-blue pinstripe suit, crisp white shirt, and burgundy paisley tie reflected total confidence. Logan stopped about halfway, adroitly seizing control of the courtroom. "Even though this is a capital case," he began, then turned and pointed to Pete, "my client retains substantial ties to this community." *Yeah,* thought Logan. *So familiar, done so many times before. Press the home court advantage.*

"Your Honor, Mr. Foster owns an office and land here, and is still a licensed attorney in the state of Alaska. Until now, he has never been charged with a crime." He turned toward the judge. "The court should note that sixteen years have expired since the alleged crime occurred. This is a totally circumstantial case. There will be no eyewitnesses testifying, no DNA test results tying my client to the crime, and the prosecution has only a partial skeleton found on the five-acre parcel of property my client has not owned in fifteen years."

Logan pointed to the Alaska state flag displayed to the left of the judge. "The Alaska Constitution states that an accused is entitled to be released on bail when the proof is not evident or the presumption is not great. In this case, neither the proof is evident nor the presumption great."

Logan knew Alaskans and the courts took great pride in enforcing the differences between their constitution and that of the United States. More individual freedoms were granted in his state's constitution. Logan knew that the judge, also born and raised in Alaska, knew that and relished every opportunity to recognize those distinctions.

Ms. Brummett was not from Alaska and failed to grasp the significance of Logan's reference to the Alaska Constitution. She argued, "A capital case is different. The defendant no longer resides in Alaska and no longer has significant ties to the community. He should not be released for any amount of bail. That will guarantee he cannot flee. The forensic evidence establishes that a murder occurred. The defendant had reason to kill the victim, and the victim's remains were buried on the defendant's property. The motive and opportunity are clear, Your Honor."

Judge Sumner leaned back. "We'll take a five-minute break, and I'll be back with my ruling. There was an audible sigh in the courtroom.

Pete leaned toward Logan. "What do ya think?"

"I think we're okay. The prosecutor may have made a mistake sending a rookie attorney to argue such a crucial motion. That may have insulted the judge. In any event, when the big government guns don't show up, it gives the judge more leeway to rule in our favor. It's just common sense, and Sumner knows this will not be appealed."

Lacey chimed in, "I think Logan's right. I now give us a fifty-fifty chance of getting you out on bail."

Judge Sumner returned to the bench and leaned forward. "I've read your briefs and I've heard and considered your arguments. All are persuasive. However, I am not convinced the proof is evident or the presumption great that the defendant committed this crime or any crime at all. I am strongly inclined to do what I believe best protects the public and will guarantee the presence of the defendant in court. I am not persuaded Mr. Foster is a significant flight risk, but I cannot predict the future."

Logan and Pete's eyes met, and Logan winked.

"Therefore, I believe a one-million-dollar bail bond, with collateral, is appropriate under the circumstances. Again, either party is free to take this matter up to the appellate court." Sumner peered over his gold reading glasses at the prosecutor again. "The trial will begin Monday, July 19, unless there is an objection or other concern. This date is set in stone and there will be no further delays or continuances except for a good cause. A darn good cause."

Once again, Logan knew an appeal would result in pissing off the judge, the last thing Brummett would want. The decision was a good one for Pete, and he had the necessary collateral to finance the bail.

"Mr. Foster, you must relinquish your passport by 6:00 p.m. tomorrow, either here in Anchorage or at the Homer PD. You must also remain within the Third Judicial District of Alaska until further order." Sumner banged the gavel. "This court is adjourned." Logan flashed a big thumbs-up to Pete who kept smiling broadly as the bailiff ushered him out of the courtroom and back to a holding cell.

Lacey was in the hallway conferring with Fred Hett the bail bondsman. She had called Fred Sunday night and had him contact a few corporate sureties trying to get the bond in place. He was told it would take a couple of weeks. In a panic, Erika called their old family friends, Perry and Gloria Green in Anchorage, who graciously agreed to post the cash bond after getting secured by a deed of trust and promissory note on the home Arrowhead Point home. Erika had already signed the legal documents and was overnighting them to the Greens as they spoke. The Greens refused to charge anything, not even interest on the cash loan.

"Besides being the most upstanding furrier family in all of Alaska, the Greens take care of their friends," Fred said. "Of course, Perry probably won enough off Pete in poker games over the years to break even on this deal."

Logan was thrilled that Fred still haunted Alaska's courthouses. This old workhorse had been a fixture in the court system for the last fifty-five years. Decades ago, Fred married a stripper, Miss Wiggles, on the condition she give up strip teasing. She said yes, so long as Fred gave up his weekend drinking at the strip clubs.

Fred remembered Logan. Years earlier, they'd shared late-evening drinks while watching Miss Wiggles wiggle. Their camaraderie also put Logan on Fred's preferred attorney referral list.

"I suspect Pete will be out of the slammer by late this afternoon," Fred said with a smile.

"Good. I mean, great. Thanks, Fred. Seems I've been saying that to you forever."

Fred nodded and disappeared back into the courtroom. Logan and Lacey exited the courthouse. An *Anchorage Daily News* photographer documented their departure by taking some photographs. "I hope you don't mind that I called Fred last night. I worked with him most of last year on two of my criminal trials," Lacey explained. "He'll return my calls anytime, day or night. He called Erika earlier this morning."

"It's all good, and thanks. Less for me to worry about." Logan smiled. "Are you ready to go to the airport?"

"Yeah, let's get going." Lacey made no attempt to conceal her excitement for her upcoming Hawaiian getaway.

"Aww, I thought you might change your mind. It's gonna be more fun here than in predictably boring Hawaii," Logan teased.

"Yeah, right. I'll miss you and all the action," Lacey mocked, then winked, "but take me to the airport anyway, and congratulations on the successful bail review hearing."

They tried to keep the conversation light en route to the airport. Logan was feeling a profound sense of loss. When Lacey turned and wheeled her carry-on through the security checkpoint, he realized how much he'd come to rely on her during the last few weeks. *Damn, her plane hasn't even left the tarmac and I already miss her!* Now that his oldest friend was leaning so hard on him for support, he wanted to lean on her.

CHAPTER

15

CARTER DROLLY ANSWERED Logan's call. "Mr. Finch, I presume. You may be happy to know I've acquired clippings from the *Anchorage Daily News* archives—and at no cost, I might add. There's a short column covering Hamlin's disappearance, and recent headline stories featuring the discovery of his skull and a few about Pete's arrest. I may acquire others, as I still have feelers out at the APD and with some *Daily News* people."

"Great. I can either come by your office or meet you at the bar of your choice."

"Darwin's," Carter enthused. "See you in ten minutes," and he hung up.

Darwin's, a.k.a. Darwin's Theory, was a hole in the wall on Fifth Avenue that had been there forever. Specialties remained canned beer and popcorn. A glossy ad in the Alaska Airlines in-flight magazine strongly suggested it was an upscale place. No, not true. Never was true. If you wanted to relive the crazed old oil pipeline days, Darwin's was the place to do it.

Carter excelled at draping his behind on a Darwin's barstool, which was where Logan found him. *His* stool didn't have his name on it but should have. Logan found Carter perched like an ageless gnome. Light blue eyes peered from behind a thick, red thatch of hair. Those eyes missed nothing, not even when Carter's reddish-gray beard grazed the froth in his stein of Guinness. Logan settled onto the next stool. "Thirty years later and it's still the same," he observed.

Carter tipped his head to the side and casually surveyed the bar's seedy interior. When that same scene was photographed for the website, patrons half-jokingly hid behind menus to dodge being identified or associated with the place. A brown manila envelope lay next to Carter's frosty stein. He quaffed his beer before sliding the envelope toward Logan. Patting it with his left hand, he whispered conspiratorially, "Review this in private."

They talked about changes in Anchorage and the meager information regarding Pete's case. Logan took a call from Fred who advised that Pete was being released in a half hour.

"Ya know, Perry Green posted Pete's bail," Logan said.

"Small world. I'm playing poker with Perry tomorrow night. Do you have time to join us?"

"Great, another fine opportunity to augment the millions I've donated to his grandchildren's college fund over the years!"

"Ah, c'mon, he usually just gives the money back to us at the end of the night."

"And that's damn embarrassing too! But I've got to take a rain check on this one, Jim, at least until the trial's over in July."

Logan was sorry to miss getting together with Perry and his family, as every gathering where Perry was present was a special occasion for sure. Perry Green won three World Series of Poker bracelets, and twice made it to the final table of the World Series of Poker Main Event. One of Alaska's last living pioneer celebrities, the infamous Perry Green was friends with everyone in Anchorage, including Jim and Pete.

The Green family history began back in New York, where Perry's grandparents were furriers. Perry's father was the youngest of five boys, and after reading Jack London's *The Call of the Wild*, his dad boarded a tramp steamer bound for Seattle and Alaska in 1922. He established his family in Seattle and created a world-renowned furrier business converting Alaskan pelts into fur coats. In 1936, Perry was born, the youngest and undisputedly most precocious of two siblings. He terrorized three high schools in Seattle before joining the military in 1954, where he found himself stationed at Fort Richardson in Anchorage.

In the retelling, Perry's adventures became and continue to be the stuff of legendary folklore. He traversed thousands of miles in merciless arctic weather to bush communities from Nome to Juneau, purchasing furs for the family business. He described narrowly surviving three plane crashes, and when socked in because of bad weather, Perry boasted that he made more money playing poker with the Indians and Eskimos than he did trading furs.

Despite a life of adventurous shenanigans, however, Perry took no chances when it came to love. He married his childhood sweetheart, Gloria, in 1956, with whom he had three beautiful daughters and two handsome sons.

It was always great talking with Jim, and Logan promised, "I'll get in touch with you at the end of the trial."

"Ah, you won't have to wait that long," Jim promised. "I'll be there watching your closing argument—but remember, if Perry could place a bet on it, he'd bet on a directed verdict of acquittal. And you know he'd win!"

Logan laughed, appreciating the vote of confidence, and finished the conversation. "I'll keep that in mind, Jim. An acquittal of any kind would be wonderful news for Pete."

Carter, Logan reflected, *is just beginning an evening at Darwin's. He's gonna outstay me. Besides, I gotta go, and he'd be holding court much longer than I would be able to attend.*

Logan effusively thanked Carter for his help and went to pay the tab. He watched Carter strike up a conversation with some sourdoughs. *Lucky folks*, Logan thought. Carter was a master raconteur with an endless stockpile of great stories. All were true, except some just hadn't happened—yet.

Logan was at the jail waiting in a cramped lobby. He greeted Pete, "Hey, guy, how you doing?" Pete's attire reminded Logan that he'd forgotten to bring clothing for him.

"Probably better when I get some warm clothes," Pete sniped irritably. He was wearing the moccasins and the T-shirt and sweats he wore when he was arrested. Logan dropped him off at J. C. Penney, gave him a couple hundred bucks, and then drove over to the prosecuting attorney's office to pick up discovery documents. He then circled back for Pete, who was now wearing a warm coat and clutching a crammed-full J. C. Penney bag. They parked in the garage at their hotel as Pete's sullen moodiness evaporated, thanks to the warm clothes and the restoration of his privacy and freedom.

Anxious to take a long shower, Pete said he'd rejoin Logan later in Fletcher's, the bar honoring Fletcher Christian of mutiny on the *Bounty* fame. The bar was a favorite of both Pete and Logan. A restorative nap lured Logan but first he called Lacey. "Hi, sweetie," Lacey softly answered. "How are you?"

"Great." Logan sighed. "I just checked Pete into the hotel with me. We'll drive down to Homer in the morning; Erika gets in tomorrow night. But, hey, enough about all the excitement here. How was your trip? It sounds like you're in a car. Where are you?"

"The flight was fine. And, yeah, I'm driving out to Maili. Thought I'd get a few groceries on my way to the cove, and I wanna get there before dark. The last time I stopped at a 7-Eleven in Maili, some Hawaiian boys snuffed their cigarettes on the hood of my rental car...evidently a very subtle secret code for: *We don't like haoles.*"

"Your red hair probably doesn't blend in a lot either, huh? Is it a gated community?"

"Everywhere but the beach. That's open to everyone, so I stay off it at night."

"Good girl."

"I'm still shocked the judge granted Pete bail. During the flight down here, I thought a lot about the case. I know you can't fathom Pete committing murder, but I think we should consider that possibility. If we don't, a conviction would be a horrible blow to all of us. And to you, most of all."

Logan knew he needed to consider that Pete might have committed the crime—in part to prepare his defense and, as Lacey suggested, to know how to respond if it was true. It's what he'd have to do as an attorney, yet every fiber of his being recoiled.

"I hear what you're saying. It's just that I've known Pete forever and he simply didn't commit this murder."

"Are you upset that I mentioned it?"

"Of course not. You want to protect me and help Pete. Can't be angry about that." Logan yawned. "Sorry, I'd love to keep talking, Lace, but I've just got to get a nap in before dinner. Okay if I call you in the morning?"

"I'm counting on it. I never thought this vacation could be lonely, but...I may be wrong."

"Hey, I'll call you every day if it'll help."

"Promise?"

"I promise." Logan's heart warmed. "Goodbye, sweetie," he said without thinking.

"Bye."

Logan couldn't nap. He knew from experience that an innocent man has a burning sense of injustice in his eyes. *Pete didn't emote an innocent man's outrage. Why? What was he hiding?* Logan had seen *the look* many times in his career. Instinctively, he probably worked a case a lot harder when he saw it. Jurors, he believed, could see that *look* unless they were blinded by prejudice. If a criminal client doesn't have *the look*, you can't risk putting them on the witness stand. You resort to training a client to appear neutral with a not-guilty demeanor at the defense table. You instruct them not to make eye contact with jurors. Even actress extraordinaire Meryl Streep couldn't mimic *the look* of innocence if she were guilty.

Damn, Pete just didn't have the look.

Fletchers was already popping when Pete and Logan arrived. They studied the menus and looked around. Unlike the Lower 48, Anchorage bars still hummed with office staff after work. Workers and bosses generally indulged at a watering hole before going home to kids and overwhelmed spouses. Logan ordered his dinner and then announced, "You've enjoyed your last stint as food tester for the government, I'm afraid."

"Mr. Finch, you sound mighty confident." Pete smiled. "Here's hoping those old instincts are alive 'n' well."

They planned the next morning's drive to Homer. "I like the idea of using Lacey's office to prepare for trial," Pete declared. "We can avoid the press and use her staff. Do Pam and Katie still work with Lacey?"

"Yeah, but only part-time, so we'll see how it goes." Logan elevated his eyebrows as he warned, "It'll cost you."

"No problem, whatever it takes. You know, it's all good with me. Are those two still easy on the eyes?"

"Oh, yeah," Logan confirmed.

Lacey's staffers, Pam and Katie, were vigorous, strong-willed, and smart. Both were in their early forties and pursued different paths to happiness.

"Pam," Logan elaborated, "is married with a couple of kids. She's a real mother hen and still the best-looking blonde in Homer."

"And Katie? She still sampling the field?"

"Yep, Katie's still gorgeous, and still happily single. I'm thinking I'd like to move this case forward as quickly as possible. You okay with that?" Logan asked.

"Sounds great."

"We've got a five-hour drive tomorrow. You'll have plenty of time to review the discovery documents." Pete nodded in agreement. They ended the night when Pete gave Logan an appreciative thump and muttered, "Thanks, buddy."

"**J**ESUS, WHAT'S ALL THIS?" Pete shouted at Logan as he handed him a banker's box of documents, then started driving the Seward Highway to Homer. Pete adjusted his seat back to review the reams of documents the prosecutor intended to use to get a first-degree murder conviction. Newspaper articles, still bundled in the manila envelope Carter had given to Logan, were on top of the files. Pete experienced a chilling *oh my God* moment as he read the first paper-clipped sheaf of papers.

Three hours later, as they passed Cooper Landing, Pete closed the file on his lap. He exhaled slowly and tilted his head back against the headrest. Logan glanced over at his weary friend. *Is Pete intimidated by the mountain of work ahead or overwhelmed by the mountain of evidence supporting the murder charge against him?*

"Sure you don't want to hire somebody younger, some rising-star attorney? For Chrissake, Pete, I haven't tried a major felony case in years."

"I'm sure."

"Pete, seriously, we need to think this through. You can afford a big law firm. Those guys can do research on every conceivable issue. They'll hire jury consultants, private investigators. They'll even hold mock jury trials."

"I know, but I want you. Matter closed."

Not to be deterred, Logan suggested, "Well...how about Bill Brison, remember him?"

"The six-foot-two, GQ-dressed Viking from Stanford Law School? That guy?"

Logan laughed. "Yeah...single, consummate babe magnet, and great trial attorney."

Pete interrupted. "Quit trying to get out of this. You're stuck with me and your minimum fee."

Logan persisted. "Still, Brison seems to be one of those rare guys who manages to weather the battles in criminal defense work without any ill effects."

"Yeah," Pete half-heartedly agreed. "Maybe."

Criminal trial attorneys crave the victorious highs generated by courtroom victories. Then, like finely tuned professional athletes, once the dust settles, depression kicks in. And the dust always settles. Logan quietly admitted, "Years ago, I wanted that life...I used to think I'd be that guy. Then I realized the price was just too high."

"I hear ya...your days are consumed by willing things to happen that the laws of nature dictate can't and won't happen. Then you're tossing and turning throughout the nights, second-guessing every legal strategic nuance, unable to unwind and let go," Pete recapped.

It was early afternoon as they crested the last hill that dropped them into Homer. The warm sun emphasized the rugged beauty of the Homer Spit as Logan drove by the Homer Police Department. "Is that where I surrender my passport?" Pete asked.

"Yeah, you can do it tomorrow, though. Just don't try flying to Morocco tonight. Why don't you bunk on *The Coral Dawn*?" Logan offered.

"Thanks, but no. You're already going above and beyond. I'll pay you back for my room when Erika gets here."

His response didn't surprise Logan. Pete had already refused Lacey's offer for him to stay in her house while she was in Hawaii. Pete never wanted to be a nuisance to anyone.

Their next stop was the Land's End Resort at the end of the spit. The J. C. Penney bag containing Pete's scanty wardrobe rustled softly as he walked into the hotel to check in to the room Logan had reserved for him for the next thirty days. He winced at the price, but since Homer was on the cusp of the summer tourist season, he was relieved Logan had found lodgings, period.

"Want to go to the office and work, or shall we put a lid on it today and go find a drink?" Logan asked.

"I never turn down a drink, but if you don't mind, I'd like to get some work done before Erika gets here. Then we can have a drink with her. She'd like that."

"Like it?" Logan snorted. "Hell, Pete, she'll need it."

CHAPTER
17

THEY ARRIVED AT LACEY'S OFFICE to a joyful homecoming. Pam and Katie hugged them exuberantly before they congregated in the ubiquitous war room. Sitting around the conference table, they listened intently to Logan's presentation of the case. They were concerned about Pete's predicament, but in the legal profession, a criminal murder case is the most exciting it ever gets. At the end of the informal briefing, Logan collected the files and newspaper articles and sat at the far end of the conference table, in front of a wall of law books. As they exited the room, he reminded Pam and Katie not to discuss the case with anyone. The women solemnly nodded.

Suddenly, Pam remembered the phone call she received shortly before Logan and Pete arrived. "Hey, some guy called about an hour ago and said you and Lacey better not get involved in the Foster case."

"Did you get a name and number?"

"No, but—and this is weird—he also said you're 'going against the will of God, my Lord and Savior.' And it was a blocked number." Pam's report instantly captured Logan's and Pete's attention, but they didn't want to appear alarmed.

"Thanks, Pam," Logan neutrally responded. "If it happens again, please try to get a name and number."

Pete gently closed the conference room door, raised his eyebrows inquisitively at Logan, and spat out, "What the hell?"

Logan nodded thoughtfully. "Yeah...remember when I represented Cinema I in Anchorage in the mid-eighties?"

"Hard to forget. You're talking about the porn shop and X-rated movie theater on Fourth Avenue. I vividly remember standing in the parking lot of our office building a couple of times due to bomb threats from the Evangelical church."

"Yeah. At least that's how they identified themselves. We never discovered exactly who made the calls."

"Think we're dealing with another nutcase?" Pete asked.

"Jesus, Pete, I hope not. Jansen and the Hamlins belonged to the same Evangelical church, but damn, that was a long time ago. We don't need any bomb threats."

"I don't know, Logan. Evangelical hypocrites have been around for hundreds of years."

They settled into the war room and began organizing materials as well as chronologically reviewing witness statements. Logan cataloged the reports while Pete matched them with photographs of the various scenes. There were ninety-three photos and multiple newspaper articles.

Pam stuck her head into the room. "Don't forget about Lacey's clients. You have two meetings tomorrow and there's paperwork to get out."

After Pete and Logan lunched at Café Cups, they returned to triplicate copies of the three-ring binders prepared by Pam. They dug in with their pens and highlighters while reading, marking, and analyzing every statement. They searched for mistakes, contradictions, misrepresentations, overstatements, or failures to follow up by the various investigative personnel. They found few errors. The entire case was based on circumstantial evidence. Would the evidence support proof of guilt beyond a reasonable doubt?

"I've had far more difficult criminal cases in my lifetime," Logan quietly opined.

"Good to know." Pete grimaced as he tossed a binder aside.

CHAPTER
18

I T WAS DARK WHEN Pam went home to her husband and Katie popped into her favorite cocktail lounge for dinner, drinks, and indulging her favorite hobby: enticing handsome Alaskan men. Her skills were exceptional.

"Erika just texted; she's in Anchorage. She'll be on the eight o'clock flight...*if* they can get all her luggage on the plane."

"Oh, right, I'd forgotten. Erika's bringing clothes to last you two for a month or more. I think we should take two cars to the airport—we may need them to haul all the luggage, and then you'll have Lacey's car to drive."

"Or I should just rent a U-Haul pickup," Pete joked.

From the Spit Road, Logan spotted the small commuter plane as it dropped down over the hillside and approached the runway. "Might be my imagination but looks like the tail's dragging a bit more than usual. Could it be due to the luggage situation?" Logan's lower back tightened up. Pete shrugged.

In most Alaskan bush towns, airport terminals had small one-room buildings with an empty cow-feeding trough installed through an opening on the side of the structure nearest the dirt runway. Arriving passengers immediately went inside the building to stay warm. The pilot or a maintenance man, barely visible through the hole in the wall, slung the luggage into the trough. The mystery of how luggage was delivered was partially preserved by black carwash-like baffles hanging down over the hole. Homer was more upscale. Luggage magically appeared in a stainless-steel trough and you never saw the delivery person.

Just feet from the still-spinning, right-wing propeller, Pete was already hugging and kissing Erika. Logan rushed into the building to escape the night chill. *There it was.* He spied...five hundred pounds of Erika's absolute essentials. Four huge bags were wedged into Lacey's car. Her fifty-pound carry-on and a purse large enough to transport rations for a dogsled team were shoved into Logan's blue Bug. Logan's back spasmed in protest, but he persevered and clung to the promise of cocktails. The luggage was successfully stashed, and there was jubilance at being together. They caravanned back to Land's End.

Pete and Erika were steering two luggage carts to their room when Logan volunteered to order drinks for everyone. His primary motive was to avoid the luggage wrangling to their room. No objections were heard. Minutes later, Erika was sipping chardonnay, her safe arrival repeatedly toasted as she savored grilled salmon and asparagus. Pete festively kept their glasses filled until the bar closed. Despite the long trip, Erika embodied Alaskan panache dressed in dark blue jeans, a black turtleneck sweater, and a faux chinchilla fur-lined vest. She snuggled up to Pete who regaled them with tales of ridiculous jail conditions inflicted on the *presumed* innocent.

Suddenly, Pete was quietly serious. "I would never have killed Hamlin. Sure, I slugged the son of a bitch. And I never forgave him, not for an instant. But that punch took the sails out of any need for retribution. Since then, my thoughts are only of Emma. Anger won't bring her back." Tears welled up as he struggled with his grief; Erika's eyes glistened with tears as she squeezed his hand.

"I know," Logan assured him. "If you're a murderer, then I'm Snow White, and I don't see any dwarfs around here. You couldn't murder anyone under any circumstances. We'll make certain you're never punished for something you didn't do."

"Emma's life and her disappearance seem like an old movie I watched years ago," Erika shared. "Bringing it all back is such heartache, and I can't believe it's consuming our lives again. Far as I'm concerned, Hamlin deserved to die."

Logan gave Pete and Erika the next day off so he could meet with Lacey's clients. If the weather held, Pete and Erika planned to boat across the bay to Halibut Cove for lunch. Back aboard *The Coral Dawn*, Logan called Lacey, grateful that Hawaii shared nearly the same time zone as Homer.

"Hey," she whispered. "What's going on, stranger?" Lacey's voice triggered a longing to be with her.

"I just left Pete and Erika at Land's End. They're doing well."

"Great! So, what's new at the office?"

"Nada...I'm just reviewing bales of documents. Oh, wait...this is kind of interesting. Pam answered a call today from some guy warning us to steer clear of Pete's case. He invoked the name of God."

"What! I'm trying to sleep. Thanks for sharing! Any direct threats?"

"No direct threats. I'm sure it's nothing to worry about, so let's change the subject. How's the weather been?"

"The weather's great. It's always great."

"I'm missing you, Lace."

"There you go, messing with my heart, and turning my life upside-down crazy again...and, yes, dammit, I'm missing you too."

"Good, right answer. Now, you get back to sleep. I'll call tomorrow. Enjoy the sunbathing, and leave some tan lines up top, okay?"

She ignored his flirting. "Good night, Logan."

CHAPTER
19

A<small>T SEVEN</small>, L<small>OGAN HEARD</small> S<small>ASHA AND</small> T<small>OBY</small> make their morning
jaunt to the pee-mail corner. Toby strode up the dock with the
ardent passion of a New World explorer, and his twitching nose guided a
thorough inspection of every signpost, fire hydrant, and shard of scraggly
grass embellishing the telephone pole at the end of the spit. The only way
Sasha ever reeled her four-legged adventurer back to the boat was with the
promise of breakfast. Logan smiled to himself as he decided to help her
out and added two more strips of bacon in the frying pan and slid the
window open. Toby spotted him immediately, crouched, and enthusiastically jumped across the water into Logan's waiting arms. *Thank God he's
dry.*

He'd always wanted a Toby in his life, but his travel and work didn't
permit him to do a dog justice. So, the little dog and his unconstrained
greetings—the quintessential "welcome home"—embodied Logan's
attachment to Homer. "Morning, Mike, Sasha," Logan yelled, louder than
intended.

Startled, they mimicked back, "GOOD MORNING, LOGAN!"

"Okay, sorry, got a little carried away." They laughed. "I'm going to
Lacey's office, so unless Toby has secret legal skills, I guess you'll have to
take him back."

"What you do is called work?" Mike irreverently gibed.

"Hey!" Logan feigned hurt feelings.

Mike was unrelenting. "Since when?"

Logan's lower back pain, mindful of the twinging from manhandling
Erika's luggage around the night before, prompted his response. "At my
advanced age, it can be work just getting out of bed."

More shared laughter. *Even with a sore back, I'm quite the humorist,*
Logan thought.

Logan was intrigued by the scent of perfume preceding the first new client Katie shepherded into his office.

The young lady nervously ran her hand through the silky black hair falling in a shining sheet past her shoulders as she pushed it away from her olive-skinned face. Delores Anne Rodriguez introduced herself in one syllable. "I'm DahlorahzaneRudreeguz. I was charged with driving while intoxicated," she softly stated. "I think the officer said something about eluding arrest too."

She was extremely distraught after spending the night in the Homer Community Jail and relieved to confide in someone. Legal pad in hand, Logan helpfully pushed the Kleenex box toward her before asking, "What happened?"

"I was living in an apartment just down the street until last month. I wasn't working, but all of my expenses were being paid by my friend."

"And what is his or her name?" Logan quickly scribbled notes.

"I'd rather not say, but the son of a bitch—sorry for my French—well, he dumped me for a nurse and terminated my apartment rental agreement. I didn't have any money, so I lived out of my car for two weeks before I found a job and rented another apartment." Her tears were now free flowing. "But I missed work yesterday and got fired this morning," she sobbed.

"Tell me about the arrest."

"Well, Ben—I love Ben, he's really a great guy." Her sobs escalated. "I miss him every second of every day. Ya know what it feels like, getting dumped for another woman by the man you love?" She then leaned forward, focusing her mascara-smudged eyes on Logan's. "I mean, *really* love?"

Logan averted his eyes from her ample cleavage and started to confess ignorance, but she continued. "It sucks. It really sucks. Big time." Logan pushed the tissue box even closer to her, but she opted for the back of her hand. "So, after work, I bought a bottle of vodka." She paused, closing her eyes momentarily at having to relive the events leading to her arrest. "I drank half. I'm sorry, but anybody else would have drunk the whole bottle," she defended belligerently.

"Anyway...so, you know, I started calling Ben, but the bastard wouldn't answer. I lost it. I grabbed the bottle, jumped in my car, and drove over to his house. He wasn't home, but the back door was open. I went in, and you wouldn't believe it! He had a fucking picture of his nurse next to his computer. Framed!

"Then, you know, cuz his computer was on, I saw their emails. Oh m'God, that killed me worse than the picture. But I saw she lived on East End Road too, so I decided to go talk to her in person. By then the vodka was gone, and I just left the bottle where it was...you know, next to his computer. So, I was driving through Homer, and I think I ran a couple of stop signs. It was just an accident, y'know?"

Logan nodded. *Yeah, accidents happen.*

"And on the East End Road, a state trooper turned on his lights." While circling her forefinger mimicking the siren and lights, she daubed the corners of her eyes with a tissue, then continued. "So, I hear this siren, but there's no place to pull over. So, you know, I had to stop in the middle of the road. I guess that's when I fell asleep. I think. Or passed out maybe. I can't remember."

Logan tried to visualize the scene. "Where were you when you woke up?"

"Parked in the middle of the same fucking road! And there the trooper was, standing next to my car, asking me to roll down my window. But I was too scared."

Logan nodded understandingly.

"So, I started driving down the road again about—she pointed to Café Cups down the street—as far as that restaurant and fell asleep again."

"Or passed out," Logan added, fascinated by the unfolding dynamics, and speculating about the trooper's thoughts. "What happened when you woke up the second time?"

"Same fucking—sorry for my French—thing! I was still in the middle of the road and, wud'ja believe it, there was the trooper again asking me to roll down my window. I rolled it down, but then I got scared and started to drive away again. Only that time, the trooper yanked open my car door and grabbed me by the arm."

Using his best poker face and keeping his stomach muscles tight to avoid unleashing a burst of laughter, Logan prodded, "And then what did you do?"

"I put on the brakes." She genteelly blotted black mascara smudges from her lower lids with another tissue. "And now I'm here with you. Happy days!" she concluded sarcastically.

"What were the results of your breath test?"

"I didn't take one. He took me to the hospital, and they took my blood and kept me quarantined for about two hours. I don't know what I registered on the Richter scale, but the next thing I know, I'm handcuffed by Trooper Blooper. The nurse told me I would have tested a lot higher if I hadn't thrown up a bunch a times in the police car." As if the thought occurred to her for the first time, she wondered aloud, "Maybe that's why he was so unfriendly."

Oh, boy. Logan's empathy drifted toward the trooper.

"Anyway, guess the good news is Nurse Susie-Q, Ben's little slut muffin, didn't poison me at the hospital and Ben said he'd pay my attorney fees. 'Within reason.'"

"Okay, then." Logan cleared his throat and refrained from slapping the table and laughing uproariously. "As you may know, I work summer months for Lacey Carpenter. Either Ms. Carpenter or I will represent you throughout the matter. She charges a flat fee of three thousand dollars up to a week before trial, and then another three thousand if the case doesn't settle by then."

"Wow. That much? What do you think will happen to me?"

"If we find a good reason for your driving away from a state trooper, we might get the eluding charge dropped. DWIs are tougher. You may end up in driving classes. You'll lose your license for a time, and you could possibly spend more time enjoying the Homer Community Jail."

"Good reason? You want a good reason why I drove away? I'll give you a good reason.

My stepdad was a police officer. He started molesting me on my eighth birthday and kept it up over the next seven years till he divorced my mom."

"I can work with that," Logan said abruptly. "I'll take you out to see Pam. She'll give you our standard fee agreement, get your contact information, and you can pay her. When the check clears the bank, I'll enter an appearance for you, get the police report from the prosecutor's office, and we'll set up a meeting before the Trial Setting Conference."

"I'll postdate a check and get cash from Ben."

"Great." Logan stood, signaling the end of their meeting. It was impossible to ignore " DahlorahzanneRudreeguz" gracefully uncross her spectacular legs.

Visibly comforted by Logan's assurances that once he received the police report he'd call her with the details, she thanked him and tucked his business card into her Gucci bag. A final toss of her hair diffused an enticing waft of Chanel, officially concluding Logan's first appointment of the season.

After the new client departed, Katie looked up from her typing and dryly affirmed Logan's speculation. "They're real...so are the Gucci purse and Christian Louboutin shoes."

Katie and Pam then looked at Logan expectantly. They had pored over the photos and news clippings from Pete's case while Logan reviewed the entire case aloud. Now, they anxiously awaited his analysis. How would he get Pete off? They wanted legal magic, and Logan didn't disappoint them. He reviewed the circumstantial evidence and identified the weaknesses in the prosecutor's case. They were impressed and relieved when he predicted a successful conclusion.

Internally, Logan wasn't certain of anything, especially after he overheard Katie answer a phone call in the outer office. "Hello? Hello? Yes, he's here. May I tell him who's calling? Hello? Hello?"

"Sorry, Logan. He hung up after I told him you were here. Guess he didn't really want to talk to you."

Pam looked up. "Hey, maybe that was the same weirdo who called yesterday, you know, the holy-roller dude."

"Let's hope it's a crackpot with too much time on his hands," Logan suggested. "But if you get any more calls, I want you to write down the times and dates, and exactly what is said. We're gonna keep a log if these calls continue."

CHAPTER
20

A FTER TWO MORNING APPOINTMENTS with Lacey's clients, Logan resumed his detailed review of the evidence in Pete's case. He jotted down some pertinent facts:

Barbara Hamlin placed a 911 call to the Anchorage PD on Monday, September 5, 1988, at 9:35 p.m. She reported that her husband, Bill, left the house with the family dog at about 3:00 p.m. Bill said he was going to the Huffman Road Dog Park. Barbara Hamlin explained he usually returned within a couple of hours.

At 9:35 p.m. Mrs. Hamlin called the police to report her missing husband. She asked the police to check the airlines to determine if her husband had left the city or state. She was informed that a forty-eight-hour wait was required before reporting a missing person. She advised that she'd check the airport in person.

Tuesday morning, an office employee at the Huffman Business Park noticed a dog sitting in a black SUV. He didn't recognize the vehicle or the dog. That afternoon, while leaving for lunch, he saw the same dog still in the SUV. He called the police.

Tuesday afternoon, Anchorage PD Officer Albright ran the SUV's license plate for the vehicle's owner's name and address. He established the vehicle was registered to Bill Hamlin and arrived at the Hamlin home at 1448 hours, where he took Mrs. Hamlin's statement.

So, the fearless Officer Albright and I cross paths again. Logan thought back to their first encounter.

When Logan began practicing law in Anchorage, he was contacted by an attorney he'd worked with at the Legal Aid Clinic in Tacoma. The attorney sent him a $32,000 judgment for back child support against Officer Albright. Logan called Albright to arrange for payment without having to garnish his wages since it might jeopardize the officer's job and thereby lessen the ex-wife's chances to receive the child support.

Officer Albright silently listened to Logan before asking, "Where's your office located?"

Good, Logan thought, *he's going to bring the checks to the office.* "Five forty-two West Third Street."

Officer Albright then asked what hours Logan worked. Logan unsuspectingly replied, "I generally leave the office about 6:00 p.m."

Officer Albright's next words were not ambiguous. "I carry a gun. I can and will sit across the street and wait for you to come out of your office. It will be the last day you ever work if you contact me again."

A remarkable threat from an officer sworn to uphold the law in the great state of Alaska. Logan weighed his three options: Report him to his supervisor; move forward with the garnishment; or return the papers to the attorney in Tacoma. *It's a no-brainer*, he reasoned. *I didn't marry this guy, nor have his kids. Not my fault he's this far behind in child support payments. And I'm sure as hell not going to die for this woman's piss-poor life decisions.*

Logan resumed preparing his list.

Albright's police report implied the Hamlin marriage was troubled. Mrs. Hamlin believed her husband had a girlfriend. She was distraught and concerned that he'd left her for another woman, whose identity was not yet known. When asked about her Labor Day afternoon whereabouts, Mrs. Hamlin said she was at the Evangelical Baptist church on Muldoon Road until early evening but didn't recall seeing anyone at the church. There was no one to corroborate her whereabouts.

Another officer arrived at the Huffman Park site at approximately 1615 hours to dust the Hamlin vehicle for prints. Everything had been wiped clean. The luminol blood test on the seats and cargo liner didn't reveal any blood, just a lot of hair and drooling slobber from a very anxious dog. The officer returned the dog and SUV to Mrs. Hamlin at 1740 hours.

APD Investigator Garrett Brent and four other officers canvassed the Huffman Park and dog park areas to no avail.

Had there been a gunshot, it most likely would have been ignored, Logan reasoned. Shooting at varmints or over the heads of moose, wolves, and black bear was a regular occurrence on the hillsides surrounding Anchorage.

Anchorage Police announced Hamlin's disappearance to the two local newspapers the following day and distributed flyers at the Huffman Business Park and the dog park. Photos of the SUV were included in the packet sent to the newspapers.

The case quickly went cold. There had been no additions to the file for almost sixteen years.

Logan finished the day's review, jammed his notes in the file, and locked up the office. His brain was fried, and it appeared not much was missing from the evidence reports.

When he returned to *The Coral Dawn* after dinner, he tried to sleep, but he was preoccupied by the absence of any misstatements of fact, missing information, or contradictions between the reports themselves and what Pete had told him. Logan's concerns about Pete's legal situation grew as he pondered the shortcomings of the American justice system. He knew that, like much in life, details were key to criminal cases. An experienced defense attorney scoured every statement for inconsistencies. That was the easy part.

The challenge was isolating the pieces of missing information from investigative reports, phone calls, physical evidence, and photographs. Then the question became: Why was it missing? Those were the questions he'd pose to witnesses at trial. Experience taught him that cops and investigators usually leave out anything that may help the defense. Logan needed to understand the timeline of events and those involved. If he could uncover a plausible alternate theory, Pete would probably be acquitted.

All defense attorneys eventually mastered the art of the Alternate Scenario. Despite the teachings of every American law school, and the judge's jury instructions, jurors usually declined to invest weeks in a courtroom to then decide there was not enough evidence to find someone guilty. It was only natural for jurors to pin it on the accused unless they were presented with a suitable alternative defendant. Logan knew his job was to find and reveal that person to the jurors.

CHAPTER
21

"THANKS FOR TAKING MY CALL, DR. ADAMS. I'm Logan Finch, and I represent Pete Foster in the Hamlin matter. Perhaps you recall the situation regarding Bill Hamlin?"

"You bet. Yeah, I think everyone in Alaska is aware of the case."

Logan chuckled. "That's the general feedback I've been getting. I'm hoping you can help me by comparing the skull's teeth to Hamlin's dental records and X-rays taken at Dr. Paine's office."

The doctor's tone became businesslike. "I suspected that I might be called upon for this. Also, I'm qualified for forensics work. If you need me at trial, I've testified in superior courts all over Alaska."

"Great." Logan mentally checked *expert witness* off his to-do list as they discussed financial details and scheduled a meeting for Monday morning at ten o'clock at the prosecutor's office, where they'd meet with the prosecutor, Christopher Branson.

Logan returned to the conference room and added to his summary list:

The statement of the homicide investigator, Crystal Sorensen, was based on her interview with arborist Cliff Echternkamp. She reported Echternkamp was hired in May of 2003 to review the plans for the construction of the new South Anchorage High School. He was marking trees for removal on the construction site when he found what appeared to be human skeletal remains. He called 9 1 1 to report finding a femur and skull and what turned out to be a bullet from a .45-caliber pistol. No shell casings were found in the vicinity.

Locating missing persons in Alaska is a serious business. Dozens of people came to the state every year to avoid prosecution or imprisonment in the Lower 48. Names and identities were changed as they tried to start new lives. Some did an admirable job of it. Some didn't.

Sorensen had the evidence bagged while she and two other state troopers searched for additional remains. The task was performed despite suspecting wild animals had probably scattered remains over many miles.

Locating graves or burial sites in Alaska was simpler than in the Lower 48. It took many years for disturbed ground cover to reestablish itself and cover clothing, bones, or any other possible evidence. This was primarily due to the impact of Alaska's frozen tundra.

In September 2003, an unnamed Alaskan trooper found disrupted ground cover with bone fragments just 150 feet southwest of the site where the skull and femur had been found. Delicate digging at the new site exposed ribs, the second femur, and tattered clothing beneath the bones.

Dr. Rebecca Wilson, the coroner, took photos and tagged and bagged the bones and the ragged clothing at the new site. She checked for possible bloodstains. Wilson generated a short report: She stated that although she was not a forensic anthropologist, the size of the femurs, the brow bone, eye sockets, teeth, and jaw were all reliable indicators that the deceased was a middle-aged male. "The bullet found near the remains," she predictably reasoned, "strongly indicates death was due to gunshot."

Further findings included that the .45 bullet that had penetrated the frontal lobe and the close-up photos of the bullet indicated its surface was sufficiently striated to match a specific revolver. Logan knew if another bullet were fired from the same gun, an investigator could match the bullet grooves using a special microscope in a side-by-side comparison of the bullets' strata.

He immediately sifted through documents to determine if a .45-caliber pistol had been removed from Pete's home. His hunch was no, because a test-fired bullet compared to the burial site bullet would have been included in the report and the statement of probable cause. Still, he was vastly relieved to find there was no such pistol on the list of search warrant items taken from the search of the Foster home.

Hamlin's dental records confirmed the skull, located in South Anchorage on September 22, 2003, was William Hamlin's, and the crime lab concluded the skeletal remains were consistent with a date of death as late as 1988.

Logan found a folded, one-page handwritten note that appeared to have been intentionally buried near the back of the file. It reflected Assistant AG Gerald Abbott's brief telephone conversation with Barbara

Hamlin. Mrs. Hamlin had been located at a trailer home in Eagle River. The note included her address and telephone number and would prove critical to the case. Logan nearly overlooked this critical note.

The last report Logan reviewed was by Alaska Trooper Mary Ann Harding. She led the search warrant and arrest team at the Foster's Arrowhead Point home in Kenmore. Included were questions asked of Erika. The most damning was her answer to whether she had ever heard of Hamlin. She said, "No, never heard of him."

Logan's thoughts raised deep concerns and he began to perspire as he took a deep, calming breath, exhaled, then entered Café Cups to meet with Pete and Erika.

CHAPTER
22

"Hey, you two." Logan pulled a chair out and sat, smiling appreciatively at the basket of warm crusty bread. "I'm starved. This looks great."

Sensing their apprehension about the information he was about to share, Logan ordered a bottle of wine. The ponytailed server, eyes sparkling with enthusiasm as she took the order, sped away on white tennis shoes. Logan began optimistically. "I have some good news. As you remember, Barbara Hamlin's former neighbors said she left town after her husband disappeared. Well, guess what, boys and girls? She's back. This morning, I found a crumpled handwritten note stashed and nearly hidden at the bottom of the files. Evidently, Barbara Hamlin is living in Eagle River. Her address and phone number were scribbled on the note. It also documents a brief phone conversation she had with AG Gerald Abbott."

Pete and Erika exchanged glances as Logan continued. "I need to interview her as soon as possible."

"Has she remarried?" Erika asked.

"The note says that she's living alone."

Logan paused a moment.before looking up from his blue cocktail napkin, his eyes met Pete's, then Erika's. "Anything you two want to tell me about the dog park and the Hamlins?"

They looked at one another, their faces inscrutable, waiting to see who wanted to go first. Before either could reply, there was a loud commotion at the door. Pam and Katie burst into the café, yelling Logan's name. "Hey, I'm over here." Logan waved his arm.

"We got a bomb threat from that guy who's been calling us." Pam's voice immediately lowered as she embarrassingly realized the impact of her statement. Too late. A wave of panic swept through the restaurant.

"Okay, settle down, Pam. Exactly what'd the guy say?"

Logan was intentionally calm and quiet. Erika, however, was not. "Oh my God. I was afraid this would happen."

Pam, ducking her head to muffle her voice, hoarsely whispered, "I answered the phone. The dude said, 'I planted a bomb in your office, and it'll go off in five minutes. There's going to be more bombs and deaths if you don't dump the Foster case. May God have mercy on your sinful souls.' Then he hung up."

"Have you called the police or anyone?" Pete questioned.

Pam looked incredulous. "Hell, no! We blew outta there so fast, we didn't even grab our cell phones." Logan was already on his cell phone as they spoke.

"This is Logan Finch, and I'm reporting a serious bomb threat at the law office of Lacey Carpenter. Yes, it's located at 542 West Pioneer Avenue. Thanks, I'll wait out front. No, believe me, I won't be too close."

The young server, oblivious to the excitement, returned to the table and plopped the wine bottle down and dug in her apron for a corkscrew. Pam wearily pulled up a stray chair to their table for four and sank down slowly, every shred of her coolheaded self-control shattered. Wide-eyed, she ticked off her past feats of composure under fire: all remarkable under any circumstances.

"I've hosted birthday parties in my house for thirty preschoolers. My mother-in-law stayed with us for a month after her hip surgery—doctor and physical therapy appointments, round-the-clock cooking, and cleaning—done, and without mixing vodka and Valium. Those cloned soccer moms in their Dorothy Hamill haircuts—no problem. I can shrivel sorority speak with just a raised eyebrow. But this afternoon's excitement, y'got me."

She pulled the uncorked bottle closer to her, looking around the table as if daring anyone to stop her. "I think I'll just drink this bottle of chardonnay. And I don't need any help, thank you all very much." Pam's performance struck Logan as hilarious but, as he was the only one laughing, it seemed prudent to lend a semblance of control.

"Okay, Pam...you, Erika, and Katie stay here. Same goes for you, Pete. We both might be targets for a shooter, and the bomb threat might be a ploy to get us out in the open."

"Not a chance," Pete protested. "We're always out in the open. You go,

I go. We'll report back here as soon as we know something. Okay, Erika?" She nodded solemnly.

As they headed to the door, they heard what they believed to be the most noise ever recorded in Homer's history: two Homer police cars, a state trooper, an aid car, and a fire pickup passed by, all with sirens blaring. They converged on Lacey's law office. The earsplitting commotion drew people from their offices and homes to investigate. Logan was tempted to duck back into the restaurant but knew the police would need information, so he and Pete continued cautiously up the road. The excitement interrupted everything from dining to pillow talk, and the gathering throng buzzed in tense whispering with all eyes avidly trained on the emergency and security personnel.

Logan and Pete knew the chief of police. He was the second to arrive on the scene and stood a careful distance across the street from the office. The chief was a plump, balding man pushing fifty-five years. The poor guy was sweating profusely. Rod Steiger's role in *In the Heat of the Night* flitted irreverently through Logan's mind. "Hey, Chief, what's going on?"

Logan's nonchalance immediately antagonized the chief's sensibilities. "Very funny. You tell me. Marge said it was you who called in the bomb threat, right?"

During their exchange, firefighters pulled hoses off their truck and the medic team removed a stretcher from their van's rear door. A state trooper captured the activity with his camera and embedded in the crowd was a *Homer Tribune* reporter.

The horde of spectators continued to grow until someone yelled, "It's a bomb threat!" As if rehearsed, the crowd retreated like lemmings, reaching into coat pockets and purses for cell phones.

"Well, Chief," Logan quietly explained, "I was eating with friends at the café when my office staff, Pam and Katie, ran over and reported that a bomb threat was phoned into the office."

"Where are they?" the chief probed.

"Still over at the Café Cups."

"Tell me exactly what they said. Was it a phone call? Email? Fax? What was it?" the chief demanded.

"According to Pam, a male caller said he planted a bomb in our office, and it'd go off in just a few minutes. Actually, I think Pam said five minutes."

"Did the caller say why?"

"We've received phone calls demanding we stop representing Pete here. But," Logan added, "this is the first mention of a bomb." Chief Lyons glanced over his shoulder as Pete shrugged with an embarrassed half smile. As they talked, Pete noticed the emergency personnel had turned into statues. They needed some direction. As the chief mulled over what steps to take next, Logan tactfully suggested calling the bomb squad in Anchorage. Chief Lyons, energized by the suggestion, announced, "That's what I intend to do."

Logan assessed the situation and concluded the roadway and immediate businesses would be closed until the law office was secured, so he casually, albeit quickly, walked across the street to the office parking lot and drove his car back down to the café. Pete noticed Logan's retreat and walked just as quickly back to the restaurant. Chief Lyons angrily pursued Logan. As Logan exited his car, the chief hotly demanded, "Hey, what in hell did you do that for?"

"Do what?"

"Go back to the office and get your car. What a stupid fucking thing to do."

"You're right, Chief, I'll never do it again."

The chief, unimpressed by the smart-ass answer, scowled at Logan before glancing down at his notepad. "So, Pam and Katrina are in the restaurant?"

"It's Pam and *Katie*, Chief. Not sure if they're still there. Let's go have a look."

As they entered and approached the table, Logan noticed there were now two empty wine bottles, and the ladies were giggling. A lot. Pete had also returned and stood behind the table. The women awaited the arrival of a just-ordered additional bottle of wine. Pete was wondering if sitting down was a good idea, given that things appeared to be going well without him.

"Chief Lyons, this is Pam Prepper, our paralegal. And Katie Wasner, our office manager," Logan said.

The chief quizzed them about the calls and took careful notes. A historic event had occurred on the chief's watch, and he didn't want to screw anything up. Meanwhile, the women were anxious to expedite the interrogation because the server was approaching with their wine. Logan heard Pam slur some words, garnering upraised eyebrows from the chief. Pam and Katie provided their cell phone numbers for follow-up questioning and then Chief Lyons slapped his notebook closed.

"I'm done here," he announced. "Thank you very much, ladies."

"Uhm, so, Chief, what happens now?" Pete interjected.

Chief Lyons straightened up and proudly proclaimed, "The FBI's sending their bomb squad and two certified bomb-disposal techs. They're also bringing down an Anchorage PD explosives technician." He noted the time on his watch and continued, "It's gonna take 'em at least five hours to get here. In the meantime, we're blocking off roads and clearing the adjacent homes and offices."

"Five hours!" Katie exclaimed. "We need our purses and our cars! Can't they just fly down here?"

"I think I just explained that. They're not going to do that because the equipment's already loaded in the FBI van. By the time they could move it all onto a plane, fly down here, and pack it into another van, it will take the same amount of time. So, ladies, your purses and cars will just have to stay right where they are. Now, I've gotta go call the utility company and have them cut power to the entire block for a few hours." Homer's valiant chief of police then did a military about-face and marched out of the restaurant without so much as a backward glance.

Logan was annoyed. *This bomb threat is costing a lot of people money and is wasting precious time. All because of a crazy caller.* Aloud, he proposed, "We'll wait and let folks disperse. Then I'll take Pam and Katie home and call Lacey with an update."

"Good," remarked a calmer Erika. "Try not to scare her. Once things clear up, maybe we get some cameras installed and the locks changed?"

"Yeah, great idea. I'll get started first thing in the morning,"

"Of course, the office could blow up tonight." Pete grinned.

"Won't happen," Logan replied. "Most threatening calls don't amount to anything. Remember the two calls we got years ago in Anchorage? Nothing. But Timothy McVeigh gave no warning before bombing the Oklahoma Federal Building. And Ted Kaczynski, likewise, didn't warn anybody before he mailed his bombs."

"You're right," Pam agreed. "And no need to drive Katie and me home. Erika called my husband and he's on his way to pick us up. And the security system sounds good. Not sure my husband would want me back at work otherwise."

Outside, Pam's husband honked his arrival. Logan declined when Pam and Katie offered to pay for their wine. *Difficult to pay with no purse.* Logan snickered to himself. *I just hope they don't sue for the on-the-job traumatic stress they've experienced.*

Out in the parking lot, Logan said to Pete and Erika, "I'll come back in about five hours to see what's going on. I'll call if there's anything new."

Pete said, "That works. We're sure sorry about all this. We don't want Lacey to lose her staff or have to cut her vacation short."

"You're right. I'd better minimize the details when I call her tonight. But Pam and Katie? Don't worry, those women are real troopers. They won't be bullied into quitting, especially not in the middle of a murder case." Logan's attempt to insert a scrap of humor was received with just polite nervous smiles.

Logan called Lacey when he climbed aboard the boat. There was a happy lilt to her voice when she answered. "Hey, you, what's up?"

Not wanting to put a total damper on her mood, Logan shared a bare-bones rendition of the day's events amid Lacey's shocked oh-my-gods. "Should I come home?" she asked.

Logan reassured her, "The office is closed, and there's really nothing you can do...but me!"

"You're not funny."

"Hey, a guy's gotta try. But, no, stick with the current game plan. If something requires your presence, other than me, of course, I'll call you. And, yeah, I get it, I'm still not funny, but I'm going to run back over there later tonight to see what's happening."

"Thanks...great thoughts to leave me with, but I'll talk to you tomorrow, you troublemaker."

"Goodbye, Lace."

Chief Lyons's phone call jolted Logan awake at two in the morning.

"I see that you and your buddy Pete own the house, but it's so old, we can't find any as-built information about the interior layout, and the FBI needs that before they enter the house."

"I can tell you," Logan sleepily volunteered, "or just come into town."

"Is the house locked up?"

"The front door is probably unlocked but the upstairs storage area door should be locked. Give me ten minutes and I'll be there with keys."

"Great, thanks."

Floodlights illuminated the entire street when Logan pulled into the café's parking lot. He walked toward the barricades and hailed the chief with a wave. Lyons, leaning against his car, gulped the last bite of his sandwich and greeted Logan. "Great, you're here! The bomb guys are waiting for you, so let's go."

They crossed the barricades and approached the office but were intercepted by two men—"Tall" and "Stocky," Logan dubbed them. They were official-looking in their black windbreakers with "FBI" stenciled on their backs in large white letters. Lyons made the introductions. "This is the owner. He brought keys to the upstairs and knows the office layout."

The agents nodded. Tall put out his hand for the keys. "The small one fits the upstairs door," Logan said.

Stocky requested the layout of the structure, and Logan quickly penciled a sketch of the rooms on the back of a gas receipt. Tall studied the sketch. "Upstairs always locked?"

"Yeah, I think so. There's a light switch on the right as you enter."

Jiggling the keys in his hand, he quizzed Logan further. "Could anyone get under the house?"

"Nope. It's built on a concrete slab. The air vents can accommodate a squirrel is about all."

The agents were in no mood for banter. Tall soberly remarked, "Some bombs are about the size of squirrels."

There was a third guy on-site encased in a bulky white protective blast suit and a bulletproof vest. *Resembles the Michelin Man*, Logan thought. The guy held a helmet in his right hand and a remote in his left. A boxy, apple-crate-sized robot was at his side. A large robot arm was folded but looked capable of reaching four feet in any direction. The man walked toward the house accompanied by the robot. *These guys are gutsy*, Logan thought. *Wonder what their pay scale is?* The man reached the steps and put on his helmet. His backup, two more agents in blast suits, joined him. One toted a large, plain globe; the other had what appeared to be a portable X-ray machine. One agent walked the exterior of the house checking the air vents. The other two entered the house and gently closed the door behind them. *Considerate*, Logan observed.

Spectators, their breaths condensing in the cold air, stood in huddled silence. Nearby were a couple of local police officers, the chief, and a guy from Homer Electric. At the other end of the block, three firemen stood guard at the barricades. *Seems like a good time to leave*, Logan instinctively thought. *But that's my house and my legal files, plus Lacey's files and furnishings.* And *those people are heroically risking their lives to save it all.* He stood alongside Chief Lyons, slightly behind the chief's donut-filled belly in case the house bomb exploded. *The chief gets overtime, and I don't*, he reasoned.

The fluorescent light fixtures up on the second floor went on. Everyone waited and waited some more. And kept waiting some more. After an excruciating thirty minutes, the Anchorage ammunition technician came out, leaving the front door wide open. Logan took that to be a good sign. The tech removed his helmet and thrust a thumb up in the air. "Clear!" he bellowed.

Cheers, clapping, and relieved exaltations greeted his declaration. The spectators left while the professionals packed up their gear for the long drive back to Anchorage. Logan's keys were returned, he secured the house, and he audibly yawned on the drive back to *The Coral Dawn*.

He was just half-awake Friday morning when he updated Lacey and began calling security companies. One company offered weekend installation of cameras, lights, video controls, and remote-access-test alerts. The initial charge was minimal but required a two-year contract, which was fine. Following that scare, no one would be quibbling about price.

He went back to sleep.

CHAPTER
23

D ELORES ANNE'S STRESSED VOICE was on his office answering
machine. "I need to see you right away. What time can I come by
your office?" He returned her call, but when she didn't answer, he left a
message suggesting a 3:00 p.m. meeting and asked her to call him back if
she couldn't make it.

The security guys were still busily installing little grommets in the windows and the two outside doors when Katie pulled into the parking lot
driving her new baby-blue Lexus SC 430. Logan met her at the door.
"Hey, Katie, your things are out in my car."

"Thanks, Logan." She was visibly relieved not to have to go inside the
office. "I think Pam's on her way." As she spoke, Pam arrived. The women
took their purses and phones and quickly left, promising to be back Monday morning. *Tough women*, Logan thought.

Pete showed up at one o'clock and Logan updated him on the bomb
squad and the security guys. Pete apologized but couldn't deny the entertainment value. "What's Lacey saying about all this hoopla?"

"She was cool. She's not gonna cut her vacation short."

"Thank God."

"But I think Pam and Katie are pretty scared. Any objections to relocating the office over to the boat? We would still use Lacey's copier and
fax machine, but I think less visibility is better."

"Yeah, fine by me. But I just don't understand why this guy is upset
that you're representing me. This case isn't wrapped up in any moral issue.
Okay, Hamlin was supposedly a God-fearing man, but why would an
Evangelical get all riled up? What do you make of it?"

"That question crossed my mind as well. I understood the Evangelical
outrage and involvement when I dared to represent Anchorage's sex theater and drug center. But this case? It makes no sense, but I'm sure going

to follow up on it. Do you remember which church made the threats the last time?"

"It was the Baptist Evangelical church out on Muldoon," Pete recalled.

"Okay. I'll start there. But I do need more information about the dog park in 1988. What do you remember?"

"Well, remember our Pekingese, Elsa Grace? When we lived next to the Huffman Dog Park, I used to walk her there in the late afternoon or early evening. There was a fenced area for large dogs and another smaller one for miniatures. One Sunday afternoon in the spring of 1988, I saw Hamlin there with his dog. Elsa Grace and I were walking toward the dog park when I saw him inside the large pen, throwing a ball for his dog to chase. Because of that scuffle in court, I about-faced and went home."

"You ever see him again?"

"Not really. He was at the dog park almost every Sunday afternoon, so I changed our walks to the late morning."

"Think they ever saw you?"

"I doubt it. You know how it is; everybody's bundled up in parkas. On Sundays, there was usually a swarm of people and their dogs at the park. I always left the minute I spotted Hamlin. And if I saw the black SUV he drove, I didn't go into the dog park. Once Erika found out Hamlin went there, I promised her I wouldn't go anymore. And that was the end of it."

"When was the last time you saw him at the park?"

"I don't remember exactly. I know it was sometime in the summer because I kinda remember being surprised that I never saw them again. I just figured maybe their dog died. Then that fall we moved to Washington."

"Okay. That's all I need to know for now. If Erika remembers anything else, let me know."

"You bet."

Logan was personally relieved by what Pete said, but professionally troubled. *Bill Hamlin couldn't say whether he had another altercation with Pete because he was dead. Meanwhile, his skeleton spoke volumes…and Pete's claim that he never again spoke to or approached Hamlin wouldn't matter to a jury.* The grim look on Pete's face suggested he shared Logan's concern.

CHAPTER

24

As Delores Anne entered the office, the stunningly beautiful woman leaned against the doorjamb looking confused.

"Afternoon, Delores Anne. Can I get you some coffee?"

"Coffee'd be niiche, an' y'ken jus' call me Lola."

Logan detected a slur in her reply and directed her into the inner office. "I'll be right there." She staggered toward the client chair. When Logan returned with her coffee, she was draping her sweater over the back of the chair. She turned gracefully to face Logan. She wore a cream-colored sheer blouse...just a blouse. No bra. Ignoring the view, Logan focused on carefully placing her coffee on a coaster.

"So, what can I do for you?"

"I jus' hadda tel'ya, Ben's not justa boyfren'. Lo'an, he's the lovvah m'life. I'm jus' s'lonely, I k'harly shtan'it." Logan walked to the credenza behind her chair for the Kleenex box. As he grabbed it and turned, she levitated to a standing position and suddenly hugged him. Her entire body trembled. *Yep, can't deny that feels great.* Still, he tried to resist the urge to be aroused. Unfortunately, his lower half wasn't cooperating. She felt the growth in his slacks and immediately grabbed hold of him. She sat back down in her chair and put her mouth to his zipper, blowing hot air while she began undoing his belt.

Logan closed his eyes momentarily as a tsunami of delicious temptation flooded all vestiges of common sense—until he noticed his Alaska Bar Association license, framed and hanging above the credenza behind her. His burgeoning desire withered as the consequences of breaking ethical rules prohibiting sex with clients swamped his fleeting lapse in judgement. He tried to back away, but she grabbed his buttocks and pulled him closer.

"Delores Anne, I cannot even begin to tell you how much I'd love to indulge my fantasies right now. But you've got to stop. I can't do this."

She looked up at him, her expressive brown eyes ablaze with passion. "Yer'na mahr'd, r'ya?"

"No, I'm not married, but the bar association frowns on sex with clients, especially when they're drunk. If you weren't a client and were sober, this could be wonderful."

"Yeah...din't feel like your cock's worried 'bout yer old bar sosh'shashun. 'Sides, we ken jus' say I'm Lacey Car'pater's client."

"That won't work either. Lying's frowned upon too." She released him and rummaged in her purse. Eventually she extracted her lipstick and reapplied it with elaborate bravado. Safely back behind his desk, Logan realized this was a familiar ploy for Delores Anne, one that undoubtedly achieved glowing results. She expected Logan to agreeably solve her legal mess if she did her usual thing. Ethics were not part of her worldview. But Logan knew a physical relationship with her could potentially destroy his career and would not improve her situation, legally or emotionally.

"I'm very sorry. You're just gorgeous, but please understand my conflict here." Lacey now entered his mind as he considered the possibilities of seeing Delores Anne when she was sober and no longer his client. *Nope, not going to* ever *happen!*

With their meeting at an impasse, Logan offered to take her home. Her apartment was a mile or so out the East End Road. His offer was colorfully rejected, but then haughtily accepted when she required help down the three front steps. On the outskirts of town, she pulled out all the stops in one last seductive bid. She slid her seat back and unbuttoned her blouse. She cupped her exquisite breasts while fingering her erect nipples. Moaning softly, she begged. "Puhleez, Lo'an...tou'sh me."

Logan's eyes drifted fleetingly from the road ahead to the vision on his right. *Damn.* He sped up, thankful that he knew the exact location of her apartment. He gripped the steering wheel with both hands while staring straight ahead, saying nothing, doing nothing. Two blocks from the Harbor Ridge Apartments, Delores Anne moved her seat back into place and rebuttoned her blouse. Her slurring seduction dissolved into whiny wheedling. "But aren't we frenz? I thought y'liked me."

Having spent his entire life as a single guy, Logan had long ago mastered the art of maneuvering emotional minefields of inebriated women. "I'm your attorney," he firmly stated. "You don't need one more person taking advantage of you. We're going to get you home, and I promise you that tomorrow will be a better day." He parked at her building, then helped her out of his VW and guided her toward the apartments. "Now where?" Logan asked.

"S'up..." She drunkenly gestured to the wooden stairwell. Depression from drinking throughout the day settled over her like a shroud and her weeping began anew. "S'ken f'oor," she bawled. "N'mer tooh-tooh-tooh." Logan struggled to maintain his footing while keeping Delores Anne upright as they navigated the stairs. When they reached her door, she flung her arms around Logan's neck...the remaining arrow in her quiver of considerable charms.

"Lo'an, I dunno what to do. I'll do any— you can do anything w'me. Jus' hol'me."

This would be an unbelievable scene in a B movie, Logan thought as he extricated himself from her stranglehold and gently directed her through the door. "Goodbye, Delores Anne. You're home. I'll see you later."

CHAPTER

25

MONDAY MORNING, AFTER FLYING TO Anchorage and checking into the Captain Cook, Logan jogged across the street to the attorney general's office and was confronted by the king himself, Gerald Abbott. "Good morning, Counselor," the reigning AG said. His white shirt strained valiantly over his belt and ample belly. "Why are you wasting your time investigating this case? You should be spending your time and your client's money negotiating a plea bargain." He puffed up his six-foot-four, three-hundred-pound frame and leaned into Logan's space. "I'll make you an offer you can't refuse."

"A misdemeanor plea with credit for time served?" Logan suggested.

"Not a chance. I was thinking twenty to thirty years with the possibility of parole. I think you have a shot at a heat-of-passion defense."

"Really?" The pompous prosecutor was easy to bait, and Logan couldn't resist. "Gosh, Gerry, hadn't thought of that, and here you go coming up with a great defense without ever having read the file."

Red splotches, signaling a rapidly rising blood pressure, crept above Abbott's shirt collar.

"It might interest you to know I *have* read the file. I know what I'm talking about and what the jury will do with you—and the murderer you're representing!"

Logan smiled coolly. "Gerry, you might be interested in reading the Universal Declaration of Human Rights, Article 11. It's about the presumption of innocence."

"The what?" Abbott's bluster deteriorated into a shrill stutter.

"Ah, never mind," Logan replied. "You're kinda wet behind the ears...you still have time to learn about criminal law and citizen rights."

On the verge of stroking out, Abbott pushed past Logan. "Get out of my face and wait for Branson." He stormed down the hall, arms vigorously churning. Logan sat down on the sturdy wooden bench in the hallway to wait for Adams and Branson. His face exuded the benign serenity seen on a cat casually batting a mouse.

Dr. Adams arrived and Logan handed him a signed blank check. He would fill in the amount when he had completed his work. They waited in silence for ten minutes. Logan kept quiet because anything he said to Adams could be introduced at trial and Dr. Adams knew the drill.

"Good morning, gentlemen," Christopher Branson greeted them as he approached. "And Dr. Adams, I presume? Let's go to the conference room and meet Cameo Navarre. She's our evidence custodian."

Evidence was maintained with a chain of custody, and a custodian is charged with properly documenting the chain. Otherwise, an attorney would insist the evidence be excluded from the trial if it wasn't verified that no one had tampered with it. A custodian is the individual tasked with oversight of the evidence.

The room was sparsely furnished. Of all the objects sitting on the metal conference table, Logan was most focused on the skull and X-rays. He glanced at the attractive young staffer standing vigil next to the table. "Good morning. Did Chris say your name was Cameo? That's a beautiful name; never heard it before."

"Thank you," she said and shyly smiled, her eyes never leaving the table. She trusted no one.

"Cameo, please identify Dr. Paine's X-rays for Dr. Adams," Chris requested. "I see he already has the skull in hand." Adams took the X-rays and placed the skull in front of him while bending over until his eyes were at table level. He noticed the large hole in the skull just above the frontal bone on the right orbital surface. He compared the skull with the X-rays, tooth by tooth. Twenty minutes elapsed before he photographed the skull from various angles with close-up photos of the teeth.

Meanwhile, Logan examined the other bone fragments, remnants of tattered clothing bagged in clear plastic baggies, and a .45-caliber slug. He tried to look like he was looking for something, but that was pure fiction. It was up to the experts to determine what they didn't have or wouldn't need. His expert, Dr. Adams, would establish if this was Hamlin. Then the question was: Who murdered the guy? Logan knew forensic evidence couldn't establish a definitive answer without a murder weapon.

After Adams completed his examination, they thanked Chris and Cameo. Logan asked Chris, with tongue-in-cheek flippancy, to tell

Abbott goodbye for him. Chris appreciated the sarcasm and winked. "Uh-huh...I'll be sure to do that."

He's probably never spoken to Chris, Logan speculated. Abbott was reputed to be a real hardass who didn't speak with subordinates. He viewed everyone as his subordinate.

Out the door and back on the street, Adams said he would compare the photos, but he believed the X-rays and teeth were a match. Logan wasn't surprised but needed to do his due diligence to establish certainty.

He called Lacey after returning to the hotel and updated her on the office and Pete's case, as well as the firm's newest client, the flamboyant Ms. Delores Anne Rodriguez. He asked Lacey for the contact information for her jury consultant. Lacey was in good spirits and on the beach.

"Clear blue skies and eighty-six degrees," she reported before providing the requested referral. "The name of the guy who helped me last year is Tim McQuigg."

"What do you know about him?"

"Former military, he was stationed at Elmendorf Air Force Base. A degree in criminology from the University of Alaska. While he was in the military, he worked with several plaintiff attorneys around town and gained a solid reputation. Joe Young, the most successful personal injury attorney in Alaska, met McQuigg years ago and hired him as his jury consultant before Young became famous. In the sixties and seventies, they collaborated and orchestrated the best personal injury verdicts in Alaska."

"I've never thought much of jury consultants. I've won a lot of cases against large firms that had hired jury consultants. What makes this guy so special?"

"He's smart, and I think as a minority in America he has a survivalist knack for detecting prejudice. Kind of a specialized radar. So, it's not a stretch for him to excel at detecting biases. He can do it within minutes of interacting with someone. It's a gift, and he's good at returning phone calls. He works out of his home on the Park Strip near the courthouse."

"Okay, I'll give him a call now and check back with you tonight. I don't want to interrupt your vacation more than is absolutely required."

"Thanks...but you're not an interruption."

"Glad to hear it. Enjoy that beach for me too!"

"Oh, you can count on it!" Lacey giggled as she hung up.

CHAPTER
26

"COME ON IN," McQUIGG INVITED. "I live alone so my living room is a good meeting place." Logan got comfortable on the couch while McQuigg settled his five-foot, ten-inch frame into a leather recliner. The muscular consultant had a short, graying beard that complemented a receding hairline. He wore a casual, Pendleton navy-plaid shirt and blue jeans and held a yellow legal pad, along with a list of information he would need plus a fee agreement for Logan.

Logan quickly launched into a condensed *Reader's Digest* version of the case. McQuigg nodded his understanding as he looked up from his note-taking.

"Need me to attend the jury selection?"

"Not sure whether it will be necessary. Okay if we leave that option open?"

"Absolutely. You'll need to provide me with the bios of your client and the witnesses—yours and theirs. I don't need personal information about the experts, but I do need the bio of the deceased, Mr. Hamlin. It should include where he's from, any criminal background, race, religion, prejudices, and biases."

Logan appreciated McQuigg's confidence and matter-of-fact recitation of needs.

"I'm more effective," McQuigg continued, "if I meet witnesses in person before the trial. My strongest skill is observing prospective jurors during voir dire and identifying those jurors who'll be most empathetic to your case."

Logan explained, "There was never a trial or hearing when the Hamlins had to testify, so I don't know much about them. I'll work on that over the coming weeks. I'll also send you a case synopsis and our probable defenses. On the next Anchorage visit, I'll introduce you to Pete. I want your thoughts about putting him on the stand. I've been trying to contact

Hamlin's ex-wife, Barbara. If I interview her, would you like to come along?"

"Sure. That would help me describe the most favorable jurors to look for in terms of gender, age, race, employment, religion, income, family, children, education, and overall attractiveness. I should be able to describe the jury foreperson you'll need. I know the jury pools around Anchorage. For some reason, there seems to be a standard pool. Been doing this over twenty years and I see the same jurors every year, while some people never get called. It's a mystery to me. I always try to find jurors who see gray areas. The prosecutor will portray your client as black. You'll portray him as white and hope the jury perceives him as gray. Gray is your reasonable doubt and leads to a possible acquittal."

"Makes sense," Logan said as he rose to leave.

"Good. It's been a pleasure meeting you, Logan. Please tell Lacey hello for me. She's one special lady."

"You have that right." Logan left with his to-do list and the contract for McQuigg's services.

As Logan pulled away from McQuigg's house, a big white pickup pulled in behind him. *Weird.* He kept one eye on the rearview mirror...a couple of guys in the cab. The pickup sped up until its front bumper and hood blocked Logan's view. *Jesus, are they trying to run me off the road?* His heart pounded as he pulled off the Glenn Highway and stopped. The pickup followed his lead. *Huh...* He took some calming deep breaths as he saw that neither guy exited the pickup.

Still looking in the rearview mirror, Logan pulled back onto the highway and took the exit at Muldoon Road. The pickup shadowed him. When he reached the church parking lot, the pickup peeled off and parked at the Shell station across the street. Logan waited a few minutes. No one got out of the pickup.

The neighborhood featured a strip mall of businesses with glaring neon signs further exposing the dilapidated storefronts: a couple bars, a gloomy gun and pawn shop with barred windows, and a selection of worn-out fast-food joints. The local bar, the Rusty Nail, was infamous for hiring bartenders who didn't know what the drink known as a Rusty Nail was. The stately, white-columned Evangelical Baptist church was out of place. Behind the church, a broken-down chain-link fence surrounded a small day-care center.

Logan bounced up the wide stairs and into the church's impressive vestibule. On his right was an information desk, and the double doors ahead presumably led into the church sanctuary. The two doors to his left were stenciled in black, "MEN" and "WOMEN." He was reaching for some literature when a tiny elderly woman carefully hobbled from the restroom to the information desk. Logan turned and offered a sheepish grin.

Her whispery voice was practiced, confident. "How may I help you?"

"Well, I'm Brian Bosworth. I just moved to Anchorage. I'm looking for a good old Baptist church."

Logan internally winced at his lies when he saw her pale blue eyes sparkle with enthusiasm.

"Why, yes, I can help you. Our church is one of the oldest Evangelical Baptist churches in Anchorage. We opened our doors in 1976 with the Reverend Dr. Ron Tasker as our pastor. These days, his oldest son, Terry, does most of the preaching, but Dr. Tasker retains control over the direction and missions of the church." She boasted shyly, "He and his son are two of the finest upstanding Christians you could ever meet."

"You don't say," Logan expressed delighted amazement.

"I'm sorry for being so rude; I haven't even introduced myself. I'm Ingrid Johansen. Please, just call me Ingrid. I'm the church historian, librarian, and executive secretary to Dr. Tasker."

"I'm so glad to meet you, Ingrid. So, you're the person in charge around here?"

"Oh, no," Ingrid demurred and shook her head. "I'm never in charge of anything. That would be the Lord and my Savior, Jesus Christ. I'm just his messenger. You know, many dignitaries around here are members of our congregation. But since you're new in town, you probably aren't familiar with their names."

"Try me. I'll remember the names and it will help me feel as if I know part of this community."

"Community first, we always say. Let's see...the photographs here on the wall should help you associate names with faces."

Logan looked toward the nearby wall plastered with large, framed photos. "Good idea, I'll look at those." He started with a photo of the Reverend Dr. Tasker. His name and the years of his pastorship were engraved on the frame. As he perused the photos, he noted the congregation's heavyweights were all white males. *Why do women, of any color, join a church where they invariably get treated as second-class citizens?*

The former mayor was there with "1978–2002" engraved on the frame. Logan stopped in his tracks. A photograph of William Hamlin was engraved with "1976–1988." Logan instinctively glanced over his shoulder. Had Ingrid seen his reaction? Nope, she was engrossed in the tattered Harlequin romance novel he'd spotted near the piles of religious tomes and flyers. He didn't recognize any other names as Anchorage dignitaries, except one. Next to the men's restroom door was a photo of Gerald Abbott. The frame was engraved with "1974–," indicating he was still an active church member.

When Logan approached the desk, Ingrid hastily stashed the romance novel, which prompted his impish apology for the interruption. "You were right, Ingrid. I don't recognize anyone, but what a delight to see so many dignitaries associated with the church."

Her face was slightly flushed while she recovered her composure. "Oh, they're more than just associated, Mr. Bosworth. They are all current or past members of the Guidance Panel."

"Oh..." That got Logan's attention. "What is the Guidance Panel?"

"The Chosen Five. They provide spiritual guidance to our congregation. They meet every Thursday night with members who seek spiritual guidance beyond that received by attending worship on Sundays. The Chosen Five are the best of the best. I hope you get to meet them."

"I'm truly impressed with your church." Logan smiled and grasped Ingrid's hand. His voice and demeanor radiated devout passion. "I was a member of an Evangelical Baptist ministry in Green Valley, Arizona. Now that I've moved here, I need a new faith community, and your church sounds great."

"Wonderful. Please take some of our literature, and if you want to meet Terry Tasker, I can see if he's available."

Oh, no! Logan hastily declined. "No, no, that won't be necessary today." He backed up toward the door. "But may I take a rain check?"

"Of course. I look forward to introducing you on Sunday morning.

We have two services, nine and eleven, scheduled to let you sleep in." Her wrinkled little face broke into a dimpled grin.

Logan smiled. "I'll be here." As he exited, the Rev. Dr. Tasker came out from behind the wall and questioned Ingrid about the visitor. She joyously recounted the entire episode. In detail. Tasker's scowl grew more pronounced when she proudly remembered the visitor's name, Brian Bosworth.

"Was he big and blond?" Tasker asked.

"No...no, he's thin, tall, athletic...with a graying mustache."

"That's not the Boz," Tasker gruffly mumbled as he slunk back into the sanctuary.

Two guys stood at the bottom of the church steps. Logan assumed they were the two pickup guys. Logan started down the stairs, noticing the tall guy on the right held an aluminum baseball bat.

"Gentlemen, no disrespect, but I need to question your driving skills. You tend to follow too closely." He stared at batman. "Were you the guy driving the pickup?" Logan, now on the last step, was almost nose to nose with batman who stood firm and fumbled for a verbal response. *Guess I'm going to see if the army boot camp was worth it,* Logan thought. He headbutted batman's nose while simultaneously landing an uppercut to the guy's chin using the open palm of his hand.

Batman tumbled backward, dropping his bat, which gave Logan the needed opening. He delivered a swift kick to the groin of his Baby Huey companion. The beefy dude doubled over in retching agony. Logan followed up with a knee slam to the chin and hurled him onto the asphalt parking lot where he landed with a thud. As the dazed men lay groaning, Logan grabbed the bat, trotted across the parking lot where he tossed it into his back seat, and jumped in his car.

He drove to Muldoon Road and then merged onto the highway. The same pickup raced down the entrance ramp and slammed into his bumper. His bumper was hit even harder the second time as he pulled off the highway. The white pickup careened past him, exhaust pipes thundering with accelerating gear changes as it disappeared. He managed to get a good look at the license plate. Shaken, Logan noisily exhaled, then resolutely continued back to Anchorage.

Logan lay flat on his hotel bed. *It must be those damned Evangelicals trying to get rid of me. A mission from God. Time to get outta this hotel, this city—hell, I'm ready to check out of Alaska altogether!*

"I've discovered paradise isn't as much fun as I thought it'd be," Lacey cooed into the phone.

"Aww, anything I can do?"

"Thought you'd never ask. Beg me to come home. I'm afraid that I'm missing all the action and excitement."

"Come home, Lacey." To her gleeful delight, he spontaneously belted out a spirited Homer-esque rendition of "Please Come to Boston." "Hey, ramblin' girl, why don't you settle down? Maili ain't your kind of town. There ain't no gold and there ain't nobody like me-eee...I'm the number-one fan of the girl from Homereee."

"What's that? Dave Loggins? There's no 'Homer-eee' and you know it." She laughed.

"I know...it's improv. Kind of a Logan/Loggins rhyme thing. But, yeah, Lace, I'd love for you to come home. You're the one I wanna talk about my day with. I've worked hard not to bother you on your vacation, but I hate it when you're not here! Besides, you're not going to believe what happened today."

"What? Tell me what I missed!"

"First, I met with McQuigg. Thanks for the introduction, by the way. He's going to be a great help. And he says hello."

"C'mon, that's not exciting. Or new."

"I'm getting to the good part. Keep your pants on."

"Never thought I'd hear that from you."

"Oh, how we digress, Lace. But listen to this." He dragged out the suspense. "I went to the Evangelical Baptist church in Muldoon today."

"And that's exciting because..."

"As you know, Hamlin and Jansen were members of that church, and guess who else?"

"Besides Jesus Christ?"

"Okay, you got me. Him too. But no. The great and powerful—as well as legend in his own mind—Gerald Abbott!"

"He's the prosecuting attorney. So, that's no surprise. His membership alone is not remarkable. But when you frame it in context with his failure to prosecute fellow members Bill and Barbara Hamlin for their false alibi, and now, sixteen years later, he's hell-bent on prosecuting Pete for Hamlin's murder, you have to ask why."

"I don't see the conflict. Abbott has complete discretion in these matters, and besides, they just found Hamlin's bones."

"I understand. But suppose Abbott had a conflict of interest that guided his decisions. Why would a prosecutor avoid charging two people who provided a false alibi that enabled at least ten more murders? And why was the Jansen case transferred to Fairbanks for the search warrants?"

"Maybe we need to hire a private investigator and dig deeper."

"It crossed my mind. I've gotta hire a PI to interview the state's witnesses. Do you have anyone in mind?"

"You bet. Call J.D. Cline in Anchorage. He graduated law school a few years back but is having trouble passing the bar exam. I think he's enjoying the PI business and playing golf whenever he wants. I hear he's the low handicap player at Elmendorf. He helped me with the two criminal trials I had last winter. I can call him and have him contact you. He's really good."

"I should meet him at the golf course and get a free lesson or two."

"J.D. would go for that."

"Let's talk about it more when you get home tonight." Logan smiled with anticipation and proposed, "Let me know when to expect you."

"Ha! Not happening. I'm hanging up and hitting the beach."

Crap. "Okay, have a great afternoon basking in the sun."

Although Logan didn't tell Lacey about the pickup incident, he did report it to the police and gave them the license number without mentioning the physical altercation. *No use complicating things with a few extraneous facts.*

"Was there any damage to your car?" the officer inquired.

"Not really. They were probably just trying to intimidate me."

"Any guns pulled?" she asked.

"Not that I saw."

"Okay. Thanks for the report. Your case number is APD-04-0365. We'll contact the owner of the vehicle and find out what's going on."

"Thanks." Logan knew there would be no follow-up. He called Mrs. Hamlin. *Damn, still no answer.*

CHAPTER
27

A S HIS FLIGHT TAXIED TO HOMER'S one-room terminal, he remembered his promise to check on Lacey's house while she was gone. Since she might return early, now was a good time to do it.

Logan was recalling the warm summer nights at Lacey's as he pulled into her dirt driveway when those fond memories instantly evaporated. The front door stood ajar. Logan, who carried a gun only when halibut fishing, wished he had one now.

Lacey's home was near the hospital above Homer on a small knoll. Her trilevel log home was perched on an acre-and-a-half lot and had a spectacular view. The property overlooked the Homer Spit, Kachemak Bay, the Alaska Range, Redoubt, Augustine, the city of Homer, several glaciers, Cook Inlet, and Beluga Lake. He cautiously approached the house. The front door had been jimmied open. He slowly, carefully entered, then gagged. The usual warm coziness and delicious smells were absent now, as the home reeked. The freezer door hung open and its contents were strewn across the kitchen floor. Bloated insects lazily maneuvered touch-and-go flybys, feasting on the bounty of rotting moose meat, fish, and crab. Intent, focused, listening, Logan stealthily moved through the house. The intruders were gone, but Lacey's home office was destroyed. Her computer was on the floor and the innards of the filing cabinet were strewn as if hit by a cyclone, obscuring the carpet. The shards of a broken lamp mingled with the mass of files and documents.

A single item remained on her desk. It was a yellow legal pad with the black Sharpie used to scribble a terse missive:

Drop the case—now!!!
All the sinners of my people shall die by the sword,
which says the evil shall not overtake nor prevent us.
A directive followed by biblical retribution. Logan shook his head in dis-

gust and stuffed the yellow sheet into his shirt pocket. He hurried outside and strode away from the stench.

A call to the police produced a rookie cop who showed up within seconds of Logan's call. He had been nearby, driving down the hillside from the hospital. The young cop took photos and filled out an incident report. "This is unusual," he commented. "We rarely get simple vandalism without a burglary."

"I don't really know if anything is missing or not. The owner gets home sometime this week. She'll have to do an inventory."

"Oh, yeah, right." The officer nodded. "Lacey's in Hawaii again, isn't she?"

So much for small-town privacy. After the cop left, Logan embarked on cleaning up. He dragged the outside garbage can into the kitchen and armed himself with a pair of rubber gloves. Spurts of Raid dispersed the swarm of flies and he tossed the rotten food into a garbage bag. When he finished throwing the rotten food out, he scrubbed the linoleum floor and then secured the door by putting larger screws in the faceplate.

Back on the boat, Logan debated whether to call Lacey. *News of the break-in would bring her home unnecessarily early...I'll wait.* He chased down a bowl of chili with a cold beer. He contemplated the last few days' events and nibbled stale popcorn before he went to bed and tossed and turned until Tuesday morning.

The sunrise found a troubled Logan. He was disturbed by the scene at Lacey's plus an unwelcome variation of his recurring earthquake nightmares: the menacing threat, attempts to flee, the looming disaster, trapped in an office, unable to get out. The threats were nonspecific—earthquake, bomb, a man...*I need some time off,* Logan decided.

He called the office and told Pam about the break-in at Lacey's house and that he was going to go fishing. "Oh my God," Pam screeched. "Don't tell Lacey or she will shorten her vacation. There's no need for that."

"I agree. I cleaned the house so there is little more she can do except an inventory of any damaged or stolen items."

By the afternoon, Logan caught his two-halibut limit and returned to the harbor. Mike, Sasha, and Toby were out sailing, so he docked *The*

Coral Dawn without Mike's usual assistance. He cleaned and fileted his 140 pounds of fresh halibut. A portion was smothered in fresh sliced onion and studded with lemon wedges, then encased in tinfoil. While the fish baked on the Sea-B-Que attached to the aft bulkhead, Logan fried potatoes on the propane stove. The chilled half bottle of chardonnay in the fridge completed a fine evening meal.

Logan thought for a moment about what life would be like without Mike, Sasha, and, of course, the lovable Toby. *They have my back—something everyone needs in Alaska.* The Last Frontier was a do-it-yourself and wherever-you-chose culture with minimal interference and regulation. Rugged mountains, gorgeous meadows, forests, grasslands, and the sea—these very resources and conditions enabled Alaskan lifestyles but increased the personal hazards and danger from an environment of brutal, subzero winters, earthquakes, and erupting volcanoes. Paradoxically, you became more dependent on others for your survival than almost anywhere else in the world. This awesome polarity between freedom and dependence, surrounded by danger, defined life in Alaska.

Pam shook the rain from her umbrella before entering the office. "Nothing happened yesterday," she reported to Logan. "No crank phone calls. By the way, I don't know how to disconnect the alarm system and then reset it again. Do you?"

"I sure hope so. If you hear sirens as I'm doing this, don't run away."

"You got it."

He approached the newly installed electronics next to the door. He managed to arm the alarm system. "Should be a slow day, unless you've lined up some new appointments for me?"

"You have two scheduled for tomorrow morning. Also, the Rodriguez lady called a couple of times."

Logan's shoulders stiffened. "Thanks, Pam." *Something's wrong with the office. Hmm, my chair!* He climbed the stairs, unlocked the door, and turned on the light. He spotted his dilapidated special executive chair amid a jumble of file boxes. *Yep, laziness, pure and simple.*

No mystery why he and Pete still owned this old house. It was mind-boggling to contemplate sorting and organizing years of legal files in storage boxes. *The cost of renting a storage unit would exceed the mortgage payment,* Logan concluded.

He moved the three stuffed banker boxes balanced on the dusty black leather chair and dragged the chair down the stairs. After dusting it off, he placed it behind Lacey's desk and ceremoniously sat down. *Home at last...*If he'd had a cigar, he would have lit it. The message pad bore just three phone messages. An Anchorage cop called to advise the plates on the white pickup were stolen. Pete had called and there was a call from Ms. Rodriguez.

Pam had completed the court documents for the Rodriguez case before the bomb threat commotion. She placed them on Lacey's desk—currently co-opted by Logan. He grabbed the file and strode off to the prosecutor's office. His objective was to obtain the police report and other documentary evidence before calling Rodriguez. The city attorney's assistant scanned the Rodriguez documents and pulled the prosecutor's file from a cabinet. She copied the police report, while advising Logan that the hospital records and blood test results weren't available yet. The arresting trooper's summary of the hospital report was being copied for him. The packet was at least an inch thick. He then sped to the courthouse and filed his original documents with the clerk before returning to the office.

Back in his chair, he read the trooper's report, which had him in stitches from the first paragraph. The trooper realized the extent of and pervasive aroma of Ms. Rodriguez's vomit when he was ready to transport her from the hospital to the jail. He drafted a city cop to transport her to the Homer jail while he drove to the local Chevron station and spent a miserable hour hosing down his patrol car's back seat. When that didn't do the trick, he bought four air fresheners. The revolting smell nevertheless assaulted his nostrils and permeated his uniform until his shift ended five hours later. By then, he was beyond pissed and researched the Homer city ordinances for a basis upon which to charge Ms. Rodriguez for puking in his patrol car. Unfortunately, he came up with zip. Logan genuinely pitied the guy.

The report also reinforced Logan's reluctance to get personally drawn into her situation. He was sorry life had not gone the way she would have liked, but he'd seen this before with clients who, mistaking their professional relationship for something more, sought his friendship *and* legal expertise. He'd also encountered other beautiful women like Delores Anne, who hoped for a knight in shining armor to rescue them from their memories, their demons, their lives.

I'm not going to call her back, Logan decided. *If it's important, she'll call again.* Also, there was nothing new to share and, frankly, he wanted no repeat of their weekend exchange. He also didn't want to give her false hope he was interested and, if Logan was honest with himself, he didn't want to subject himself to her temptations. A personal relationship could not end well for either of them.

"HELLO. THIS IS LOGAN FINCH, ATTORNEY for Peter Foster. May I speak to either Ron or Terry Tasker?"

"This is Dr. Ron Tasker. What can I do for you?"

"I was wondering if you recall who William Hamlin was dating at the time of his disappearance?"

"I don't know what you're talking about." The phone went dead.

Then he answered a call from J.D. Cline.

"Hey, J.D. I could use a little help."

"No problem, chief. You come highly recommended by my favorite attorney."

"She's my favorite too."

"So, what exactly needs done. Lacey briefed me on the case. Murder cases are becoming her forte, I guess."

"I'll have Pam send you the statements of six state witnesses, and I would like you to interview them and make sure their statements are consistent with what they tell you."

"Piece of cake, chief. How soon do you need a report?"

"A week before trial, which is now scheduled for July 25."

"Great. That should give me plenty of time. Are the witnesses all local?"

"Yes. I'll have Pam alert the prosecutor that you're on our team and will be interviewing their witnesses. You should get everything tomorrow.

"Do you need a retainer?"

"Nah. I know you're good for it."

When Pete and Erika arrived at the Homestead Restaurant, they were more animated than usual. "Before we get into the church on Muldoon, tell us how this information might help our defense," Pete said. Logan was pleased they were finally taking an active interest in the case.

"We have to find out who had a motive to want Hamlin dead," Logan answered. "We know his jealous wife qualifies. So, focusing on the church seems like another viable possibility, considering the recent threats to our property and safety. I mean, what if someone at the church wanted Hamlin dead? I think someone from the church has been trying to stop us from representing you. I was attacked at Hamlin's Evangelical church in Muldoon by a couple big guys in a pickup who then rear-ended my rental car on the Glenn Highway. Alternatively, we should consider that maybe it was the husband of the woman Hamlin was having the affair with. Or maybe it was a guy friend. Or a church member who didn't like him giving the alibi to Jansen. Or a relative of one of the ten girls murdered after the alibi. And there's the five-man spiritual Guidance Panel."

"What's a Guidance Panel?" Erika asked.

"Ron Tasker, the minister, appoints members he considers worthy to a five-man Guidance Panel who counsel other members about things that trouble them. And get this: both Hamlin and our esteemed prosecuting attorney, Gerald Abbott, are church members and served together on the Guidance Panel when Jansen was killing young women."

"Okay, so we're looking for someone to point the finger at within the church community?" Erika asked.

"Exactly," Logan replied. "Now, fill me in on your research."

Before they could answer, the server arrived to take drink orders and Logan ordered martini number two. "Well," Pete began, while handing Logan a copy of his printed notes, "Dr. Ron Tasker is, by far, the most conservative Evangelical pastor in Alaska. He hates gays, lesbians, transsexuals, fornicators," Pete winked, "and masturbators. He directs church members to stand outside houses of prostitution in Anchorage to take photos of the men entering or exiting these establishments of ill repute. Then, upstanding guy that he is, he prints the pictures and names the poor doofuses in the church's weekly bulletin and the *Anchorage Daily News*."

"Where does he get the names?" Logan asked.

"Don't know, but likely from the license plates. Probably has a contact in law enforcement.

"Anyway, he's a fraud. Tasker's not a doctor. He doesn't have a doctorate in anything. He claims on his church's website to have earned a Doctor of Divinity degree from Pyles Anders College. The problem is, Pyles College isn't accredited anywhere in the United States and, according to its website, doesn't even offer doctorates."

"He's a complete scam artist," Erika interjected after thanking the server for the drinks.

"It gets worse," added Pete. "He also claims to have a doctorate degree from American Baptist Theological Seminary, but the seminary is completely online, so he couldn't have physically attended classes there. The Southern Association of Colleges and Schools is the only commission or organization in the world that accredits the seminary. Furthermore, the Southern Association website is unclear whether the American Baptist Theological Seminary is even accredited by them because Tasker's online seminary uses a bunch of different names. Last, the American Baptist Theological Seminary guarantees that anyone who agrees to be baptized by them can buy a doctor of divinity and call themselves *doctor.*"

"Is the Pyles Anders College still in business?" Logan asked.

"Just barely. Membership's dwindling. Probably because of how backward the school is by today's standards. There are separate requirements for male and female students for the same degree. The Bachelor of Science degree program, for example, has a special curriculum for women that requires classes like Home Decorating, Clothing Design, and—get this—Understanding Your Husband! Also, I have an idea that prospective students aren't enthusiastic about the school policies: prohibiting long hair for men, drinking alcohol, smoking, dancing, Hollywood movies, playing cards, having fellowship with liberals, or 'participating in other questionable amusements,' whatever those might be," Pete snorted.

"Whoa." Logan laughed. "We wouldn't have made it through day one!"

"Tasker supposedly obtained a doctorate from this nonaccredited school in 1974. It was the same time the Bible instructor at Pyles Anders College was charged with kidnapping, aggravated assault, perjury, and seven counts of rape."

"Busy guy," smirked Logan.

"He and his wife were convicted in 1980 of kidnapping, child abuse, and aggravated assault. They were sentenced to 179 years for the rape and torture of their adopted daughter, and the story was featured on ABC's *Primetime*."

"If there's much more on this fascinating topic, can we order dinner first? I can't take all this on an empty stomach."

"Not a lot more, but let's go ahead and order. Pete never feeds me unless we're with you," Erika kidded as she beckoned the server their table.

They ordered various types of seafood. Homer had some good steak houses but ordering steak in Homer was like ordering seafood in Kansas City.

"We also found more recent allegations about their illegal shenanigans," Pete added.

"Murder doesn't seem like such a large step from there," Logan volunteered. "At least, it wasn't in Alaska back in the early 1980s. Let's see if we can tie some of this together. I'm still trying to get in touch with Barbara Hamlin out in Eagle River. We have her address and phone number. She may be helpful since she's no longer a church member. She's essentially gone into hiding since her husband disappeared."

"So, how can we help?" Pete asked.

"Research is about all you can do. We need to limit your involvement because you don't want to be a rebuttal witness at your own trial. That testimony wouldn't be very believable. "If I get an interview with Mrs. Hamlin, I'll take a private investigator along who can testify about what she says. The jury consultant, McQuigg, also wants to see her. I think I can keep the initial cost for the PI at less than a thousand dollars, but it may triple if he or she testifies at trial.

"Would that be a problem?"

"Nah...if we have to do it, then let's do it," Pete replied.

Upon returning to *The Coral Dawn*, Logan sank into the mattress and checked his laptop for messages. His mind was restless, and despite being tired, it took a long time to fall asleep.

CHAPTER
29

THE ROCKING OF THE BOAT SUDDENLY awakened Logan. Not the deep pitching felt in stormy weather, but the off-kilter dips announcing *you have company*. His mind momentarily reeled before a cool focus kicked in. He reached for the Glock stashed in the drawer at the side of the bed. He held his breath as he heard the salon door slide open as he unlocked the safety. Light footsteps sounded on the carpeted stairs. He saw the door latch begin to turn. Logan rolled away from the door and awkwardly slid down against the starboard wall. He aimed the Glock at the dimly lit door.

"Logan," a hoarse voice whispered from the other side of the door, "are you here?"

"Oh my God! *Yes*! I'm here! Do you know how close you were to getting shot!"

Lacey entered the aft cabin. "What's the matter?" she whispered, tossing her jacket on the side chair. "And why are we whispering?"

"Never mind. What are you doing here?"

"Not exactly the greeting I was anticipating."

"I'm so sorry. We've been on edge. Things have been dicey around here."

He stiffly unfolded his long legs from his crouched position behind the bed, and in one step enveloped Lacey in his arms, hugging her tightly. "I'll explain everything in the morning."

They kissed as he sat on the side of the bed and pulled her close, his face buried between her breasts. "God," he whispered huskily, lifting her sweater. "It's good to see you."

Friday morning, Logan mentally revisited the delightful challenge of peeling Lacey out of her tight skirt. There was no talk of commitments or feelings. They'd reverted to a time past, and the unquestioned passion of lovers whose bodies, finely attuned to each other, never missed a beat. Still, something was unmistakably different. Logan was different. *I love this one woman more than ever.* He felt unfamiliar twinges of optimism about their future together. *I haven't been optimistic about a relationship in years. Hell,* he told himself, *probably never.*

In the past, Logan invariably latched onto women with bipolar leanings. *Incredible in bed, but forming an attachment was like adopting a feral cat.* Interestingly, his therapist had discerned a pattern. It was a—*how'd the guy put it?*—a self-sabotaging technique. No surprise that those relationships usually ended abruptly, and sometimes with calls to the police and pistols pointed in his general direction. *Maybe I'm done with the body piercings, vaginal paintings, handcuffs, and recreational drugs.*

His relationship with Lacey was different. It had *always* been different and normal. Logan had assiduously avoided normal. He innately understood that the long-ago earthquake drove his avoidance of a long-term, healthy, committed relationship. His relationship with his parents was enough emotional risk. However, he had to admit, those alley cat relationships had been exciting, albeit brief, liaisons.

Lacey exited the aft cabin. "Good morning, sunshine," Logan hollered from the galley. "Ready for coffee on the lido deck?"

"Sounds wonderful."

The sun was shining, promising a beautiful clear day in South central Alaska. Logan, comfortably dressed in baggy cargo shorts, a Seattle Seahawks sweatshirt, and flip-flops, grabbed his aviator sunglasses on his way from the galley to the aft deck with their coffee. Lacey followed, her lithe figure obscured by a white T-shirt. One of his. Nothing else. She smiled and kissed him as he reached under her shirt. "Whoa...you, Mister, are on a twenty-four-hour shutdown, or however long it takes me to recover. Now, fill me in on what's been going on, and why the Glock?"

"You haven't been home yet, have you?"

"No. My priority was you, especially after a six-hour flight with free drinks in first class. They upgraded me because of my cuteness."

"Hey, no surprise there. Then another upgrade when you got here."

Lacey nuzzled his neck, kissing his cheek. "Your upgrade was the best."

Logan sighed. "I am so happy about you coming back early that I almost can't bear to give you any bad news."

"Oh, no, what else could have gone wrong while I was gone?"

"Well, there was a break-in at your house. It doesn't appear that anything was stolen, but a few things were broken. On your desk, I found a threatening note demanding that you stop representing Pete."

"Jesus, that's horrible. We can deal with that when we get there."

Toby interrupted with a loud bark followed by pathetic whining. Logan went down to the swim step. Toby jumped and Logan caught him. Lacey had witnessed their routine many times over the years. "Okay, buddy. This morning it's just the dry treat, no chili."

Logan carried him up the steps to the deck before he disappeared into the galley. Lacey scratched Toby's ears and he reciprocated her thoughtfulness by thoroughly licking her hand before standing patiently at the sliding door to await his treat. Since Mike and Sasha were still asleep, Toby watched Logan start breakfast, raptly absorbing the enticing fragrance of bacon wafting across the boat harbor. After sharing a leisurely breakfast, Lacey and Logan quietly left the boat, and Toby jumped back onto his sailboat, circling briefly before fluffing up his bed and quietly resuming his guard dog duties.

"You're not going to like what you're about to see," Logan warned as they drove up the hillside.

"I can handle it as long as the smell's gone."

"I think I took care of the smell, but I didn't touch your office. Homer PD wants to know if anything's missing." They entered Lacey's front door, grateful that the only lingering smell was the air freshener Logan had sprayed during the cleanup. He followed Lacey into her office.

"My God," she whispered as she surveyed the room. She picked a lamp and her computer off the floor and gloomily looked at the scattered books and photographs in shattered frames dispersed across the hardwood.

"Can you tell if anything is missing?"

"Right now, I don't care. This is an invasion. Whether stuff's missing or not, I don't know if I'll ever feel safe in my own home again. It's...it's like being physically attacked." Lacey leaned into Logan's arms and sobbed. Eventually, she stiffened her shoulders, pulled away, and sat at her desk, too shocked to move.

Logan began straightening Lacey's papers and files and picked up smashed family pictures. There was one of Rusty, the beloved cocker spaniel who'd grown up with Lacey's children, and a photo of Lacey and Logan smiling at sunset aboard *The Coral Dawn*. Lacey watched for a moment. "I know you're trying to help, but I just can't face this right now. Let's go down to the office. I'll do cleanup later in my own time. I'm anxious to see Pam and Katie, and it'll be nice to see my desk and computer there, all in one piece."

Pam was furiously typing away when they entered the office. Surprised to see Lacey back, she blurted out, "Hey, what are you doing home so soon? I thought you weren't coming back until Monday." Lacey responded by hugging Pam as tears began cascading down her face.

Pam looked anxiously at Logan. "What happened?"

"Lacey came in late last night and just saw her vandalized house."

"Oh, I'm so sorry you came back to that, Lacey."

"I have to sit down." Lacey regained control of her emotions and walked toward her office. Logan rushed ahead, yanked his chair from behind her desk, and quickly rolled hers into place. She plunked down, yanked a tissue from the Kleenex box, and blew her nose. "It's really good to be home."

Pam and Logan burst out laughing until Lacey had to join in. They were all teary-eyed before the laughter died away. Pam and Logan settled into the client chairs opposite Lacey's desk. "Before we go over our clients' files," Lacey said, "what's been happening with Pete's case."

"A ton, if you ask me," Pam said.

Logan's summary of the investigation concluded with, "So there's a lot to digest."

"Huh...nothing exciting, then." Lacey's eyes twinkled above a Kleenex as she blew her nose again.

"Nope, just a bomb threat closed our fair city for half a day and that little break-in at your house. Oh, yeah, and I was followed and rear-ended while driving a rental car in Anchorage. Twice. In one day."

"You guys sandbagged me! I can't believe I missed all that!"

"But wait," Logan added cheerfully, "there's more. Pam and Katie got drunk on company time. At office expense."

"Logan! We were coping with a possible bomb going off in the office! Besides, we did offer to pay for our wine. You declined."

"Okay, okay, just don't sue us." And they all laughed some more.

"But what about Hamlin," Lacey asked. "Do you have any idea who killed him?"

"Not yet," Logan responded. "At this point, my best guess is it's either Barbara Hamlin, Bill Hamlin's lover, or maybe even the lover's husband, or some poor schmuck from the church."

"Sheesh, I leave for ten days and that's all ya got? Good thing I came back early. We've gotta get this show on the road."

"Exactly." Logan pointedly looked at Pam as if the words were directed to her and not him.

"Okay, okay, I'm on it." Pam laughed, holding her hands up in surrender, and returned to her desk.

"Anything else I need to know? New clients? Deaths? Unpaid bills?"

"Yeah, one new client. No deaths. Ask Katie about the bills. Pete gave her a $5,000

check to cover some initial overhead, and he'll pay for the security system that I had installed."

"He doesn't have to do that. I've always wanted a system to protect us. And the oh-so-valuable contents abandoned in the attic," she added sarcastically.

"You'll have to spar with Pete about the alarm system. He was adamant about paying for it."

"That sounds like Pete. Now, who's the new client? Pam said she's charming and way younger than you are."

"Uh-huh...women do talk."

"You bet. There are three monumental communication devices: the telegraph, telephone, and telling a woman."

Logan chuckled. "Can't argue with that. And, yes, Ms. Delores Anne Rodriguez retained your firm to represent her in a DWI case. And, yes, she is pretty. Unfortunately, she's also very troubled. Her mental condition and actions are sufficiently bizarre that it might provide a defense to the charges against her."

"Charges plural?"

"Yep, there's also an eluding arrest charge."

"Sounds like you have a handle on it. Why don't you take the case until you head back south? Just make sure she understands there will probably be a transfer of her case within the office. And, Logan, it might be a good idea for someone to lose the braless look and miniskirts."

"I haven't owned a bra or worn miniskirts in years."

"Uh-huh...grab your old chair and find a workspace in the war room."

30

A GRAVELLY, CIGARETTE-THROATED voice croaked, "Hello?"
"Hi...Barbara Hamlin?" Logan asked in a pleasant, cordial tone.
"Who's this?"

"Logan Finch. I represent Pete Foster."

Click. The dial tone buzzed loudly in his ear.

A frustrated Logan immediately called Chris Branson.

"Christopher Branson here. To what do I owe the pleasure of your call this beautiful Wednesday morning, Mr. Finch?"

"The beautiful morning just clouded over, Chris. Your key witness, Barbara Hamlin, hung up on me. You know I have the right to interview the state's witnesses. I can subpoena her and get a court order and depose her for twenty hours if I see fit."

"Whoa, settle down, Counsel. We both know your legal rights...just give me a chance to cooperate with you."

"Sorry, you're right. Obviously I'm not a fan of getting hung up on."

"Look at it from her point of view. She may have excellent reasons for hanging up on you if she believes *your* client killed *her* husband. But, Logan, I'll contact her and set up a meeting with the three of us. Do you want to depose her or just ask her some preliminary questions?"

"I want to interview her with my private investigator present to take notes. I'd also like to have my jury consultant present."

"Jury consultant? Huh...it's unorthodox, but I'll do my best to arrange it."

"Okay, give me a call when you put something together. And thanks."

Pam entered the war room. "How's Lacey doing?"

"She'll be all right. A lot has happened to impact her safe, quiet life. She needs a little time to chill out."

"Take her to lunch. Mexican. Mucho margaritas!"

"Great idea...now, why didn't I think of that?"

"Oh, could it be you're a typically unaware guy?" Pam laughed, then rushed to grab the phone ringing at the reception desk. Within seconds, she transferred Branson's call to Logan.

"Hey, Chris, that was quick. Did she hang up on you too?"

"Not hardly, but she did throw me a curveball I've never seen before. She'll meet with you. Just you. Not me. Not your PI. Not your jury consultant. No recording devices either. Be at her home, 2:00 p.m. tomorrow in Eagle River. If you want to depose her later, she says that will be difficult because she travels a lot. I seriously doubt that, but you'll have to agree in advance that you will not serve her with a subpoena between now and 5:00 p.m. Saturday."

Logan didn't hesitate. "Agreed. I'll be there."

Their call ended and Logan slapped his desk loudly. "Yes!"

Lacey burst through the door. "What happened?"

"Great news." Logan winked.

"We could use some great news on this case. Looks like I brought good luck from the sands of Hawaii! So, what's the good news?"

"You won't believe this, but Mrs. Hamlin wants to meet with me. Alone. No one else. No tape recorders and no prosecutor."

"An exclusive interview, as they say in the news business?"

"Exactly!"

"When?"

"Tomorrow afternoon. I was thinking if you come to Anchorage with me today, I'd take you out for dinner and then follow up with the *Whale Fat Follies* at the Fly By Night Club in Spenard on the southern outskirts of Anchorage."

"Really! Oh...wait a minute. I've *heard* of the *Whale Fat Follies*, just never thought I'd actually *see* the *Whale Fat Follies*." Lacey winked.

"Lacey, you are in for a rare treat. Skinny Dick and his wife are the guests of honor at Mr. Whitekeys's extravaganza. Skinny Dick operates an old roadhouse on the Parks Highway between Anchorage and Fairbanks called—I kid you not—Skinny Dick's Halfway Inn."

Lacey, visibly unimpressed, said, "Ooh, this just keeps getting better. Any chance female mud wrestling will be added to the evening's events?"

"Yeah," Logan deadpanned. "But I thought I'd save that for another time."

"I'm sorry you missed out on this great slice of historical Alaskan schtick."

Every summer for over twenty years, Mr. Whitekeys, a piano player, assembled an Alaska show poking fun at tourists and Alaskans. He used to stage it at the Fly By Night Club in Spenard, but when the state legislature started meeting in Spenard, Whitekeys looked to relocate his piano-playing extravaganza to downtown Anchorage. According to legend, Whitekeys gibed, "The place got too sleazy, even for us."

"Okay, I'm in. If it's half as entertaining as it sounds, it should be fun. Go ahead, get our tickets. What time do you want to fly to Anchorage?"

"I'm thinking about four o'clock. I want to meet with Ms. Rodriguez in about an hour."

Logan then called Rodriguez. "Good morning, Delores Anne."

"Hello," she said demurely.

"Can I meet you in about an hour and review the police report and discuss my recommended approach for defending you?"

"Yes. I have a job interview in Kenai at three thirty, so that will work."

"Great, see you in an hour."

Katie entered the office and shrieked, "Wow, Lacey, what are you doing here?"

"Had to come back where the action is."

"Are you doing okay?" Lacey asked, referring to the bomb threat.

"Oh, yeah, we're good. Especially since we learned how to work the security system."

The phone rang and they lowered their voices as Pam answered. "Law offices of Lacey Carpenter. How may I help you?"

There was a slight pause and Pam smoothly stated, "I'll give them your message. They both look forward to meeting you in person. May I say who is calling, please? Hello? Hello?"

Pam's side of the conversation had caught everyone's attention. She looked up and shook her head before reaching for the telephone message pad and dutifully filling out the top of the page: *Same voice. Same guy.*

"Good job, Pam." Lacey looked around the room. "Anybody want to quit?"

Pam and Katie responded in unison, "Hell, no."

CHAPTER
31

L OGAN GLANCED INTO the reception area. Yep, Pam was covertly
monitoring the hallway. Not a chance in hell Ms. Rodriguez would
take an unexamined step through the office. *Opportunity was a'knocking*,
Logan thought as he walked out of the war room and announced, "By the
way, my appointment with Ms. Rodriguez will be at Café Cups this afternoon."

Lacey's head snapped around, and her green eyes sparked and nar-
rowed.

Pam's eyebrows nearly touched her hairline.

Logan enjoyed their reactions, "Just kidding, ladies."

"All right, you got us," Pam admitted.

Lacey declined to comment. She kept reading, but Logan read her
broadcast loud and clear: *You are so not funny, Finch!*

Thirty minutes later, Logan's intercom buzzed, and Pam announced,
"Ms. Rodriguez has arrived." When he emerged from the war room,
Lacey was ostensibly searching for a document in Pam's desk drawer. Pam
stood sentinel next to her. They presented a formidable team. Delores
Anne Rodriguez rose gracefully from the guest chair and, feeling the
inspection heat, was circumspect. "Good afternoon, Mr. Finch, how are
you?"

"I'm great, thanks, Ms. Rodriguez."

After entering the war room, he visualized Lacey and Pam with their
ears pinned against the door. "I've read the police report. Good news
is that it mirrors your statements to me. Still, I need more information
about your background and why you fear men."

"I'd rather not talk about it."

"Delores Anne, I don't want to invade your privacy, but your history
may provide a defense to the evading arrest charge. If you have had some

experiences or situations that make you want to avoid a trooper, then bring it on. I need to know."

"Okay...if you must know, I suffer from PTSD. I was molested by my stepfather for seven years when I was a little girl. He was a cop. I get counseling for that."

Bingo. Logan pounced at the possibility of burying the evading charge. "I'll have to discuss this with your counselor and get a letter for the prosecutor. Last, the counselor may need to testify in court if we wind up going to trial. You're okay with that, right?"

"No!"

Logan looked up at her calmly until she caved.

"Okay, yeah, fine. Whatever," she said forlornly.

"Great, I'll line it up. Do you have any other questions?"

"Well, I got a notice in the mail. My license is going to be suspended next week for ninety days. What's that all about?"

"I'm sorry, but not surprised. It's standard. After thirty days, you can get a limited license allowing you to travel to and from work and to any necessary appointments. I'll help you with that."

Although her case was looking better, she looked defeated.

"I'll wait for your call, then."

CHAPTER
32

"**L**OGAN AND I ARE GOING to Anchorage this afternoon," Lacey told Pam.

"What's up?"

"Logan's interviewing Barbara Hamlin tomorrow. He wants her version of events before she changes her mind."

"Okay...so, why are you going too? Besides the obvious?"

"*Obvious*, is it? I thought my secret was in the vault."

"I heard you cry and mope all winter, vowing to never get romantically involved with Logan again. Ever. Good job, kiddo. You held out almost a month after he returned."

"A whole month, huh? Wow, I must have been crazy to have left him alone so long.

Besides, while I was in Hawaii, I decided that this time, I'd protect myself. I'm emotionally okay to say goodbye when he leaves."

"Uh-huh...I've heard those words before too."

"I swear, I'll keep my emotional distance. But it's nice to have a man in my life even..." She stopped at Pam's eyeroll and pointed a forefinger at Pam. "*Even* when it's just temporary." Lacey then added the fateful words spoken by every woman immersed in a dead-end relationship. "Besides, I'm not interested in anyone else right now."

Pam shrugged. "*Not* my business. So, what are you going to do in Anchorage while he's working?"

"Are you kidding? Shop! And wait, there's more! We're going to see the *Whale Fat Follies* tonight at the Fly By Night Club!"

"Ooh, doesn't get better than that! I've even heard that the audience participates in a raffle at the end of the night. The winner gets a one-week, all-expenses-paid vacation to Fairbanks."

Not one to let her happiness bubble burst, Lacey quipped, "See, told ya it was going to be fun!"

"Yeah," Pam deadpanned. "And the loser gets two weeks in Fairbanks!"

"Very funny."

Hearing their laughter drew Logan out of his office. "Glad everyone's having such a good time this afternoon. There must not be any more phone threats."

"I have a few more things to do before we leave for the airport, but I'll be ready in about an hour."

Logan reserved two rooms in Anchorage for that night and Saturday. His room was once again on the bottom floor, due to his earthquake PTSD, but he reserved a room for Lacey on the tenth floor with a view of the inlet and Mount Susitna. *God, I hope she doesn't use it.*

"Guess we're not saving our appetites for the great dining experience at the Fly By Night later this evening," Lacey observed as Logan ordered halibut cheeks and fries at the Whale's Tail restaurant.

"How perceptive, but this is just an appetizer, Ms. Carpenter. Tonight, it's Fly By Night Spam and cheeseburgers all the way, baby! Let's go back to the room. We'll work up an appetite for that gastronomical dining experience."

"Mmmm." Lacey touched her nose to Logan's, her green eyes dancing. "You drive a hard bargain."

They cabbed the mile to the Club and entered amidst a boatload of excited tourists. "Can't wait till you see Skinny Dick and his wife," Logan said.

"Neither can I," Lacey responded dryly.

"Hey, do I detect a lack of sincerity?" Logan laughed as they entered the establishment. To their right, between the bar and dining area, sat an old couple surrounded by hats, shirts, and kites. Next to them, the marquee read:

"The Alaskan Show the Department of Tourism does NOT want you to see!"

"What's that all about?" questioned Lacey.

"Satire...pure political satire. We'll see hundreds of slides of Alaskans and tourists doing stupid things, along with stand-up comedy and hilarious skits."

The cover page of the program read:

"This year's centennial edition of the *Whale Fat Follies* will be a glorification of a town that, in only one hundred years, has grown from a backwater boondock into a metropolis where people are more afraid of gluten than they are of grizzly bears."

Laughing and reliving the hilarity of the evening's *Follies*, Logan and Lacey sauntered back to the hotel. Lacey was a convert and an ardent fan.

"Every tourist should see this stuff."

Alaska Magazine is a promotional magazine for the state and once hired Mr. Whitekeys to write a monthly column about Alaska. In an early column, he used Alaska's fishing statistics, applied them to the expenses incurred on a fishing trip to Alaska, and determined the average sport fishing tourist spent over $500 for a single salmon. It was the last column 'Keys wrote for the tourist industry in the great state of Alaska. 'Key's termination notice stated, "*Alaska Magazine's* mission is to encourage people to come to see Alaska, to promote tourism. Everything about your piece trashes the state we love.'"

"The *Follies* are Alaska in a nutshell," Lacey laughed.

Logan nodded. "I know, I loved it! Especially the fat lady in the bikini. When the crowd yelled at her to 'put it back on!' to stripper music, she did!"

Lacey giggled as she opened the hotel room door. "She sure did. Then she put her ski pants, parka, and her boots back on too!"

"Now, young lady, let's see if I can inspire you by yelling, 'Take it off,' without the music!"

Lacey responded by jumping onto the ottoman and seductively humming, *Ta da, da, da...ta da, da, da.* She slowly peeled off her jacket, one sleeve at a time. She threw it on the bed while Logan tugged off her belt...

CHAPTER
33

L OGAN LEFT FOR EAGLE RIVER THE NEXT DAY. The same white pickup came up behind him. *How the hell did these guys know he was going to Eagle River? I thought only our office and Chris Branson knew about the meeting.*

Logan slowed at the entrance to the trailer park subdivision. The pickup slowed down and dropped back fifty yards. He spotted the word *Hamlin* on a dented mailbox and pulled into the driveway. A faded 1972 red Toyota Celica crouched in the carport adjacent to the dilapidated remnants of a tin storage shed. When Logan got out of his car, the pickup sped past, its tires churning gravel. Mrs. Hamlin observed the warning shot as she peered out a smoke-stained window.

Before he could knock, the front door opened slightly to reveal a tall, decaying woman in worn house slippers. She clutched a baggy, dingy brown sweater around her thin shoulders. Stale cigarette smoke saturated the trailer and assaulted his nostrils. "Mrs. Hamlin? Barbara Hamlin?"

Barbara Hamlin didn't waste her time on pleasantries. "Hurry up, get in here. They're going to kill me."

"Who's going to kill you, ma'am?"

Her demeanor softened and her lips curled up in an almost forgotten gesture of friendliness, reminding Logan of someone who'd just sucked the lime after a tequila shot. "Call me Barbara. It's those nutty church guys. They're trying to get rid of me before the trial. They're afraid I'll rat out the Guidance Panel for what they did to my husband." Grim-faced, she added, "And your client's daughter."

"Whoa . . . okay if I sit down and take some notes?"

"Not in this lifetime! No tape recording. No notes. And if I'm ever in court, I'll deny I ever talked to you."

"What are you afraid of?"

"Not what. *Who.* If what I tell you gets to the wrong people, I'm dead and after you hear my story, you'll understand, but I want to get this off my chest. Once I'm gone, you can do anything you want to with the information. But s'long as I'm alive, I'll deny all of it. "Eagle River's my last stand," she declared. "I'm tired of runnin' and hidin'. Those bastards don't know it, but I'm still pretty good with a gun and a helluva lot stronger than I look." Cloudy gray eyes scrutinized Logan. "You're my last contact. I'm sorry, but that's the way it's gotta be."

Logan recognized the futility in pressing the issue. He sat gingerly on what had once been a plush velveteen gold couch. He pushed aside a crocheted afghan, its frayed multicolored squares carpeted in cat hair. He placed his file on the floor to reassure her there'd be no notetaking.

"Okay, why don't we start at the beginning . . . if you could please take me through it chronologically."

She settled into a matching recliner across from Logan. It was threadbare with a host of cigarette burns from a millennium of use.

"Okay, then, from the beginning. Hope you got lots of time."

"I have all the time you'll need."

She nervously launched into her story. In 1978, she and Bill moved to Alaska. "It was a real struggle at first, you know, making ends meet. We joined the Evangelical church in Muldoon to find some friends. Weren't so many members back then. But Tasker grew the congregation with a lot of pipeline workers from down south who were flocking into Anchorage back then." She interrupted herself. "Mind if I fix a drink and get a cigarette, Logan?"

Logan shook his head and gracefully lied. "Not at all."

She shuffled the few feet to her four-by-eight kitchen, reached above the tiny refrigerator, and pulled down a nearly full half-gallon bottle of Johnnie Walker Black. Logan's right eyebrow raised when she grabbed two glasses and primly set them on the coffee table. "Wud'ja like a shot?"

"No. No, thank you. Maybe later."

"You're gonna need one before I finish talkin'," she predicted.

Logan stifled a laugh. "Okay, I'll keep that in mind." Although the smell in the house couldn't get much worse, Logan noticed with immense relief that she didn't light the cigarette.

"Ron Tasker insisted we call him *Doctor.*" She paused for a long sip of scotch before confiding, "We all had our doubts about him being any kinda doctor, you understand. Anyway, Jansen and his family was already there. The two kids were bright enough. So was Darla, his wife. Jack'd come to church every Sunday, but he was just another butt in the pew— pardon my French. He never said or did shit."

Logan visualized a jury's response to Barbara Hamlin's colorfully constructed narrative and struggled to maintain an impassively neutral expression.

"Not very long after we arrived in Anchorage, Tasker put together this five-member club. He called it the Guidance Panel and the members acted like they was judges. They'd punish the parishioners for wrongdoing—you know, the blasphemers and them folks. Bill was drafted on to that Guidance Panel in 1979. Tasker's the one who really made all the decisions. The rest of the panel was only there so's they'd learn the teachings of God according to Mister High and Mighty Tasker. Then, I think it was sometime in eighty-two, Bill comes home all upset. He said Jansen asked for a special meetin' where he talked about cleaning up Anchorage's Fourth Avenue trash. He said whenever he saw a whore or anybody doing the devil's work, they'd all be forced to act in the name of God. Tasker was at that meetin'.

"Bill told me Tasker quoted the Old Testament scripture, mostly the Book of Isaiah, where it says:
'And the destruction of the transgressors and
the sinners shall be together, and
they that forsake the LORD shall be consumed . . .'
"Blah, blah, blah—it was somethin' like that. I looked that part up so's I'd remember when I talked to you. I'm not real good about quoting from the Good Book. Anyway, t'way Bill put it, Jansen talked about taking whores up in his plane and flying out over to the mudflats where he'd release 'em. He hunted them poor girls down 'like the animals they was,' Jansen said. 'Just as God wanted.'"

"You're not making this up, are you?"

Seeing Logan's incredulous stare, she repeated Jansen's words. "Swear t'God, that's exactly what Bill told me. It's the Lord's truth. After that, Jansen left the room while the guys on the panel talked it over. Bill wanted to report Jansen to the police, but Tasker told 'em s'long as Jansen didn't say he was gonna keep on killin' them girls, they was good ta go. Bill said a lawyer on the panel agreed with Tasker."

"Any idea who the lawyer was?" Logan pretended not to know.

"Gerald Abbott."

She spat out his name and then poured two more shots. With her watery gray eyes turned upward, she nearly drained the glass before slamming it back down onto the coffee table. Logan was tempted to ask for that shot of whiskey. *Why is it Gerald Abbott seems to be at the heart of this mess—which was looking less like a run-of-the-mill murder case and becoming something far more sinister: a conspiracy between church and state, with vulnerable young girls as the victims.*

"Early one morning, Tasker called and talked to Bill. He wanted us to tell the police that Jansen was playin' cards at our house the night before. Tasker said some whore was tryin' to frame Jansen and bilk him out of a few thousand dollars. She was threatenin' to lie to his wife and ruin his marriage. Bill din't like getting involved, but . . ." She looked at Logan pleadingly, hoping he'd understand why they made the terrible decision to go along with Tasker.

"Neither of us wanted t'do it, but Bill was afraid not to do what Tasker said. He made me lie too."

"Did the cops ever ask you about Jansen?"

"You bet. Early that morning, we heard a knock at the door. Two cops asked us if we knew Jansen. We did what Tasker told us to do. You know, told 'em he was upstanding and religious, he was a great family guy. Bill said we knew his wife was on vacation in Europe with the kids, so's we'd invited him over to play cards with us. We told 'em we played into the wee hours of the night."

"What happened next?"

"Tasker kept on a'runnin' his private posse within the congregation . . . all believers savin' the world, according to Tasker. Bill and the other Guidance guys had to take pictures of people's cars parked in front of the stripper bars and the whorehouses. Back then, they called 'em *massage parlors.*"

"What happened next?"

"The whole damned lie blew up in our faces, is what happened next!"

"How so?"

"Sick bastard murdered more girls 'tween the time we give our alibi story in June till October. *He's* the son of a bitch who needed to die. Not my husband. Anyway, it was 'bout then I started suspectin' Bill was seein' some gal. The meetin' time he was spendin' at the church got real long. He never done that before. Bill hated being around Tasker. Of course, Tasker was a real phony, if you ask me. But still n'all, truth is, we was afraid of him."

"What'd you do?"

"I asked Bill if he was seein' somebody. He said I was crazy as a loon. So I started checking out his car, cuz'... ...." She paused for another a gulp of scotch whiskey, then daintily wiped her mouth. "I ain't no loon. Bill would come home from those meetin's smelling like a goddamn cologne factory—same thing after walkin' our dog, Layla, on Sunday afternoons."

"So, you thought that Bill saw this someone on Sunday afternoons?"

"Thought? Hell, no. I know he did!" She nodded sagely, her wrinkled lips clenched in tight resignation against nicotine-stained teeth. "Women know that shit."

"Would you be willing to testify to that?"

"Maybe." She wrestled momentarily with her decision. "How much ya paying?"

"I'm sorry, Mrs. Hamlin, but I can't pay you for your testimony. I'd get disbarred," Logan explained.

"But no one would ever know. You could give me cash."

"Damn." Logan shook his head in frustration. "You're the second person this month who wanted payment for testimony. Barbara, here's the deal—I will know. I will know, and just maybe someone else will too. It'd be the end of my law career as well as my reputation in the state where I grew up. Won't you, please, just tell the truth because it's the right thing to do?"

Barbara sat back in the recliner. "I'll think about it. Now, you wanna hear the rest of the story, or not?"

"Of course."

"When Jansen was arrested, Bill went to the next meetin'. He told 'em about us being 'fraid we'd get arrested too, that we was accomplices. Tasker and Abbott promised that'd never happen. Turned out they was right. We was overlooked. Always figured that Abbott fellow had some pull somewhere."

That's an understatement. "What happened next?"

"We hung round town till February when Jansen got sentenced."

"Really?" Logan hoped he sounded surprised. "You were at the sentencing hearing?"

"You bet. We din't wanna miss that for the world, till your client cold-cocked my husband. He shoulda punched the Taskers, don't cha think?"

"Probably. But no one knew the Taskers were involved."

"Don't get me wrong, I can't put blame on your client. But then the next week, at the church meetin', Bill got told to leave town right away."

"Would you testify to that?"

"Maybe. We was so pissed off at the church, we couldn't see straight. As if trying to withdraw from the past, she slumped back and muttered softly. "I still can't believe I kept workin' there on Sundays . . . And Bill? He kept up his goddamn foolin' around."

"What's her name? Any idea where she is now?"

"I don't know. I asked Tasker who she was. 'Just leave it alone,' he said. 'Everything'll be all right.' From what Tasker said, sounded like he doubted that it was a woman. Of all things, can you imagine him thinking Bill was a queer? I snooped around but nobody in the congregation would tell me anything about the affair. Then Tasker up and gives us round-trip tickets and all 'spenses paid for two weeks in Maui! We couldn't believe it. 'Bout this time, the cabinet business in Anchorage had gone t'hell. We had a huge house with a big garage where he built the cabinets. Still n'all, we managed to get by okay. We even took vacations . . . Europe, Africa, Asia, South America."

"Wow."

"Yeah, sounds great, don't it? Till y'know Bill went on several vacations without me. He was s'posed to be goin' with the Guidance Panel, but I know he was with . . . whoever." Anger crossed her face and she paused for a last gulp that emptied her glass. "Four years later, the fall of eighty-eight, Bill up and disappears. That finished it for me. I had no more tears left, not 'bout his affair or anything else."

"Did you or Bill ever see my client at the dog park on Huffman?"

"I never did. I don't know about Bill. After Bill disappeared, wasn't too much longer afterward though, Tasker called me into his office. The son of a bitch demanded that I get outta Dodge and forget all about Bill. But Anchorage was my home. I din't wanna leave, but he made it clear I had to make a clean break. He said if I din't leave, I'd be a sinner and deserve punishment. Tasker threatened me, said Abbott'd charge me for giving that false alibi if I didn't leave. The false alibi that son of a bitch *made* Bill and me give! Then, the bastard got down on his fucking knees and quoted scripture outta the Bible:

'Let the sinners be consumed out of the earth

and let the wicked be no more. Bless thou the LORD,

O my soul. Praise ye, the LORD.'"

She bore down with a stare that would scare the devil himself. "He was one crazy fucker. With Bill gone, I was all alone and damn afraid. Nobody had to tell me twice that I had to leave the state, pronto. So, I quick-like sold our house, packed up my shit, and moved down to North Phoenix. Little town called Cave Creek, to be exact."

"So, why'd you come back?"

"Phoenix is too fuckin' hot. Alaska's home. Besides, the time limit's probably up on anything they could charge me with. So I'm not afraid of Tasker or Abbott or anybody else no more. I figure I could make more trouble for them than they could for me."

"Not if they killed you."

"Yeah . . . I'm just starting to get that. It weren't no problem when I first moved back here. But when they ID'd Bill's bones and the prosecutor decided your buddy kilt him, things changed. Tasker and Abbott found me up here, told me, 'Stay silent or else,'" she said as she mimicked Abbott's voice. "Y'know what, though? Fuck 'em. I'm old. I've got a bad liver and a heavy heart. They can't make my life more miserable than it already is, and I don't give a rat's ass anymore if I live or die. I just want a little say-so as to when. I wanna clear my conscience by telling t'truth to someone that'll make it better, s'all. Then . . . let the chips fall wherever."

She poured two more shots of whiskey and neatly downed them.

"Can I see you again before the trial?" Logan carefully asked.

"Yeah, sure. But I still don't know what I'm gonna say on the witness stand. And y'gotta think about the money too. Not much. Just enough to get me by."

Logan stood at the door. "Fair enough. Thanks again for talking to me, Barbara. I know this wasn't easy for you. Please, be safe. Call the cops if you see that truck again, promise?"

"Don't worry 'bout me, I'll be okay," she said with the cigarette still dangling from her lips.

❖

"Lacey, the woman's a gold mine and she had some ideas about who killed her husband," Logan said after returning to the hotel room.

"Great. What'd she say?"

Logan recounted the highlights of her story.

"Wow! I guess I'm not shocked. Then again, I am totally stunned by the depth and scope of the wrongdoing. So, now whom do you consider alternate suspects?"

"Well, there's Mrs. Hamlin. She's a mess but knew her husband was fooling around on her. She was fed up with him and his lover, and—her words, not mine—'the fucking church.'"

"Who was his lover?"

"Still don't know. Tasker implied it may be a guy. So, add Bill's lover to the suspect list."

"Good. So, who else?"

"The church. I mean, someone from the church."

"Why would anyone from his church want him dead?"

"The Hamlins were unhappy and nervous about their alibi. Someone may have feared they would cut a deal with the prosecutors and tell them all about the Guidance Panel and Jansen. Plus, their marriage was on the rocks. Barbara was extremely pissed that Tasker wouldn't tell her who her husband was seeing. It's also possible the Guidance Panel got jittery. They risked exposure by propping up Jansen's alibi, and they were the ones who strongly encouraged the Hamlins to leave Alaska. Can you imagine their immense displeasure when they didn't leave town?"

"So, you think they could have arranged to have him killed? Seems farfetched. Flimsy, really, without a specific murderer in mind. I mean, it couldn't be Tasker or anyone on the panel, right?"

"Nah . . . it'd be a church soldier. Someone trying to pave their way to heaven via the Old

Testament. There's plenty of church members willing to do that job. Even without pay."

Lacey smirked. "Small price for a shot at the pearly gates, I suppose. Your theories need work, but they're better than nothing. You might also consider Pete as a suspect. He had the motive and opportunity. Don't shake your head at me. For God's sake, they found the man's bones on Pete's property."

"No. No, I can't accept it. I know the guy like a brother. He wouldn't put me through this if he were guilty."

"Maybe not, but it's early. He might want you to find an alternative suspect that lets you cut him a better deal with the prosecutor. He might be planning to come clean after your investigation is complete. If I'd murdered Hamlin, that's what I'd do."

Logan's phone buzzed. He flipped it open and mouthed to Lacey, Miss-sus Ham-lin.

"Hey, Barbara, everything okay?"

"Yes. Yes, it is. But I forgot to tell ya one thing."

"What? What is it?"

"I forgot to tell you about Bill's findin' out Jansen was confessing privately to Tasker the whole fuckin' time. Every time Jansen confessed to another murder, Tasker did his little absolution shtick and marched him into the church where he splashed him with holy water. Tasker 'cleansed and forgave the bastard,' is how Bill put it."

"Those poor girls . . . I've been all torn up 'bout what we did. That's why Jansen never fessed up to murdering and raping the girls who weren't prostitutes. He knew Tasker and the panel wouldn't protect him for raping and killing girls they considered innocent and good with God. I just wanted you to know your client won't never find out what happened to his daughter cuz she wasn't a hooker. Jansen'll never admit killin' her or even tell where she's buried."

"Oh, God! Damn! Thanks for the update, Barbara. That's very helpful. I appreciate it."

"No problem," she said and hung up.

"Lacey, how would you like to drive over to the Spring Creek Correctional facility in Seward early tomorrow morning and have a visit with Jack Jansen?"

"Can we just do that without an appointment?"

"I know some of the people over there. Namely, the warden. Used to play rec basketball with him. We played the inmates in Anchorage about a dozen times, and they took out their frustration on all of us, but mostly on the warden."

"We can do that, but why?"

"I'd like to see if Jansen will confirm he killed Emma even if it's off the record. I think Pete and Erika want to know that, once and for all, despite the fact there's no other possibilities. I'll call the warden. He'll get it arranged and, if we're lucky, Jansen will cooperate. For some reason, once they're locked away, serial killers always have 'one more thing' they want to get off their chests."

Logan and Lacey arrived at the penitentiary at 10 am. They were greeted by the warden, Sam Stockman, at the outer gate. After the introductions, Stockman directed two guards to take Logan and Lacey to the confined cells reserved for the worst of the worst. They were seated in a spacious room with multiple tables and chairs.

Lacey nudged Logan. "Looks like this is where all their fine dining takes place."

Logan stifled a laugh when he saw the guard enter with a smallish, bespeckled man. He was unshaven and appeared almost ghostly. "Hello, Mr. Jansen. I'm Logan Finch, attorney, and this is Lacey Carpenter, my associate."

"I know who you are. What do y'want?"

"We represent a former partner of mine, Pete Foster."

"I know that too. What do y'want?"

"We want you to confirm that Pete's daughter, Emma, was in your presence when she died."

"Who?"

"A young, blonde girl by the name of Emma. In October of 1983 she worked in a restaurant across from the Bush Company. She disappeared that night and we were just wondering if you saw her and were with her. Maybe took her for a plane ride or something? It happened just before you were arrested. She was maybe your last victim."

"Are you recording this?"

"No, we're not. I assure you."

"Okay. One of you needs to get out of hearing range and the other has to prove to me you are not wired."

Lacey rose and walked to the far side of the room while Logan opened his shirt and pants and pulled out his pockets. "Anything else?"

"Nah, but anything I say is off the record and I will deny it. You got that?"

"Of course. I only intend to disclose what you say to Pete and his wife. They're suffering by not knowing what happened to their daughter."

"I get it. Jansen, looking defeated, glanced across the room at Lacey. "I'm only going to say that I was the last person to see her alive... that's it."

"That's enough. Hope we don't see each other in hell."

With that, Logan rose, and Lacey followed him out the door. Neither looked back.

"He did it, didn't he? Lacey asked.

"Of course. Mrs. Hamlin was right."

Lacey and Logan arrived back in Homer Sunday afternoon. Clouds hid the sun and the wind swept from the south into Cook Inlet. Logan decided it was a no-go fishing day. He'd witnessed boats overwhelmed by sudden gusts and had no intention of being another casualty. He drove Lacey to the office and, since fishing wasn't an option, contacted Pete and Erika. *They need to hear Mrs. Hamlin's story—at least most of it.*

They agreed to meet at the Salty Dawg Saloon near the end of the Homer Spit. Bald eagles circled lazily overhead as Logan walked past the signage outside the bar:

"HUSBAND DAY-CARE CENTER
Need to go shopping? Need some time alone? Need to relax?
Leave your husband with us."

Memorabilia, including women's bras and panties and one-dollar bills, plastered the Saloon's low ceiling and walls. Names and numbers were gouged into the wooden bar, walls, and tables by locals and drunken tourists eager to test their new fish filet knives. Sunlight barely filtered through the smoke-filled haze and grimy windows. Behind the bar stood a wooly gentleman about sixty-five years old with a scraggily beard and full sleeves of tattoos on his arms. He appeared hungover.

The Salty Dawg was a drinker's bar. The shelves behind the bartender boasted an impressive array of bourbon and whiskey. And beer. But scant other beverages. Most of the late-night patrons didn't worry about the drunk driving laws—they lived aboard their boats and just walked the few steps to the harbor where they slept off the night's excesses. It'd been that way for years. Logan found Pete seated alone in the back corner, away from the four Sunday-afternoon patrons.

"Hey, where's Erika?"

"She didn't want to hear what Mrs. Hamlin had to say. I'll tell her an edited version later."

"Probably just as well. But the good news is she did come up with some alternative suspects, and that's what we need."

"Such as?"

Logan described his meeting with Mrs. Hamlin and her statements. He excluded her comments about never finding Emma or learning what happened to her.

"Think it'll sell to a jury?" Pete asked.

"You know, it'll depend on the jury and the prosecutor's presentation. But I'm feeling confident. Lacey firmly believes our jury expert will give us a fighting chance at an acquittal."

Pete didn't respond. *Pete has never insisted the murderer would be found. And never includes Erika in our discussions. Why? Does she think he's guilty?* Logan mulled over these disquieting thoughts while they nibbled the bar food.

A fight broke out near the front door.

"How in the hell can there be a brawl during the day with only four people in the bar?" Pete asked rhetorically.

"It's Alaska, buddy."

And being Alaskans, Pete and Logan ignored it. The bartender glanced at the brawl, then returned to washing glassware. The biggest guy in the bar hit the deck with a spectacular thud.

"How are your parents doing these days?" Pete asked.

"Not well."

"Ah, Logan, I'm sorry. Your folks are such great people. Parents to be proud of."

"Yeah, they are. And I am. It's just tough knowing that their days are numbered. Even tougher when they can't remember me. Reminds me of the song 'If I Could Turn Back Time'..."

"No question...but, Logan, you've been a great son. Their lives have been so much easier because of you."

"Thanks, Pete."

The fight at the door subsided. Pete and Logan stepped around the big guy moaning on the floor next to the front door as they left the bar.

CHAPTER
35

"**P**AM, PETE, AND I ARE GOING FISHING TODAY, so no phone calls or interruptions, unless there's another bomb threat."

"Whoa, buddy, don't even mention that. But you betcha, we'll hold down the fort. You guys go snag that prize-winning halibut so we can eat, drink, and be merry on your tab!"

"Will do. Thanks, Pam."

Logan hung up and immediately called Pete. "Hey, what d'ya say we forget about our worries and catch the winning halibut today? The sun's out. Maybe you can win the derby again. It'll be like the good ole days!"

"I'm on my way. Erika's still asleep but wouldn't be interested anyway."

"Okay. Bring some chow from the restaurant. I have coffee brewing."

Ahhh, warm and sunny. Logan inhaled the invigorating, crisp salt air. The weather report warned of changing conditions in the afternoon, but the slack tide was before noon—an excellent time to hit the halibut grounds.

Pete boarded *The Coral Dawn*, hollering, "Hey, Logan, all I could get were a couple of donuts and the Land's End version of Egg McMuffins with bacon."

"Permission to come aboard *denied*. We need a mixer too."

"Oh, perhaps I should mention," Pete amended, "I brought two liters of tonic water."

"Permission to come aboard is *granted*."

They reached the hundred-foot water depth an hour after heading due west out of the harbor. Pete refreshed their vodka tonics and turned on the CD player while Logan baited the hooks and cast the lines. "Okay, El Capitan, which pole's mine?"

"Whichever one doesn't snag the winner. You don't have a ticket, do you?"

"Nope, but I'm still going to reel the monster up to the side of the boat."

"Okay, Mister Optimistic...have a drink and settle down."

It was noon with not a single bite when Logan noticed the clouds amassing and the wind blowing from the east.

"Uh-oh, here's the easterly they were predicting. It's early. The seagulls are heading to shore."

"Damn, I wanted to catch the big one today. What d'ya think about staying just a little bit longer?"

"You're singing to the choir, Pete."

They fished for another thirty minutes before they were engulfed in a full-blown storm with wailing winds and waves whipped into whitecaps.

"Let's get outta here!" Logan bellowed.

Pete began the arduous task of reeling in the lines while Logan turned the key on one of the engines from the upper helm. Nothing. Not even a sputter. "Shit! Batteries are low. I've gotta start the generator."

"Hurry, the waves are really picking up." Logan didn't need Pete's weather update. The boat rolled and slammed against the sea. It was a struggle to keep his footing down the steps as he stumbled into the salon. They needed to turn into the waves fast or they'd get swamped. Logan lifted the floorboard covering the engines and generator. He bent over to switch the electrical starter to the single battery when a huge wave hit the starboard side. The force threw him into the hold, and he immediately felt a sharp pain. He looked down where blood gushed out of his slashed right forearm. "Fuck!" He pressed down on the gash but couldn't stop the bleeding.

Pete heard his scream of pain and stumbled down to help. Below deck, they were tossed about as waves pummeled the boat. Dishes crashed, curtain shades and pictures flew. The refrigerator door flung open, dumping its contents. The TV dropped off the counter, dangling from the coaxial cable as the boat pitched crazily from side to side and lurched up and down. The engines were dead, and they were adrift in a tempest. "You need a fucking tourniquet," Pete hollered.

"A shirt might work."

"Got it!" Pete careened his way to the aft cabin to find a shirt. Logan reached down and tried the generator again. It started, providing enough power to start one engine, then the other from the lower helm. Sweet, welcome music to his ears! They'd navigate from belowdecks because the rocking up top was too dangerous. Pete returned with a T-shirt to see Logan put both engines in gear as the heavy seas crashed over the front starboard bow. Neither of them could see through the salty froth coating the windows. The beautiful day of an hour ago had evaporated.

"Jesus, can you believe this wind? Pete, wrap that T-shirt around my arm and grab the walrus *oosik* over there by the TV. Use it to twist the T-shirt ends snug around my forearm. I've gotta head us into the waves before this fucker flips over."

Pete picked up the *oosik*. "You've lost a lot of blood. How are you feeling?"

"Scared shitless. Now, twist that sucker!"

Pete twisted until the blood ceased flowing. "Logan, my friend, you've just been saved by a walrus cock."

Logan's face was grim. "I'm not saved yet."

Pete dulled the din from the roaring engines by dropping the floorboards back into place. Still, it was nearly impossible to hear one another, and they needed to figure out where they were. "I'll go above," Pete shouted. "Maybe I can see more from there, and I'll check the GPS. We'll talk by radio."

"Great. I'll steer east to the shoreline."

"Be better to bear northeast," Pete yelled. "Otherwise, we could wind up going down Kachemak Bay and run out of gas. Or run aground."

"Right."

Logan took the waves at forty-five-degree to sixty-degree angles heading mostly northeast and grimly waited for Pete's navigation report. Loud retching caused him to look back through the sliding door. Pete hung over the back rail, violently vomiting onto the swim step. Logan shouted, "Good job! Wait till the dry heaves kick in."

Facing the stern, Pete raised his left arm with a middle finger extended. "Fuck you, Finch." *It has a beautiful ring to it.* Logan cheerfully smiled and reciprocated the salute. His arm throbbed, so he released some of the twist pressure from the *oosik* and the bleeding didn't restart. *So far, so good.* Pete was now lying on his back next to the aft railing. "Sink this motherfucker and just kill me now."

The five-foot swells only permitted eight miles an hour. At this rate, they wouldn't see land for a couple of hours. Unfortunately, the gas gauges showed less than quarter-full tanks. Success getting home hinged on their proximity to Homer once they spotted land. They needed to end up southwest toward the Homer Spit. Too far north and they might have to beach the boat at the Anchor River, ending in considerable damage to the hull. If they ran out of gas before getting to shore, the boat would capsize.

Pete and I would survive the frigid water for about ten minutes, Logan grimly thought. *Shit! The life jackets were up top on the skybridge.* Logan couldn't leave the helm to retrieve them, and a glance at Pete—prone on the aft deck—confirmed he was out of commission. *Hell, he won't want a fucking life jacket anyway.* With his crew prone on the aft deck, Logan wouldn't get a GPS reading anytime soon. He considered his cell phone, then remembered it too was on the upper deck. *Pete's wish just might be granted.*

Logan had lost a lot of blood and he was cold. It was difficult to stay focused and his attention wavered. One colossal wave nearly spun *The Coral Dawn* around. Had that happened, the tailing winds and waves would probably have delivered them to eternal lounging in Davy Jones's locker. When the hull of the boat hit the bottom of the swell, Logan quickly spun the wheel and rotated the boat 180 degrees. The maneuver got the boat up atop the wave and heading again in an easterly direction. It was a masterful move under incredibly rough conditions, but there was no time to applaud nor praise his skill. It was urgent to broadcast an immediate Mayday, although he knew no one would come before they capsized or ran out of fuel before they reached the shoreline.

I'm in Alaska, Logan reminded himself. *The strong and the lucky survive.* Dangerous weather often descended with little or no warning and showed no mercy for anyone. Will Rogers, Wiley Post, and Louisiana Congressman Hale Boggs were among the unlucky who'd died in the state. *If we go down, at least we'll die in good company.* The gas situation was looking bad when Pete abruptly bellowed, "Land ho!"

"Woo-hoo!" Logan shrieked. "Where are we?"

"I see Anchor Point and some lights on the spit. We're halfway between. Head southwest if you can. If you can't, we're a mile offshore, so go in closer where the swells look smaller."

Logan changed course and knew that heading closer to shore would conserve their fuel.

"Tell me when we're a half mile offshore." Blood had begun seeping through the T-shirt tourniquet.

"Want me to pull up the GPS?" Pete asked.

"Nah...we can see land. I don't even want to know distance or speed." Logan twisted the tourniquet and the bleeding stopped, but the ache grew worse. Heading south by southeast, Logan gained new appreciation for the Homer Spit's reach into the bay. Four and a half miles was agonizing to traverse at eight miles an hour in stormy seas. The waves were less violent, so Logan pushed the throttles forward. *If we run out of gas, I'll try beaching the boat. That'll cause hull damage and the inevitable embarrassment from neighbors driving by and seeing us run aground on the rocky beach. But at least we won't drown.*

"Hey, Pete! I'll throw you an oar; you can save us a little fuel."

"Great idea, Maestro. Make sure to throw me the left-handed one!"

They'd entered the harbor, finally sheltered from the wind and waves, when the starboard engine choked and shut down. Logan put the port engine in neutral and moved to the upper helm. He cranked the wheel portside and steered toward their boat slip. Pete held the aluminum pole, prepared to fend off Mike's sailboat.

Standing on the dock were Mike, Sasha, and a barking, tail-wagging Toby. The bad weather had them worried. They'd been anxiously watching for *The Coral Dawn* for the last two hours. "Ahoy, Cap'n Logan. Good to have ye back safe 'n' sound thar, matey," Mike hollered.

"Ah, shaddup or I'll give ye a taste a'me broadsword," Logan yelled, disguising his relief.

Pete gestured to the bloody T-shirt on Logan's arm. "We're off to the hospital for that."

Mike camouflaged his relief to see them safely back by exhibiting zero empathy. "Ay, them halibuts be a dangerous breed of fish. Ye get a bit gummed thar, matey?"

"Very funny. We'll tell the tale when we get back," Logan added.

"It'll definitely be funnier in the retelling," Pete promised. "At first, I was afraid I was gonna die," Pete confessed. "Then I was afraid I wouldn't."

Mike laughed, waving them off. "I've got this, you two get going. We'll get the lines secured."

Still battling queasiness, Pete gingerly jumped off the boat and wobbled his way down the dock. On their way to the emergency room, he kidded with Logan to keep his mind off the pain. "Try to keep your blood off me...I can't wait for the nurses to get a look at the *oosik* you're carrying around."

"I hurt too bad for any of this to be funny," groaned Logan.

TWENTY-ONE STITCHES LATER, Pete drove Logan back to *The Coral Dawn* where he wearily leaned back against the headrest, waiting for his pain meds to kick in. His phone buzzed. "Hello. Yes, this is Logan Finch. Yes, she's my mother. What? Aw, damn…okay. I'll be there on the next plane. I'm in Alaska, so you probably won't see me until tomorrow afternoon. Yes, and thanks for letting me know. Good night."

"What was that?" Pete asked.

"It was the hospital. Mom's not eating. She's in a semi coma and has pneumonia. Dad doesn't know what's happening, and they want her next of kin with her as soon as possible."

"Anything I can do?" Pete asked.

"Could you and Erika get me the earliest possible plane reservations to Anchorage, then on to Tucson? That'd help a ton."

He rested his head back on the headrest again. "If I can get some sleep, I'll be able to think more clearly."

"I'll call Erika so she can get a jump start on those reservations."

Logan exited the car, waved thanks to Pete, and walked down the dock. He had almost reached the boat as Sasha and Toby approached. They were beginning their nightly trek to the fire hydrant. Excited at the unexpected encounter, Toby wagged his tail, generously bathed Logan's hands, and cautiously inspected the bandages. Logan laughed. "The healing welcome of a dog. But I'm glad I ran into you, Sasha. Could you guys watch over the boat for a while? My mom's not doing well, and I'm flying back to Arizona."

"Not a problem. Sorry things haven't gone the way they usually do for you, Logan, but don't worry about your boat. Mike and I are staying in the harbor until after the Fourth. The fish aren't expected until mid-July."

"Thanks! You're a lifesaver. You've got my cell number. Call if there's a problem or you guys wanna leave the harbor for a few days. Pete and Erika can always step in. I'm leaving the keys with them. They might take a short cruise over to the Glacier Spit or back to Halibut Cove." Logan winked. "Unless you and Mike decide to go out on a gas-guzzler."

"You know Mike. No chance, but thanks all the same."

Logan boarded *The Coral Dawn* and descended to the aft cabin bed. The picture of his parents had tumbled off the nightstand during the storm. He picked it up and stared into their faces from a happier time. He eased himself onto the bed while tears trickled down his cheeks and onto his pillow. The adrenaline surge from the nearly fatal storm, his slashed forearm, the stitches, and the pain meds were exacting a toll. He called Lacey.

"Mom has pneumonia and she's in the hospital."

"Oh, I'm so sorry. Do you need to get down there?"

"Yeah. I hope it won't be a problem for you."

"Absolutely not. I go fishing after the Fourth of July this year. And, for heaven's sake, don't worry about the office. We'll handle Pete's case. Take as much time as you need. When do you leave?"

"Not sure yet. Pete and Erika are making my reservations. I wanted to call you and kick this around before I go."

"Are you up for a little company? I'd like to be with you."

"Sounds great. We can talk while waiting to hear from Pete about my flight arrangements and go from there."

Twenty minutes later, Lacey came aboard. "Hey, handsome, how ya doing?"

"You may not want to be around me." He felt trapped, incapable of moving his weary, exhausted body.

"Are you kidding? Slide over. What's up with the arm?"

"Ahh, a few stitches, but they plied me with legal drugs. I can't feel anything."

His seafarer's harrowing tale was interrupted by the phone.

"Hey, Pete...Okay, thanks. Lacey'll take me in the morning. We'll stop by Land's End and have coffee with you guys. Does seven o'clock work? Great, see you in the morning."

❖

"What's up with Erika, doesn't she like us anymore?" joked Lacey the next morning as Logan handed over the car keys to Pete.

"She's back to crying herself to sleep. This has triggered all the bad memories of Emma's disappearance. It's been pretty tough on both of us."

"I get it. If there's anything I can do while Logan's gone, just call," Lacey offered.

"Thanks. I may encourage her to go back to Seattle and see her doctor."

After goodbye hugs, Logan and Lacey walked out of the restaurant, leaving Pete to stare out the windows at the inlet and the Alaska Range. Logan caught Lacey's eye and knew she was thinking the same thing. *Is this a guy about to go to prison for life, a guilty man? Or just an innocent victim of circumstances and a distraught husband?*

Following the cab ride from Tucson to Green Valley, Logan picked up his car keys at the reception desk and stuck his head into his father's room. He smiled at his dad, who didn't seem to recognize him. His mom's bed was empty. She was still at the hospital. It was a short drive from the nursing home to the hospital.

Dr. Jerry Petrino greeted him at the nurses' station.

"Dr. Petrino, I'm Logan Finch, Sarah Finch's son."

The handsome, gray-haired doctor in his mid-sixties reminded Logan of Seattle golfer Freddie Couples. "Good to meet you, Logan. I understand you flew down from Alaska today."

"Pretty long trip worrying about Mom and her situation."

"I can imagine. Well, come into my office where I can update you on her status. I want to prepare you before you see her."

What kind of "preparing" do I need to see my own mom? Logan wondered.

He was impressed by the surroundings. The building was relatively small, new, modern, and not depressing—for a hospital.

"Okay, then...your mother is an eighty-eight-year-old woman with six years of Alzheimer's. As you know, the disease has a four-to-six-year life expectancy, and she's contracted pneumonia. We now have to confront some tough decisions."

Logan took a deep breath. "Okay...so what are our options?"

"First, we're treating the pneumonia and she's breathing through a ventilator. She was admitted with rapid breathing, low blood pressure, and confusion. We checked her vital organs and her kidney functions have declined significantly. She's being fed intravenously but we hope to add spoonfuls of soft foods soon."

"What's her prognosis?"

"Assuming the antibiotics work, she'll become a prime candidate for hospice care within a few days to a week. The Prestige Assisted Living Facility, where your mother resides, offers excellent hospice care."

Hospice care, Logan knew, provided end-of-life care to those in the last stages of terminal illness or for the fragile elderly nearing the end of life. Hospice also provided support services to the families of those in hospice. The care focused on the dignity and quality of life remaining, instead of seeking to cure illness or prolong life.

They discussed his mom's religious preferences, artificial life support, respirators, feeding tubes, IV hydration, and CPR.

"Okay, Logan. I support your decisions and have entered them in your mother's file. If you'd like to see her now, I'll begin my evening rounds at her room. Be prepared for tubes in her nose and mouth, and she's hooked up to a heart monitor and an IV. It can be distressing, but hopefully it's temporary."

"Let's do it."

"I have to ask, what happened to your arm?"

"Oh, it's a long story. I was out trying to catch Moby Dick. But I'm okay."

Logan had watched his parents' health relentlessly deteriorate over the past few years. Nonetheless, he was unprepared to see his frail mother's beautiful spirit tethered to this world by a pulsating life-support machine. She was sleeping. He sat at her bedside and caressed her hair, hoping for a response.

"Mom, it's Logan. I'm back from Alaska, and I'll be here whenever you need me," he softly vowed.

No response.

"We can talk for a while. I'll put on your favorite CD; let you listen to some good music."

No response. But he squeezed her hand and wanted to believe she squeezed back.

Logan unintentionally began speaking louder than necessary. "Okay, Mom. Dad's doing fine. As soon as they get this nasty cold taken care of, you'll get to see him again."

Still no response.

Her breathing slowed and Logan pulled his chair closer. He gently held her hand before he eventually nodded off. A nurse woke him when she came in to take his mother's vitals.

"Hi," she whispered. "I didn't mean to wake you. I'm Wendy. I'll be on duty tonight until 2:00 a.m. Do you have any questions?"

"Yes. How long has she been like this, I mean, uncommunicative?"

"About thirty-six hours."

"Can she hear what I say?"

"I always assume patients hear everything being said. So, if you want to speak confidentially, we could talk in the hallway. Are you hungry? I'll be happy to bring you some food."

"Will you be feeding Mom?"

"No. Right now she's being nourished through the IV line. We hope she improves in the next day or two so she can be fed soft foods."

"Good, thank you. I think I'll go get something to eat, check on my dad, and come back to say good night to Mom."

"Sound like a good idea. See you later."

"Okay, Mom. I'm going to go see Dad and get something to eat, but I'll be back."

No response.

He pulled a CD out of his pocket and inserted it in the CD player beside her bed. It was one of her favorites, crooner Frank Sinatra, but there was no response when the music played.

"I'll replay it," Wendy offered.

"Great."

Logan returned to the hospital two hours later. The room was quiet.

"Thanks, Mom, for everything...you're the best mom and you always got us through the hard times," Logan whispered. "And sometimes you accomplished that by being a toughie yourself. I remember the day you refused to come to my high school and meet with the principal. "Do you remember?"

No response. She was resting quietly, and Logan patted her hand and continued.

"Spring of my senior year, four of us did the senior skip and went fishing for three school days. We got caught and were suspended for another three days. The principal said we couldn't come back to school until our parents met with him. Remember that, Mom?"

No response.

"The other parents came in, but you refused. You asked me what you'd done wrong. When I said, 'Nothing,' you asked why you had to go to the school if you hadn't done anything wrong. I said it was because they weren't going to let me come back unless you came and met the principal. Remember? I'll never forget you saying, 'Now, that's a dumb rule. You got yourself kicked out without my help, and you need to figure out how to get yourself back in without my help.'"

He felt a slight squeeze on his hand.

"I knew you'd remember! I went into the principal's office and apologized. I told him what you said, and he unexpectedly agreed. 'You know, your mom's right. I accept your apology. You can come back to school.'"

He felt another squeeze to his hand.

They sat quietly for another hour or so before Logan fell asleep until after 2:00 a.m. The shift changed so a different nurse entered to take his mother's vitals. "You might think about sleeping in a real bed and come back later in the morning," she suggested.

Logan stretched, then slowly stood. His wounded arm and the metal in his knees made it more difficult than usual. "Good idea." He reached over and stroked his mother's hair. "Good night, Mom. I'll be back later."

The next morning, he called Lacey on his way to the hospital. "It's not so good down here. Mom and Dad are worse than I'd expected."

"What's going on with them?"

"Dad doesn't recognize me and doesn't talk. They have to feed him by hand."

"And your mom?"

"She's still in a coma. She's been that way for two days. It's pitiful. They're treating her for pneumonia, and she has tubes hooked up everywhere, from every angle. I think she hears me, but she can't talk and hasn't opened her eyes. I'm driving back to the hospital now."

"I'm so sorry."

"Anything happening up there?"

"Yeah, a couple of things. When you have time, give Pete and Erika a call. They don't want to bother you, but Erika wants to go home to Washington for a couple of weeks."

"Sure. I don't see a problem with it, do you?"

"No, none whatsoever."

"Anything else?"

"Yeah...I didn't want to worry you, but we got another crank call, probably from the same guy, warning us not to represent Pete, but he didn't say anything about bombs. Katie documented the call. Oh, and the final witness list in Pete's case arrived yesterday from the prosecutor's office."

"Great. The next witness I want to talk to is Crystal Sorensen, the homicide investigator for the state troopers. Do we have contact information for her?"

"Let me look...Oh, wow. She retired last month and is living in Apache Junction,

Arizona. What a coincidence!"

"Great. I think that's between here and Phoenix. Message me her phone number and address. I'll give her a call today."

"You bet, soon as we hang up. Now, most importantly, how much do you miss me?"

"Tons! Wish I could haul you here by private jet."

"Wish you could too. Any idea when you might be back?"

"Not yet, Lace. But if Mom recovers, I might return as early as next week. Right now, we're taking this a day at a time, but her doctor wasn't very encouraging last night."

"I know we could get a continuance of the trial date," Lacey suggested.

"Probably, but no. Just make sure Pete and Erika know we're on target to try this case in late July."

"Okay. Call me later when you can."

"Will do."

When he reached the second floor, his mother was being wheeled to the coronary care unit. He was instantly alarmed. "What's going on?"

Wendy Lee was back on duty and explained, "She suffered a mild stroke, and we don't want to take any chances. Don't worry, she'll be okay. We're taking her for testing. We want to look for blockages, and she'll be back real soon."

"Can I go with her?"

"No. It's a small space." She smiled. "And we don't want to have another patient on our hands if you faint." Logan slumped into the nearest hallway chair. He searched the face of everyone who walked past in hopes of getting an update. After four hours of waiting and skimming outdated magazines, he walked to the nurses' desk.

Wendy reappeared. "She's doing fine, Mr. Finch. She has a small hole in the back of her heart—probably something she was born with—but air bubbles passed through it and into her brain. She's resting comfortably but won't return to her room for a few hours."

"Okay. I want to grab a bite to eat, but I'll leave my phone number. Would you please call me when she gets back to her room?"

"Absolutely."

Logan made a beeline back to the nursing home, hoping to find his dad lucid. He wasn't. He brought his dad up to date on their favorite baseball team and, with a wink, added some salacious gossip from the *Whale Fat Follies* performance. He detected a smidgeon of a smile. A nurse delivered his dad's dinner, so Logan left for a nearby Mexican restaurant. He was savoring a margarita and munching chips and salsa when Nurse Wendy called. His mom was back in her hospital room. When he arrived, Wendy was gently checking her vitals. She carefully and efficiently maneuvered around the ventilator, a feeding tube, and antibiotic drip. Wendy's shiny dark hair was pulled back into a perky ponytail. *Nurses and doctors look so incredibly young these days*, Logan thought.

"I'll stay with your mom for the next six hours. It's hospital protocol after a stroke. She doesn't seem worse than before the stroke, but we won't know of any memory loss or physical impairments until she's out of the coma."

"Did they get the hole in her heart patched, or whatever they decided to do?"

"No patch, Mr. Finch. She's too fragile to survive the surgery. If no air enters her bloodstream, she should be just fine."

How, Logan frowned, *did the air get into her heart in the first place?* He considered asking then decided it would make no difference. "If anything changes, can you call me again?"

"Of course. And I'll leave a note so the next shift nurse can follow up with you."

CHAPTER
37

"HELLO. DETECTIVE SORENSEN?

"Yes, this is Crystal Sorensen."

"This is Logan Finch, attorney for Pete Foster in the Hamlin case. I have a few questions to ask you. I'm visiting my parents in Green Valley, and I hoped we could meet if you have time. But if not, no problem, we can talk on the phone."

"I received the trial subpoena for mid-July. Chris Branson said you might be calling, and I could speak freely with you. I could meet you this Saturday in Green Valley. My mother's in a nursing home there, and I visit her every Saturday morning. Would the afternoon work for you?"

"Yes, of course. I won't take more than an hour of your time. If you like Italian food, how about meeting at Ragazzi's on the west side of the highway?"

"I know the place. I'll be there at two on Saturday. See you then."

Logan researched pneumonia and Alzheimer's on the internet after he arrived home. He didn't like what he read. Pneumonia could be deadly to an Alzheimer's patient. He called Pete for a little levity. "Hey there, buddy, how are y'doing?"

"God, you're way too cheerful. What's wrong?"

"Ah, you always could read me like a book. I think Mom's dying."

"Logan, we're all dying. But what's all the worry about her today?"

"She had a stroke. It's minor, so they say. But she's not recovering from the pneumonia and hasn't opened her eyes in over two days. Outside of—"

"Jesus, I'm sorry," Pete interrupted. "What about your dad, how's he doing?"

"Yeah. Dad hasn't recognized me nor talked to me since I got back here."

"Okay, hold on. Dr. Foster prescribes scotch."

"Very funny. It's going to take more than scotch. But let's talk about something positive. Oh, I know, your murder trial!"

"Hey, my dream team's optimistic, haven't you heard?"

"Yeah, I think I'm the one who said that. Lace mentioned that Erika wants to go home for a few weeks. I think that'll be good for her."

"Glad to hear that. I wanted to put her on a plane tomorrow. Waiting here for the trial to start is further dampening her spirit. I asked her to focus on keeping the home fires burning for when we both get home."

"Sounds like an excellent approach. Did it work?"

"Maybe. She's been a nervous wreck and is constantly asking how she can help. Damn, Logan, I sure's hell don't know what to tell her."

"Well, take it day by day if you can. That's what I'm doing."

"Yeah...like we have a choice, right?"

"By the way, Saturday I'm meeting with the homicide detective who investigated the case in 1983."

"Is that good or bad?"

"I won't know till I talk to her, but she sounded friendly enough on the phone. We need to figure out how Hamlin's body got to the burial site. Can you review the reports, see if you can discover anything? Very possible I overlooked that information."

"You bet. I'll get back to you tomorrow if I come up with anything. Where did you dig up the detective?"

"You're not going to believe it, but she lives just northwest of here, in Apache Junction. She's driving down to Green Valley this Saturday."

"Well, obviously, she's no hottie after you because *you* ain't driving to see her," Pete charged.

"Hey, I *am* a hottie! She *could* be after me! Or...maybe she's driving down because her mother's in a nursing home here in Green Valley."

"Uh-huh...and the ugly truth comes out. But, seriously, I'm sorry about your folks. My money's on your feisty mom. She'll get through this. Don't forget, she weathered a 9.2 quake."

"You're right, if anyone can beat the odds, it would be Mom. Thanks, Pete. I'll catch up with you again tomorrow."

CHAPTER
38

L OGAN IMAGINED SHARING HIS TUBAC home with Lacey as he ate cereal, drank a beer, and watched the news before conking out on the sofa. He loved his home in Arizona. It was a Southwest stucco with high ceilings, granite floors, and bull-nosed corner walls throughout the structure. It was a former model home and furnished casually in Native American décor, as was the casita. Most importantly, there were no earthquakes in Arizona. His daily anxiety levels almost disappeared, much like when he was boating in Alaska.

When he arrived at the hospital Thursday morning, his mother was in the same condition. Logan pulled a chair up next to her bed and offered to relieve the nurse monitoring her. "I'm staying for at least an hour if you want to take a break."

"Great. I'll be back in forty-five minutes. Hit the red buzzer if you need help."

Logan sat in the chair at his mother's bedside. He fondly stroked her forehead and hair.

"Hey, Mom. It's me again. Just stopped by to see you before you decide to go shopping. Or surfing."

No response.

"Remember what you used to call Dad? 'Mister Moneybags.' When he dressed up, he nervously rattled his change around in his pocket. You told me he was showing off his immense wealth and that's why you nicknamed him Moneybags." He thought he felt her fingers tightening on his hand. "Mom, I love you so much. I miss your voice and I want you to get better. Please fight. Fight the pneumonia and shake off that stinkin' little stroke. You've got lots a great stories to tell and I don't want to lose you. Oh, by the way, Mom, I'm defending Pete up in Anchorage on some false charge. I'm meeting a detective at your favorite Italian restaurant here in Green Valley. Do you remember Ragazzi? I know they remember you. After my meeting, I'll bring Dad over. He misses you big time and wants you back with him."

Her hand squeezed his. *She wants to see Dad.*

The nurse entered and gestured Logan into the hallway.

"Okay, Mom. I've gotta go and run some errands. I'll see you tomorrow afternoon. Dad's determined to bring your favorite ice cream, the chocolate stuff with marshmallows and nuts. Do you remember?"

Again, he felt a slight hand squeeze.

Out in the hall, the nurse said Dr. Petrino wanted to see him before he left for the day. "He's in his office right now, so this is a good time."

Logan knocked on Dr. Petrino's office door. "Come in," the doctor invited.

"You wanted to see me?"

The doctor looked up from his computer, his face pinched and tired-looking.

"Yes, Mr. Finch."

"Call me Logan, please."

"Logan, I have some bad news. Your mother's stroke set her back. She doesn't have the strength to fight the effects of a stroke, pneumonia, and Alzheimer's disease."

An avalanche of anger and frustration swamped Logan. *No, no, no! Mom's gotten worse since she arrived at this hospital. The hospital's job, this doctor's job, is to* help *Mom!* Logan willfully tamped down his feelings and carefully asked, "What exactly does that mean? Is she going to die? There's got to be a solution for keeping the air bubbles out of her veins. She deserves the care and solutions to get her well." Logan's self-control slipped. "This is bullshit. My mom's a fighter! No way she's at death's door!"

"Logan, please...your mother came to us as a very sick, elderly woman," Dr. Petrino gently reminded. "We're doing all we can for her. And doing that around the clock. She's a lovely person and a wonderful patient. But, Logan, time runs out on all of us at some point. I believe time has run out on your mother. We can keep her alive a bit longer but you've already, and clearly, said you don't want that done by artificial means."

Logan was stunned. He had no words and could no longer look away from the horrible reality confronting him. *My mom is dying.*

"The congestion in her lungs causes her some pain. It's difficult for her to breathe, even assisted by the breathing tube. Unfortunately, the tube itself is very uncomfortable. My recommendation for the next twenty-four hours is we keep her comfortable, continue what we're doing, and watch over her."

"What else can I do?"

"I'd like you to meet with a hospice nurse here in the morning. Would ten o'clock work for you?"

"A hospice nurse, why?"

"She'll help make what's coming easier for you and your mother. Do you want to try that?"

"Of course. Did you say ten?"

"Yes, ten in your mom's room. I'll be there to introduce you."

"Thanks, Doctor. Thank you very much. I apologize. This is so much harder than I ever thought."

"You're losing your mother. You wouldn't be much of a son if you didn't respond emotionally." Dr. Petrino stood, shook Logan's hand, and added with a smile. "See you in the morning."

Logan numbly climbed into his car. The tears came. Suddenly a loneliness swept over him. He was alone in his car, alone in his Tubac home, alone in Homer, and alone in the world. He sat and wept for over an hour. Eventually, he turned the key, put his car in gear, and drove home.

The next morning, Logan sat with his mom, held her hand as he stroked her hair, and recalled aloud more stories of his childhood. At some point, an attractive, mature woman entered the room and silently watched him interact with his mother. Shortly thereafter, Dr. Petrino arrived and introduced the watching woman.

"Debbie Turner is one of the best hospice nurses in the world. She's been helping care for your mother."

"Nice to meet you, Logan," she said with a warm smile and calm blue eyes. They politely shook hands, each using a strong, firm grip.

"The pleasure's all mine, Ms. Turner."

"Please, just call me Debbie."

"Then Debbie it is." They walked out into the hallway and Dr. Petrino excused himself.

"All right, Logan, do you have relatives in the area who would like to visit your mother today?" Debbie asked.

"Today? Mom has a sister and brother in California but they're in retirement homes. It's difficult for them to visit."

"What about your father, is he still alive?"

"Yeah. Dad's just down the street in an assisted-living facility. He also has Alzheimer's and hasn't recognized me since I arrived a few days ago."

"Oh, I'm sorry. But could you go get your dad?"

"Now?"

"Yes, I think now would be a good time."

"Sure. Of course."

"How long will it take you?" Debbie asked.

"Thirty minutes, maybe."

"Great, come straight to your mother's room."

"And, Logan, earlier I watched you. There's nothing I can teach you about caring for and comforting your mother."

"We're going to see Mom," Logan said as he helped his dad into his slippers and blue-striped robe. He didn't notice his dad grab coins off the dresser and stuff them into his pocket. They arrived at the hospital and went directly to his mother's room. His mom wore her pink pajamas and robe. Her hair was combed and makeup applied. The drip line and feeding tube were gone. Only a small oxygen tube in her nose remained. Her face was serene.

"Dad, c'mon over and say hi to Mom."

His dad shuffled over to her bedside and smiled down on her. He rattled the coins in his pocket and smiled. *Mister Moneybags*, Logan remembered. His mother's eyes fluttered open, and she smiled. Logan's dad tenderly kissed her on the lips. She took a deep breath...

Tears welled up in Logan's eyes. His dad sat down on the bed and caressed his wife's hand. His mind no longer recognized his son, but somehow that mind understood that his wife was gone. Strong feelings bombarded Logan. He was grateful that he'd been present at his mom's passing. It helped lessen his grief knowing that she was no longer in pain and seeing his parents share those precious last moments together. It was a fitting end to their lifetime of devotion. He silently stood, absorbing the solemnity of what had taken place.

An arm encircled his shoulders. It was Debbie. "Doesn't she look beautiful," Logan reverently whispered.

Debbie smiled. "Your mother was a beautiful woman. Getting your dad here in time to see her was a challenge. It's an extraordinary gift when two hearts grow old together. She waited for the two of you." She reached into her sweater and retrieved a ring. "This is your mother's wedding ring. About a week ago, she took it off and asked me to give it to you at the right time. This is the right time."

Logan couldn't fight the tears anymore. He mumbled thanks and took the diamond and midnight-blue sapphire ring from Debbie. His dad remained sitting and caressing his wife's hand. Debbie stepped back, silently standing as a tear ran down her cheek. Logan quietly strode from the room. *So, this is what being utterly alone in the world feels like. Dad's...missing. And, for the first time in my life, my mom is truly gone.*

Logan leaned on the wall, examining the ring. It had been in his father's family since the mid-1800s. His dad had placed it on his mother's finger on their wedding day, and she had never taken it off. *That's why the heirloom ring survived the 1964 Good Friday earthquake,* Logan realized. It brought a glimmer of a smile to Logan's face.

The staff at the retirement home had shifted his dad's belongings to the memory care unit. Logan escorted him to his new room at the retirement home. *Dad will be much safer in this new environment.* Logan gave instructions for his mother's cremation. He would honor her request, voiced long ago, to disperse her ashes over the Chugach Mountains overlooking Anchorage.

Once back home, Logan opened a special bottle he'd squirreled away. The death of his beloved mother was a solemn, special occasion, worthy of a fine, smooth scotch. Glass in hand, he called Lacey first, then Pete. Commiserating with close friends made it official. *Mom is gone.* After they hung up, exhaustion slammed Logan. He toppled into bed.

The next morning, breakfast was a quick snack. His afternoon meeting with Detective Sorensen included a heavy dose of Italian food. On the way to Regazzi, he stopped at Best Buy and bought his dad some CDs: orchestral music by Michel Legrand from *Summer of '42*; Frank Sinatra's *World on a String*; Nat King Cole's *Love Is the Thing*; *The Very Best of the Andrews Sisters*; and *Tommy Dorsey, Limited Edition, Great Arrangements* and a *Billie Holiday CD*.

Next was a quick stop to check on his dad and leave the CDs. He asked the duty nurse to keep the music going...he left to the sound of Billie Holiday singing "Stormy Monday."

How fitting, he thought despondently.

CHAPTER
39

THERE WAS NO ONE ELSE in the restaurant when a slender woman walked directly to his table. Logan politely stood. "Hello, Mr. Finch, I'm Crystal Sorensen." Logan suspected she was at least sixty, but her long, dark-blond hair falling to her waist contributed to her classic ageless appearance.

"Good to meet you. How'd your visit go with your mother?"

"Mom wasn't feeling adventurous, so we stayed in her room and she had soup; I had tea. Thank you for asking."

"Which facility is she in?"

"The Prestige. It's aptly named. She's well-cared for."

"Amazing, that's where my father lives. They just transferred him to the memory care unit. I too am really impressed with their care."

Logan was relieved that she didn't ask about his mother.

"I'm surprised we haven't run into each other before."

"Well, recently I've been spending a lot of time in Alaska," Logan replied.

"Right, that explains it. So, how can I help you? I'm totally neutral and the state can't fire me if they don't like my testimony. I worked hard to be a straight shooter in every case I investigated."

"That's good to know." Still, Logan remained suspicious.

They looked over the menu. Sorensen ordered calzone and a glass of Chianti. Logan settled on sautéed prawns, salad, and a vodka tonic.

"I'm curious how Hamlin's body got to the gravesite. None of the reports mentioned anything about this."

"Nothing's mentioned because none of us had a clue how the body got there. We assumed the body must have been dragged or it was driven. It's even possible that Hamlin was shot right there. But it's all pure speculation."

"Did you find any evidence of a dragged body or tire tracks embedded in the area?"

"We didn't. Sixteen years had passed, so we weren't surprised there were no clues to explain how a three-hundred-pound body arrived at that gravesite. What was odd was the absence of blood in Hamlin's SUV or other forensic evidence to help solve his disappearance back in 1988. It was surprising that his bones and a gravesite were found all those years later. We figured the sitework for the new high school scared off animals that might have violated the grave. Even so, some bones were strewn about, as I recall."

"How good is your recollection of the investigation?"

"Very good. Chris sent me my reports, and I reviewed them. The case loomed large for me because I was involved in the initial Jansen investigations."

"Why?"

"I'll have to go off the record to answer that question."

"Do you trust me enough to do that?"

"I do. For one thing, I'd deny saying it and you'd have to withdraw your representation of Pete Foster if you took the stand to rebut my testimony."

Logan smiled. "I assure you, we're off the record. So, why does this investigation have a greater meaning for you?"

"I was just a rookie cop with the APD when they sent me to the Hamlins' house to verify Jansen's alibi. To this day, I regret the quality of my investigation."

"Because?"

"Because the Hamlins' alibi for Jansen wasn't credible. But I dutifully wrote down their statements in my crappy report and the powers above took it as gospel and released Jansen."

"Who then killed more girls," Logan contributed.

"I know. I think about it often. I believe that's when Jansen went on to kill your client's daughter. Now, that wouldn't happen if I were investigating today. I'd never just accept Jansen's and the Hamlins' alibi on face value."

"Don't feel guilty. I mean, you were a rookie. People in far superior positions of power made those decisions."

She smiled ruefully. "You know what? I need a stiffer drink to delve into this. What are you drinking?"

"Vodka tonic."

Logan warmed up to Ms. Sorensen. She waved the server over and ordered a Grey Goose double on the rocks.

"I was a rookie, but I wasn't stupid. It was the worst alibi in the world. I didn't follow up and inquire about the kind of card games they played, the food they ate, whether anyone had drinks or smoked, nor the specific times of arrival and departure for Jansen. I mean, the guy was in custody. If the Hamlins were lying, I could have gone back and questioned Jansen about the specifics. But I didn't. It was a terrible error that I deeply regret."

"It was inexperience, not incompetence," Logan said.

Yes, Logan silently agreed, *she made terrible mistakes handling her small, but vital, role in the investigation.* He also knew the environment she had been operating in.

Logan volunteered, "A rookie officer assigned to that investigation was highly questionable in and of itself. Someone wanted it hushed up, no digging, no questions asked."

"Huh...thank you, that never occurred to me. But to make matters worse, once we found the alibi was false, I prepared a second report strongly urging the prosecutor to charge the Hamlins with serious crimes, including aiding and abetting first-degree murder."

"Who was the prosecutor?"

"I'm sure it's no secret. It was that asshole, Gerald Abbott."

"Did you ever talk to him about your report?"

"Talk? No. I listened. He informed me that my career was over at the APD and I'd never get another promotion. He also said, and I quote, 'You have a lot of fucking audacity to recommend that charges be brought against the Hamlins when I didn't request a follow-up report, much less recommendations from a rookie cop.'"

"So, what'd you do?"

"I applied with the state troopers and got a new job. I worked my way up to homicide detective. I'm sure Abbott wasn't happy when I was assigned to this case last September. It was a sad day for the AG's office when Abbott began working in the state's Criminal Division in Anchorage. Neither Abbott nor the Anchorage prosecuting attorney's office would get involved in our investigation back in eighty-three. We finally went to Fairbanks for a search warrant for Jansen's house and, later, an indictment. So, no thanks to Abbott, that was where we found the hunting rifles and a map showing where he buried some of the girls."

"Did Abbott, the Hamlins, and Jansen all belong to the same Evangelical church back in the eighties?"

"Oh, shit! That's something I don't think you want to hear from me."

"You're right. A direct answer from you might require me to take the witness stand at trial. Let's do this. I'll ask you a question, and if the answer's 'yes,' then say, 'No comment.' If the answer's no, say 'no.'"

"Interesting...sure, let's give it a try."

The former trooper exhibited no signs of ever having been a homicide detective until the vodka arrived. Sorensen took a small sip and then pounded the two shots like a seasoned sailor. Her tour with the state troopers had induced a genuine appreciation for the value of a drink.

Logan repeated his question whether Abbott, the Hamlins, and Jansen belonged to the same church, and Sorensen replied, "No comment."

"Did Abbott know the Hamlins personally?"

"No comment."

"Did Abbott know the Jansens personally?"

"No comment."

"Did Abbott make the final decision not to prosecute the Hamlins?"

"No comment."

"Do you think Pete Foster killed Hamlin?"

"Probably, but I hope you can get him off. Hamlin and a few others deserved to die, but not your client's daughter."

"Do you think Abbott's affiliation with the church influenced his decision to fire you and his decision not to charge the Hamlins with crimes?"

"I have no comment to both questions."

The entrées arrived and they ate in near silence.

Is Pete guilty? nagged at Logan. *Sorenson was someone with no connection to Pete. This experienced, intelligent, and honest woman of the law was guided by facts, and she just nominated Pete as the killer.*

Logan paid the server and thanked Ms. Sorensen for her time.

"When are you going back to Alaska?" she asked as they left the restaurant.

"Probably early next week. I have some personal business to finish here. I have a home down in Tubac but will spend the next couple of months in Homer and Anchorage."

"It's a great time of year to do that. Okay, then...I'll see you at the trial in July. I'm looking forward to escaping Arizona's 110-degree heat."

"I hear you! Again, really appreciate your time, Crystal. See you in Anchorage."

"I'll be there. And I mean it when I say, 'Good luck.'"

"Thanks, we may need a good bit of luck." *A bit was a giant understatement.*

CHAPTER
40

LACEY GREETED LOGAN AT THE AIRPORT. "Hi, sweetie," she hollered as he stepped away from the twin-engine Beechcraft, cradling his mother's urn against his chest with his left hand. He dropped his luggage to the ground and wrapped his right arm around Lacey's shoulders.

"Hi, yourself. Think we can spread these ashes over the Chugach Mountains after the trial?"

"No problem. I'll fly us up. If the weather holds, we can come back without stopping in Anchorage."

Lacey had pulled Chinook salmon out of the freezer on *The Coral Dawn* and broiled it to perfection. They ate dinner on the bow, Toby happily sprawled between them until Sasha retrieved him for their evening walk. Logan and Lacey sat silently and watched the glowing sun slip beneath the horizon, two friends sharing moments of grief.

"There are four calls from Ms. Rodriguez and one from the prosecutor on her case. Do you want me to handle them?" Lacey asked Logan the next morning at the office.

"Very funny. Did I detect a twinge of jealousy?"

Lacey didn't wholly kick dirt on the thought. "Maybe. Maybe not."

Once seated in the conference room, Logan began working the phone. His first call was to Zach Zimmerman, the psychologist counseling Ms. Rodriguez. He arranged for him to write a diagnostic and prognostic letter regarding Rodriguez's mental health.

The next call was to Ms. Rodriguez. "Hi, Delores Anne. I'm returning your calls."

"Thank you. I don't know when my hearing is. I know I wrote it down somewhere, but I can't find my paperwork."

"Not a problem. We're due in court at 9:00 this Friday, July 2nd. Can you be in my office at eight thirty?"

"Yes."

"So, I'll see you in a couple of days."

He called Pete. "Sorry about my disappearance."

"No apology needed. I'm just so sorry about your mom. What a great woman she was. She was always there for you. Savvy city planner and zoning expert—beauty, wit, charm—your mom had it all."

"She was the best."

"As you asked, I researched the records to find out if investigators knew how Hamlin's body got to the gravesite. I came up with zip."

"You're just a little late, Mister!" Logan chided. "As you know, I interviewed the homicide detective. She gave me some interesting theories but didn't know how the body got there either."

"If you ask me, the body must have been dragged, carried, or driven. It's even possible Hamlin was ordered to walk there at gunpoint, shot, and buried on the spot," Pete surmised.

Pete's head was back in the game. *Thank God, Pete seems more like himself tonight; more than the last time I saw him. Maybe Erika staying in Seattle was good for him.* "If you'd buried the body, you'd remember, right" Logan joked.

"Maybe I'd remember but I'd keep it a secret from you because I just don't like you,"

Pete countered. "And Mrs. Hamlin had the motive and opportunity to kill her husband."

"Seriously, Pete, a prosecutor could argue you're capable of dragging, carrying, or coercing Hamlin to walk to his gravesite. It wouldn't look good."

Pete agreed, "Well, he'd be right. He had to have been carried, dragged, or escorted down the trail. If Mrs. Hamlin killed him, she would have had walk to his gravesite. She had the motive and opportunity, but she sure's hell couldn't carry or drag him. She'd be challenged just digging the hole. On the other hand, I'm capable of digging a much deeper grave than the killer did, especially since I could have gotten a pick, shovel, and steel bar from our nearby house."

"But wait, I know you're a lazy slob who'd never dig a deep grave if you could avoid it."

"Hey, don't dis your client. Whose side are you on anyway?" They both laughed. "Did Sorensen give you anything else?"

"She sympathized with your situation and hopes you 'get off even if you did kill Hamlin.'"

"Wow, and she calls herself a detective?" Pete chuckled.

"One with a beating heart. Sorensen hated Jansen and the Hamlins. She interviewed the Hamlins when they gave their alibi and is guilt-ridden. If she'd done a better job, Jansen would have never been free again. She's extremely remorseful."

"Huh, really...well, I won't lose any sleep because Sorensen has remorse. Anything else?"

"Yeah. Sorensen also hates our boy Abbott."

"Who doesn't? But seriously, why?"

"He fired her after she dared suggest he charge the Hamlins with being accessories to the subsequent murders."

"Did Sorensen know why Abbott didn't prosecute them?"

"Like us, she's sure it was Abbott's relationship with Jansen and the Hamlins, and their mutual affiliation with the Evangelical church."

"That's all great. But, at trial, the only real issue will be whether I killed Hamlin."

Logan agreed. *It was going to be difficult to find someone to pin this murder on. Pete's guilt was emerging as the most logical conclusion.* Logan reminded Pete, "Still, it helps to know a key prosecution witness who doesn't like the government's case or the victim."

"How did you get her to talk?"

Logan dodged the question by cryptically responding. "Vee have our veys." He then changed the subject by asking about Erika.

"She's a wreck. Her mind keeps going around and around in a nightmare loop about the night Emma disappeared, searching for her, and the horror of how she must have suffered before she was killed. I wonder if it'd be easier for me to plead guilty and put her out of her misery."

An extraordinary comment. "C'mon, Pete, that won't help. Only getting acquitted will help her."

"You're right. It's hard to keep the faith, but I'll keep working on additional defenses."

"Have you thought about taking the stand?"

"Hell, yes. A lot. I'm going to wait until everyone's testified before I make that decision."

"One more thing, Pete...tomorrow, we have to get the biographical information and pay our jury wizard, Tim McQuigg. He needs twelve hundred dollars and another twelve hundred if he has to attend the trial."

"No problem. Here's my credit card number."

The next morning, Logan summarized what he knew about the witnesses on the state's lengthy list. For Tim, he wrote a complete description of Pete and who he was. Logan's list of witnesses consisted of precisely one person, Erika Foster. And Erika was evolving into a total basket case. *To win this case,* Logan strategized, *I'll have to do it through the jury consultant, a lethal cross-examination, a good opening statement, and an even better closing argument...the best closing argument I've ever delivered.*

Logan called McQuigg, paid him, and arranged to forward his list of witnesses and their bios. McQuigg thanked him and advised, "My schedule is pretty open now, so I should be able to get right on it. When is the trial, and do I get to meet any of the witnesses?"

"The trial should begin on July 19. Unfortunately, the state's key witness refused to meet with anyone but me, but her statements to me are included in the fax I'm sending you. You'll, of course, meet Pete and his wife, Erika. She's currently in Seattle but will be back in a couple of weeks."

"Is she going to testify?"

"She's on both witness lists, so I'm guessing they will probably subpoena her. She wants to testify. Potential problems with her testimony are in my synopsis of the case. I interviewed the state's expert witness, Detective Sorensen, when I was in Arizona. My PI will interview the state's witnesses. They'll be here before the trial, and if needed, we can talk to them at that time. They're all government employees. You probably know the coroner, Rebecca Wilson, and the head of forensics for the state, Dr. Frederick G. White?"

"I do. They'll make convincing witnesses."

"I think so too. There's also an arborist, Cliff Echternkamp, and an Anchorage cop by the name of Albright and a Trooper Harding."

"I don't recognize any of those names. I'm surprised they're all available to testify after so many years. They must be all over the country. This trial will cost the state a pretty penny in travel."

"Yeah...my guess is some of them won't show. Anyway, thanks, Tim. Let me know if you need anything else. Pete and I can come up anytime, although we'll be driving. Pete doesn't like to fly. On second thought, you might enjoy coming down to Homer and fishing with us for a day. You could get to know Pete and Erika and have a good time too, all expenses paid!"

Tim's eyes lit up. "Now, that's an offer I can't refuse. I'll get my report done and come down...let's see here. My calendar says Saturday, July 9, would be a good day to see you guys. We could discuss the report and fish on Sunday. It'll be good to see Lacey too."

"Perfect. We'll be in touch in the next couple of weeks."

"Great, thanks. Goodbye."

"THANK YOU FOR THE WAKE-UP call this morning, Pam. I'd for-gotten all about the hearing," Delores said.

"You're welcome. We're glad you made it."

Logan overheard Rodriguez's comments when she entered the office Friday morning. *Zimmerman's right. This woman can't remember any-thing.* Logan shrugged. *Thank God Pam's on the job.*

Logan and Ms. Rodriguez, "please, call me Lola," discussed the Zim-merman letter, its attachments, and whether she wanted it to remain con-fidential. "Of course I do. I have to live and work in this town, but thanks for asking."

They arrived in the courtroom ten minutes early. Logan asked Ms. Rodriguez to hang back, thinking her good looks would generate lit-tle sympathy from the prosecutor, Grace Berger.

"I'm so sorry, Mr. Finch, for not getting back to you," said the athletic young lawyer.

Logan flashed her what he hoped was his most charming smile. "Not a problem. I knew I'd be seeing you today."

"I have a written offer for you and your client to consider." She handed him a one-page form with some check marks. *This case is going to be easier than I thought,* Logan surmised. *The city was treating this as just a run-of-the-mill DUI. Knowing the severity of his client's problems, it was anything but.*

"Good. I'll have to let my client consider this for a day or two and get back to you next week. Can we agree to a continuance for thirty days?"

"Yes, of course."

When they were back at the office, Logan and Delores Anne reviewed the offer. "They want me to plead guilty to both charges but no more jail time?" she asked.

"And you're required to continue treatment for alcohol abuse as well as pay to install an ignition interlock device on your car. The lock stays in place for ninety days. The state will yank your license for three months, and you'll have to buy SR-22 insurance before you get your driving privileges back. It's nearly double what you're paying now. Oh, and you have to pay a fifteen-hundred-dollar fine."

Delores Anne held her hands up in pathetic surrender. "Okay, go ahead and do it. It's better than going to trial or spending more time in jail. I can't stand jail!"

"Right answer. I'll talk with the prosecutor next week and show her Zimmerman's letter. I'll tell her we'll use it at trial if she doesn't dismiss the eluding charge. I think a jury might conclude that you couldn't intentionally elude arrest if you're too frightened to form the thought."

"Yes, exactly. Thanks."

Logan was tepidly empathetic. In his line of work, he'd seen people destroy their lives because of addictions or the lure of false dreams. But he couldn't help but feel some tough love for those poor souls. *Steep road for Delores Anne,* Logan reflected. *She's disorganized and only Pam's phone call got her to court. If she fails to stay on top of needed paperwork, fails to jump through required hoops, it's likely she's gonna end up before a judge.* Logan grimaced. *And there may be precious little I can do to help her.*

Logan set aside his reflections. "I'll keep you posted on the plea bargain," he told her.

She exited the conference room just as she'd entered, with poise and dignity despite her situation. Logan escorted her out of the office and watched her negotiate the steps.

Like so many struggling souls, she wants more in her life—not just for herself but for those around her. However, she failed to understand how her past imprisoned her. I should try to soften the bumps in the road.

CHAPTER
42

Pete and Logan stood on the Land's End patio deck with binoculars in hand and tracked Lacey's return from a fisherman's association meeting in Kenai. She expertly touched down in her white, red-trimmed Cessna. A few yards away, a mama grizzly and her two cubs lumbered down the beach toward the end of the spit. "It's fishing lesson day," observed Logan.

Lacey had just completed her postflight inspection when Logan grabbed her from behind and hugged the wind out of her lungs. "So, you did miss me!" she exclaimed while catching her breath.

"You better believe I did. Pete's joining us for lunch, and we want to hear all about your trip. Let's see if we can get into the Little Mermaid. It's close to the harbor."

"And the boat!" She smiled mischievously.

"Okay, then, let's get this plane unloaded."

"Nah, go calm Pete down. I think being this close to a plane has him all worked up." Once they arrived at the restaurant, since it was the Fourth of July, there was just one narrow table left. Everyone was in town and they could watch over the dock and *The Coral Dawn* from their window seats.

"Great landing, Lacey!" Pete gave her a heartfelt salute. "How was your trip?"

"Oh, you know...uneventful haggling over the price of fish that haven't been caught yet," she replied sarcastically and thumped Pete on the shoulder. They were all aware how deadly serious those discussions could become. "What's going on with the trial and what have you two been up to?"

Logan began, "I provided Tim with the summary of the case and biographical sketches of the witnesses. The state has eleven experienced witnesses planned. We have one very inexperienced witness unless we include Pete."

"Are you thinking Erika is our star witness?" Lacey asked.

"She could be our alibi witness and say Pete was at home all day, but we'd have to overcome her statement to the trooper claiming she'd never heard of Hamlin. We could only explain it as her questionable memory after so many years have passed," Logan responded.

"Her testimony would have the same value as calling his loving mother to the stand," Lacey added.

"Hadn't thought of that, but you're right," Pete agreed.

"Tim's coming to Homer next Saturday to deliver his initial report. He wants to go fishing Sunday."

"Good...but is that all I missed? What's happening with your favorite client?"

Logan leaned back in his chair. "Pete's right here."

"You know...the beautiful Ms. Rodreeeeeeeguez, a.k.a. Lo-lah."

"That's a confidential matter that I'm not at liberty to disclose in Pete's presence," Logan responded in wry legalese. He casually stirred the vodka floating atop his drink.

Lacey raised her eyebrows. "Uh-huh..."

"But, overall, since you've asked, she's doing well under the circumstances. We received a good initial offer from the prosecutor, and I should be able to resolve the matter without a trial."

"I'm more concerned about initial offers from *her*," smirked Lacey.

Logan raised his hands in surrender. "As usual, I got nuthin'."

Pete intervened. "Not to change the subject, which I find fascinating, by the way, but I want to offer my free services as to any contract, corporate questions, or research you need for the office, Lacey. Also, I left a check with Pam to cover some of your office expenses. Your rent is waived from May through July and keep track of your hours. I'll pay you at the end of the trial. Logan's pro bono, but don't tell him until after the trial."

"It works for me, Pete, and thank you," Lacey said, ignoring Logan's feigned disappointment. "Are you joining us at the office for the parade?"

"You bet. Thought we'd meet you at about 6:00 p.m. later today."

After lunch, Pete left for Land's End and Lacey and Logan strolled to the boat. "Can I just shower and take a short nap without any interventions?" she asked as they boarded.

"How, exactly, do you expect to pay for the water you're about to use?"

"Pay for the water? If I charged you properly, I'd own the whole damn boat!"

"A shower and nap it will be. A short nap, hopefully!" Humming the theme from *Happy Days,* Logan walked out the sliding door in search of the garden hose to refill the water tanks.

Lacey's nap was short.

CHAPTER
43

H OMER'S FOURTH OF JULY FESTIVITIES BEGAN with a 6:00 p.m.
parade through downtown and past their office. Then the entire
city pushed and shoved cars and bodies onto the four-mile spit for the
annual extravaganza. There was a fireworks display staged in front of the
Land's End Resort and restaurant. The twenty-year tradition was funded
and promoted by the city of Homer.

The four of them—Lacey, Logan, Pete, and Erika—gathered at the
office to pre-function and watch the parade: floats, bands, vintage auto-
mobiles, horses, motorcycles, and bagpipe bands with guys in kilts. In the
past, the festivities had included VIPs like US Senator Ted Stevens.

At 8:00 p.m., they crammed into Logan's faithful Volkswagen, as it was
the best way to score a parking place at the boat harbor. Once parked, they
met up with Mike, Sasha, and Toby, who remembered the Fourth of July
and all its frightening ramifications. Toby was securely tied to the aft starboard cleat and not happy about it. Mike explained Toby could go below
if he wanted, but he chose to remain up top where the people were.

"We'll leave him here for a couple of hours, max. It's tough to listen to
him howl during the fireworks, especially when there's absolutely nothing I can do for him," Mike elaborated. Then, like almost every man in
Homer, he tucked his pistol into a shoulder holster.

Logan went belowdecks and started making vodka martinis. Lacey
patted Toby's head and passed a martini to Mike. "When the fireworks
start, it's like having a baby with an earache. A helpless feeling is all I can
say. I feel helpless, utterly helpless," Mike lamented.

They toasted the day and decided to go to Land's End to people watch
on the patio where Pete had reserved a table. Toby was crying pitifully
when they left. "We'll be right back," Sasha told him.

Once again, the fireworks display was spectacular. When the last
sparkling burst of red, white, and blue exploded over the bay, Mike and

Sasha excused themselves. "Sorry to cut the evening short, but we're worried about Toby and all the noise."

"No problem," Logan said. "We'll be back after we finish these drinks."

A rock band began playing somewhere in the distance. It was a beautiful evening and they all felt fortunate to be in Homer.

As Mike and Sasha strolled casually down the dock, they heard a gunshot. *Or was it just fireworks?* Mike reached for his shoulder holster. As they approached their sailboat, they didn't see or hear Toby. They heard another muffled gunshot coming from inside Logan's boat. Mike noticed Logan's salon door was open, and someone was in the engine hold. "Who's there?" he shouted.

Then Sasha screamed. "Oh my God. Toby's been shot!"

Mike whipped his pistol out and took a defensive position on the dock and shouted to Sasha, "Get belowdecks!" He then focused on Logan's boat. A man was coming out of the hold. Mike aimed his sight through the window and directly at the guy's head.

"Throw the gun on the deck and come outta there with your hands behind your head if you wanna live."

"My gun is on the table behind me. I'm going to come up with my hands behind my head. Just don't shoot me."

Mike moved with him from the dock to the stern as a beefy, bald guy came up the stairwell. "Jump down here on the dock. Keep your hands behind your head."

The intruder jumped and stumbled slightly as he landed on the dock. At the same instant, Mike hit him flush in the face with the butt of his gun, launching him into the water. He came up gasping for air and swam toward an old wooden ladder. "Now, get on that sailboat and sit down next to the steering wheel." Shivering in his cold wet flannel shirt, the guy warily kept his eyes on Mike's gun and quickly complied.

Mike yelled at Sasha to come up top. Grief-stricken and sobbing over Toby's death, her face left no doubt she'd not hesitate to use the gun Mike handed her. He then wrenched the prowler's hands above his head and tied them onto the steering wheel. "Sit very still, or you'll be taking your last breath," Mike warned. Leaving Sasha to stand guard, he went to check out Logan's vessel.

Five minutes after Mike and Sasha left, Logan's cell phone buzzed. "Hey, Sasha. Yeah. What? We'll be right there!" He hung up. "Lacey, take care of the bill. Mike needs help. Pete and I will meet you and Erika at the boat." Logan swiftly moved from his chair and across the deck. Pete followed close behind.

"What's going on?" Lacey hollered after them as they disappeared into the night.

Jogging toward the dock, Logan huffed, "I don't know much, but some guy killed Toby and blew a hole in my boat. Mike has the guy hog-tied on his sailboat."

"Jesus."

As they ran down the dock, Sasha stepped off the sailboat and waved to them. The pistol in her hand was pointed toward the freezing hulk tied up on their boat. "Mike's on your boat plugging the hole this asshole shot in it."

Pete took the gun from Sasha and pointed it at the soaking-wet guy sitting awkwardly on the deck. "I got this," Pete assured Logan. "Go help Mike."

As Logan dropped belowdecks on *The Coral Dawn*, Sasha climbed aboard the sailboat and bent down beside the starboard rail. It was too dark for Pete to see anything, but he heard her crying uncontrollably.

"What is it?" Pete asked. "What's the matter, Sasha?"

"He shot our Toby. Toby's dead!"

Turning to the killer, Pete asked in disbelief, "What the fuck, man? Did you shoot their dog?"

Water dripped from the man's head as he looked down at the deck. He didn't respond.

"You son of a bitch, I'll fucking pull this trigger if you don't tell me right this second what the hell you're doing here!"

"God's will."

"God willed that you kill their dog and sink my friend's boat?"

"I don't know. I think so. I mean...shit, I'm sorry."

"You're sorry?" Sasha asked. She stood and walked over to the guy and slugged him in the nose. Pete heard the cartilage crack. The guy's head snapped back and stayed there. Blood spurted from his nose and streamed down his lips and chin. Sasha sat silently on the railing, petting Toby's lifeless body.

As Pete's eyes adjusted to the gloom, he saw Toby, his sweet face distorted and bloody from the cruel gunshot. "If you hadn't done that, Sasha, I swear I would have."

She couldn't respond. Tears ran down her face onto Toby's back as she cradled her beloved companion, stroking his fur and crooning softly.

Mike and Logan, having plugged the bullet hole, came back to the sailboat. Mike tenderly picked up Toby's body from Sasha's arms, tears streaming down his face as he embraced his dog. Logan threw some water on the guy's face and he regained consciousness. "Who are you?" Logan demanded.

"My name's Joe. Joe Deter."

"Why the fuck did you do this, man?"

"I don't know."

"Don't give me that shit," Logan yelled.

"Figure it out fast, asshole, or I'm gonna blow your fuckin' head off," Mike hollered. Pete underscored the question by pressing the barrel of the gun hard against Joe's ear.

"I work for the Baptist church in Anchorage. I'm their maintenance guy. I got a message in my mailbox at the church yesterday telling me to wait for someone there at noon today."

"Who was the note from?" Logan asked.

"I don't know."

"We're going to ask you just one more time. Who was the goddamn note from?" Mike growled.

"It just said I'd been ordered to do it by the Guidance Panel."

"Are you a church member?" Logan asked.

"Yes."

"Then you know who and what the Guidance Panel is?" Logan asked.

"I do."

"Who picked you up this afternoon?" Mike asked.

"I don't know the guy's name."

"Where is he now?" Mike asked.

"I don't know. He stayed in the pickup but must have taken off when you guys showed up. He fucking left me!"

The word *pickup* caught Logan's attention. "Are you the guys who followed me up in Anchorage?"

Joe looked confused. "I don't know anything about that."

Logan believed him. He wouldn't lie with a gun pressed against his head.

Mike, however, still wanted more answers. Handing Toby back to Sasha, he took the gun from Pete and pushed it up Joe's nose until it started bleeding again. "Listen to me, Joe. We need the guy's name and a description of the pickup he's driving. And we need it now."

"I can't tell you. He made it clear, if things went bad, they'd kill me if I said anything. I've already told you too much."

"You haven't told us jack shit," Mike yelled.

"Call the police. All I did was blow a hole in your boat to scare you. Malicious mischief.

A couple of days in jail. The boat didn't even sink."

"You forgot something else," Mike hissed.

"The dog? I'll pay you for the damn dog. What'd it cost you?"

"More than you'll ever...fucking...have," Mike said as he started to squeeze the trigger before thinking better of it.

"Should I call the police?" Logan asked.

"Nah, not yet." Mike sounded calm. Deadly calm.

After Sasha lay a fur blanket over Toby's body, she went belowdecks for duct tape. She gave it to Mike, and he handed his gun to her. Mike then duct-taped Joe's mouth shut, bound his legs together with the unused port-stern line, and dragged him to the port-side rail where he tied him to the cleat.

"Sasha and I are going for an evening boat ride. We want to bury Toby at sea, and we want our pal Joey here to watch. We'll, uhm, call the police when we get back."

Joe began to squirm, his eyes darting about wildly as Mike started up the engine and Sasha pushed the sailboat clear of the dock. They were backing out of the slip when Lacey and Erika arrived.

"What's all the commotion?" Lacey asked.

Logan shot Pete a quick look, and his friend nodded silently. "Nothing," Logan said. "Mike and Sasha thought the boat was leaking water and, sure enough, one of the plugs came free and the aft bilge pump wasn't doing the job. Everything's okay now."

"Yay, Mike. He keeps an eye out," Lacey noted.

"Where are they going this time of night?" Erika asked.

"They just want some privacy, I think," Pete said as he glanced at Logan. They both knew not to open this Pandora's box. Erika was already a basket case, and they didn't want to compound Lacey's worries.

Once out of the boat harbor, Mike ran the sailboat at full throttle in a southerly direction. He just wanted to get out of sight from Land's End.

"Sasha," Mike whispered, looking directly at Joe, "disconnect the anchor."

"With pleasure," Sasha sneered at Joe.

When Joe realized what was about to happen, he began to thrash around like a two-hundred-pound halibut. Mike observed his obvious distress dispassionately. *Wonder if Pal Joey here will have to be treated like a dangerous halibut and calmed down with a bullet.*

Mike turned the engine off and tied the anchor chain around Joe's ankles before throwing it overboard. Mike then went to the port-side rail and unemotionally lengthened the line on the cleat to about twenty feet. Joe tried to jump free from Mike's grasp but was unable to do so with the chain around his ankles. "Sweet dreams, you son of a bitch." With one determined shove, Sasha pushed Joe over the side the boat.

The couple both had tears in their eyes as they watched and waited for Pal Joey to submerge. It only took a few seconds. Mike counted to ten before hauling him up and back onto the deck. Pal Joey, hysterically grateful to be alive, gasped for air, shaking uncontrollably as he witnessed Sasha sorrowfully wrap their beloved Toby in an Athabascan fur blanket and lovingly slip him into the sea.

When they returned to the dock, the last they saw of Pal Joey, he looked like a fat drowned rat scuttling up the dock.

CHAPTER
44

AᴠFTER TWO RINGS, a voice answered. "Good morn-ing...Mr. Albright?"

"This is Jason Albright."

Before tackling his list of "Things to Do," Logan was eager to call Officer Albright, if for no other reason than to harass the jackass for threatening to kill him all those years ago. "Mr. Albright, this is Logan Finch. I'm representing Pete Foster. I understand you'll be a witness in the upcoming trial, sir?"

"Yeah, I think so. They subpoenaed me for the trial."

"Good, but I'd like to ask you a few questions right now, if I may?"

"Of course, but y'know, this happened a long time ago and my memory's not getting better with time."

"Neither is mine, but I do recall talking to you back in the early eighties. Do you remember?"

"No, not at all."

"Well, it's hard for me to forget that conversation because you threatened to kill me."

"Very funny. What the fuck are you talking about?"

"I called you to collect over thirty thousand dollars in back child support for your two children that you abandoned in Tacoma."

Silence.

"Hello? Mr. Albright? Hello?" The line was dead. Logan smiled. *I guess he remembered me. One less witness.*

McQuigg waved exuberantly to Pete and Logan as he crossed the small tarmac. Just in case Pete and Logan missed Tim's state-of-the-art fishing vest and attached lures, he waved a new pristine fly rod tube case in the air. A closer examination of the rugged attire would have revealed plastic thread barbs protruding from hastily removed sales tags. His entire look flawlessly mirrored the glossy covers of *Fish Alaska Magazine*. Pete, hands jammed in an ancient leather bomber jacket, nudged Logan with a succinct assessment. "All righty, then."

Logan smiled, "Yeah...at least he's not wearing hip waders."

The ensemble wasn't the only extraordinary thing about McQuigg's appearance. The Beechcraft was taxiing to the baggage claim office when Pete abruptly realized, "You know, I don't think I ever saw a black person in Homer when we practiced here."

"Never thought about it, but you're right. Once again, we're on the cutting edge of social change, Pete." They were still chuckling as Tim enthusiastically shook Logan's hand. "I assume this is Mr. Foster?"

"It's Pete. Just call me Pete."

"Good enough, Pete. You can call me Mr. McQuigg." They laughed, remembering Sidney Portier's sophistication in the 1970 movie *They Call Me Mister Tibbs!* "So, where's our red-haired beauty? You guys didn't think I came all the way to Homer just to see you, did ya?"

Pete was surprised. "You mean Lacey?"

Logan explained, "Yeah, he does. Guess I forgot to tell you, but Tim worked with Lacey on her trials last year in Anchorage." Logan then good-naturedly assured Tim, "Lacey's waiting for us at the office. Let's grab your bag and get over there."

Lacey let out a squeal when Tim entered the office. She hurried over and hugged him, her arms barely spanning his burly girth. "Tim, it's so great to have you here!"

"It's good to see you again, darlin'. How are things treatin' you?"

"Things are good."

"Great. Now, where's the coffee and donuts I heard about?"

"It's all in the conference room, just waiting for you," Lacey said.

Tim pulled out his twenty-eight-page preliminary report and distributed copies. "Go ahead, take a few minutes to read it over—or I could summarize the contents, then we can get right to discussing the recommendations and tentative conclusions. There might be changes and updates after I spend some time with Pete and Erika over the weekend."

"Good. Erika's at the hotel and I'll check on her in an hour or two," Pete said.

"Shall we discuss my preliminary recommendations?"

Logan was eager to hear Tim's thoughts. "Great, yeah."

"In general, we all know the kind of jurors we want on the panel. Thinkers, not soldiers. We want people who can understand what 'beyond a reasonable doubt' means. We don't want people who blindly follow authority figures and rules. Those people live in black-and-white worlds, and that's not good for Pete. The dominant fact for an Alaskan jury is Pete is no longer an Alaskan and lived here for a mere thirteen years."

"Can't change that, so how do we combat it?" Logan asked.

"Good question. The answer? We don't want an Alaskan jury."

"How would that happen? The judge won't allow moving this case to another state," Pete said.

"I know. So, we shoot for jurors who've been in Alaska thirteen years or less. Their Alaskan bias won't be as ingrained. Politics, religion—probably even sexual preferences—take a back seat to born-'n'-bred Alaskan sourdoughs. Mr. Hamlin was an Alaskan. Mrs. Hamlin still lives here. You don't. All the state's key witnesses live here, except Sorensen, and since she has a good reason to be in Arizona, she'll be excused for her shortsightedness.

"Sociologically speaking, and since the beginning of time, when people live in geographically isolated or segregated societies, they bond over their shared isolation. They may fight amongst themselves, but woe be the outsider. The fact that Pete's an attorney isn't nearly as damaging as his non-Alaskan ties."

"What are our chances of having a jury pool full of outsiders?" Lacey asked.

"You don't need a jury pool filled with them. You just need one strong outsider in a criminal case. But, obviously, the more, the better."

"Okay, besides outsiders, what other characteristics do we want?" Logan asked.

"First, we want parents and mothers of teenage girls—no divorced men who don't have custody of their daughters. Professional people are best because blue-collar workers generally hate attorneys, believe cops, and tend to be more tied to Alaska, physically and emotionally. Takes money to get outta here in the winter, and most of those folks can't afford to leave very often."

"What about cops and religious fanatics?" Logan asked.

"Surprisingly, a cop on this jury may be good. Their inherent morality radar is comfortably undeterred by legalities. They're frequently inclined to exact their own form of justice. In this case, it's possible they'd ignore legal technicalities and disregard the motive and opportunity arguments because Hamlin gave officers a false alibi that freed Jansen. It might be in character for them to consider Hamlin's murder as justice served. Most jurors would blame the police for a shoddy investigation; the cop juror will not hesitate to place the blame on Mr. Hamlin."

"Got it. A woman cop with twin teenage daughters who just moved to Alaska. No problem. I bet we see a lot of them," Pete sarcastically summarized.

"No one promised easy pickin's, Pete. It's a crapshoot, pure and simple. I'm just trying to improve your odds, and I think we have a good shot at doing that."

"I hear you. Thanks, these are great suggestions. Sorry for being so negative."

"It's okay. And, keep in mind, the lead homicide detective, Sorensen, is on your side. She may rub off on the jury, especially if a juror or two is a cop, or a wannabe cop, or even a security guard. Firefighters are similarly wired, so they're potentially a good choice."

"And the religious nutballs?" Pete asked gloomily.

"If you keep Hamlin's religion out of the trial, absorbing a Bible thumper or two in the jury pool may not be a death knell. They're inoculated every day, and" Tim winked, "twice on Sundays, with biblical doctrine about *heaven-sent* retribution. So, they might conclude Hamlin got what he deserved because Emma wasn't a prostitute and didn't deserve to die. But it's nevertheless a tougher call than the cop juror." The room fell silent.

Pete's face was somber as he looked directly at Tim. "So, what do you think of the case?"

"I think you have a real uphill battle. The circumstantial evidence is overwhelmingly in the state's favor. Your wife will testify that you were home all day, but her credibility was muddied when she denied knowing Hamlin when they arrested you."

Logan sounded defeated. "I was afraid you'd see it that way."

The meeting concluded with plans for predinner drinks on *The Coral Dawn*. Tim left with Pete to meet Erika while Logan and Lacey remained at the office to review the details of Tim's report.

"Damn, Lace, I'm not sure I'm up to this."

"What are you talking about? I know it's been a while since you tried a case, but you were a great trial attorney. It's like riding a bike; it'll all come back."

"Thanks for the vote of confidence, but if I screw up, Pete ships out to Sing Sing. Maybe we need to talk him into swapping me for an attorney with current trial experience. Somebody who has a strong litigation track record."

"He won't do that. Also, you can't withdraw at this late date. If I didn't think you could handle this case, I would tell you. Cross my heart." Lacey smiled at Logan's abject doubt. Cupping his face in her hands, she pulled him close to her, eye-to-eye, and slowly enunciated, "You. Can. Do. This."

Tim was onboard and studying his laptop when Logan and Lacey arrived at *The Coral Dawn*. "Pete said he'd meet us at Land's End for dinner," Tim said without looking up.

Lacey was curious about what monopolized Tim. "Reading some interesting stuff?" she probed.

"Yeah. Jansen's murders fascinate me. I'm looking for more background information to understand Ms. Sorensen's rabid dislike for the Hamlins and how we might capitalize on it."

"Great idea," Logan said. "Did you meet Erika?"

"Kind of. We went to their hotel room. The drapes were closed, lights off, and she was in bed. Whether she's timid, depressed, or petrified doesn't matter. She won't make a good witness," Tim flatly informed. "She's polite but literally hides under the covers." Tim frowned and continued, "It's been my experience that most innocent people in Pete's situation are fiercely focused on fighting. I find Pete oddly preoccupied, almost disoriented by his wife's condition. Before you can risk putting him on the stand, he needs preparation, and that requires a commitment Pete isn't delivering."

Lacey responded, "Erika's traumatized. She's having to relive the nightmare of having their only child ripped from their lives while worrying about Pete's chances of prison as a new lifestyle, and her being alone."

Tim shrugged noncommittally and continued. "It's also my experience that if you must put your client on the stand in a criminal case to assert his innocence, you've already lost the case."

As they left the boat, Lacey looked around the dock. "Hey, where's Mike and Sasha? And I haven't seen or heard Toby barking either."

Logan looked out over the harbor and sighed. "Remember on the Fourth when Pete and I left the restaurant because of a leak in the boat?" Lacey nodded as Logan looked across the bay before continuing. "Well...you were already worried about the crank calls and your house getting vandalized, so I didn't have the guts to give you the unabridged version. That night, some holy roller fanatic shot and killed Toby, and then he climbed aboard my boat and shot a hole in the hull."

"Aww, Jesus...how are they doing?"

"I really don't know. I haven't seen them since that night."

"Did you or Mike report it to the police?"

"Mike was going to after they buried Toby at sea."

"How are you doing? I know how much you loved the little guy."

"God, Lace, we all loved him. I just didn't realize..." Logan's jaw tightened as he paused. Lacey saw a tear trail down his cheek before he continued, his voice husky and strained. "I didn't realize how much I'd miss cooking those extra pieces of bacon and seeing him wait for me to catch him in the mornings. And Mike and Sasha, I can't imagine...Toby was their baby."

CHAPTER 45

L ACEY JUMPED OUT of the aft-cabin bed and scrambled to the upper deck for better reception when her cell phone rang early Wednesday morning. Logan, assuming they were now up for the day, got out of the bed to fill their coffee mugs. A few minutes later, Lacey joined him in the main salon. "That was E. J. Little, skipper of the *Dixie Normus*. He's the guy I worked for last season."

Logan wondered, *Should I tell her about the boat's name?* "What'd he want?"

"He wants me in King Cove tomorrow afternoon. He's there now. I told him about the trial on Monday, the nineteenth. He'll drop me off in Adak on Saturday and I'll get to Anchorage by 9:00 p.m."

"Hmm...well, today you could work on your cross-examination questions, fly to Anchorage in the morning, and then out to King Cove in the afternoon," Logan suggested.

"Yeah. E. J. said there's a flight out of Anchorage tomorrow at noon. He'll meet me at three on the Peter Pan Seafoods dock."

"We're as prepared as we'll ever be for the trial, and your cross-examination should be short and sweet, if at all."

"I agree."

"Then let's get to work," Logan said with a smile.

They grabbed a quick breakfast at Café Cups on their way to the office. Logan went straight to the conference room and called the Homer prosecutor. He wanted to arrange a meeting on the Rodriguez matter and show her Zach Zimmerman's professional assessment.

"Ms. Berger, would you be available for a short meeting to discuss the Rodriguez case? Maybe fifteen minutes sometime today?"

"I was hoping you'd take my offer. I don't have the file in front of me. When are we back in court?"

"Tomorrow. I have a letter from her psychologist and her evaluation reports."

"Okay. How does one o'clock today sound?"

"Perfect, see you then."

When Logan stuck his head into Lacey's office, she was reading through the witness statements and scribbling notes on a yellow pad. "Hey, can I interrupt for a minute?"

She looked up smiling. "Now that you have, sure, what's up?"

"What's the weather like in Bristol Bay this week? And tell me how safe the *Dixie Normus* might be."

"Why, Mistuh Finch, I do d'clah," Lacey responded in her best Southern belle voice. "Don't tell me you're concerned about this damsel's safety in the most dangerous water habitat on the face o'this lil'ole earth? How ver' chiv'lrus of you." Lacey's Scarlett O'Hara impersonation was a solid performance.

Logan's Clark Gable rendition, not so much. "Why, Ms. Carpenter. Your safety is of the utmost importance to me in my current condition. Your safe return is my most fervent desire."

"And pray tell, what is it about your current condition that you find so disconcerting? I was led to believe your condition was completely," Lacey batted her eyelashes, "satisfied last night."

"Now, ma'am, it was. It mos' certainly was. But the quality of that satisfaction only leaves this gentleman wanting more in the immediate future. So, surely, you understand this gentleman's extreme apprehension regarding your safety."

"Well, suh, your trep'dashun is duly noted. Ah'll do everything within my considerable pow'r to satisfy your every need upon my safe return from the sea."

"Thank you, ma'am, I am mos' grateful for all your kind assurances, but goddamn it, Lacey," Logan asserted, "exactly how big is that fucking boat you'll be on?"

Lacey gave Logan a benign Cheshire cat smile. "I guess we can dispense with the word *gentleman* in this conversation. It's a 125-foot house-aft crabber with a 28-foot beam and a 13-foot draft, built in 1981. It has twin Cummins diesel engines rated at 640 horse, a bulbous bow with a bow thruster, knuckle-boom crane, a picking boom, and a new chiller. She's fully rigged for crab and tendering and packs 300,000 pounds of salmon or 240,000 pounds of crab in the two holds. And I'm in love with every layer of paint, every disgusting crevice in the bilge, every creak and groan and rumble. So best watch what you imply about my other love!"

"Geez, okay! Sorry I asked. I feel like I stumbled onto the set of *My Cousin Vinny*. See you Saturday night, then."

"I'll be the super-hot seductress at the airport who scraped the fish scales off her Grundens bibs and Xtratufs!"

CHAPTER
46

L OGAN ARRIVED AT a precisely one o'clock, and Grace Berger gestured him down the short hallway to her office. The place reeked of
government surplus, which Logan, a tax-paying citizen, appreciated. He
grouched inwardly. *Government employees receive good salaries, incredible
retirement, six-week paid vacations, sick leave, maternity leave, and semi-
nars in warm cities. Too many also enjoy the best offices in the tallest buildings with incredible views—all on the taxpayers' dime. Zillions of taxpayers'
dimes.* "Good afternoon, and thanks for seeing me on such short notice."

"You're welcome. It worked out for both of us. I had a trial scheduled
for today that settled."

"Great. I wanted to give you the alcohol and drug assessment for
Ms. Rodriguez, a confidential letter from her psychologist, and photos of
her prescription bottles."

Within seconds, Ms. Berger had expertly scanned them. Obviously,
not her first rodeo, as she knew what Logan was going to say before he
said it. And she knew what she was willing to negotiate. "What are you
proposing, Mr. Finch?"

"As you can see from Zimmerman's letter, this woman was incapable
of the criminal intent required to substantiate an eluding arrest charge.
He'll testify to that. But, more importantly, Ms. Rodriguez loves Homer
and wants to stay here. If her private psychological issues are aired in the
open forum of the court, she'll have a tough time finding employment."

"That might be, but does Homer love her? Maybe a move to Anchorage, where her misconduct could be better hidden from the authorities,
would be best for her."

"Now, I'll pretend you didn't say that. I know the city of Homer
wouldn't appreciate Anchorage judges and prosecutors negotiating plea
deals requiring criminals to move to Homer."

"Okay, you have me there. I'm not negotiating anything that requires your client to relocate to Anchorage."

"Of course, I know that. And, based on our mutual desire for Ms. Rodriguez to continue residing here, may I suggest that we dismiss the evading charge and she'll plead guilty to the DUI charge—which is her first ever—and she will continue weekly counseling with Zimmerman for at least one more year or until an assessment determines she's no longer in need of alcohol counseling. Two years' probation seems appropriate under the circumstances. Given the PTSD diagnosis, an additional day in jail is problematic. She was extremely distraught in my office when she learned she might spend another twenty-four hours in jail."

Logan asked for more than he could get. He knew the two years would be rejected; five years was the norm. Ms. Berger knew it as well. "I think we can dismiss the evading charge, but a two-year probation's out of the question. This case requires five years."

"As long as a probation officer doesn't have to supervise probation. She doesn't have a job right now and has no money to pay for the supervision."

"I'm not happy with this agreement," Ms. Berger advised. "But if we can close the case tomorrow with a change of plea and immediate sentencing, I'll do it. I have an overabundance of cases and most of those defendants present far more danger to the fine folks of Homer than your Ms. Rodriquez—especially if she isn't drinking and driving."

"My client will be equally unhappy with this agreement," Logan asserted.

"Do you have the authority from your client to enter into this agreement? Because, if not, I'll withdraw the deal tomorrow. No more continuances."

"I have authority so long as there's no additional jail time."

"Excellent. Have a good day, Mr. Finch."

"You too, Ms. Berger."

He walked out of the courthouse smiling. Not because he had outfoxed the prosecutor—he hadn't—but because his client was so emotionally compromised that any additional incarceration would make progress with her psychologist that much more difficult. At the office, he left a message on Delores Anne's phone. "Please come to my office tomorrow at 10:00. We are due in court at eleven." *And a well-timed reminder call from Pam might be good.*

"I guess I'm getting tired of seafood," Logan said as he and Lacey entered AJ's Steakhouse and Tavern. He held the door as they entered the rustic country restaurant and bar.

"I'm with ya. Filet mignon and red wine sound perfect."

"Wine? Did you say wine?" Logan asked with exaggerated optimism.

"You are utterly hopeless at subtle."

They ordered steak and fries and a bottle of Smoking Loon Syrah from Chile.

"Before I forget, thanks again for the introduction to McQuigg. Without him, I don't think we'd have a chance."

"Even with him, we may not have a chance." No joking, no light-hearted delivery. Lacey was somber and deadly serious.

"Don't say that," Logan pleaded. "This case is causing me more anxiety than you can imagine."

"Okay, and I'm sorry, but the jury's decision is only partially under your control."

"I know. Does it seem like we're not getting much help from Pete or Erika? Tim said the same thing. What's your take, Lace?"

"I'm not sure, but I guess until we lose a child and get charged with murder, we'll never understand."

"You're right." Logan finished the wine dregs. They walked back to the boat, joined at the hips and with an arm around each other. Logan broke the comfortable quiet by abruptly asking, "Why don't we stay at your house anymore?"

"I don't want to remember you being there after you leave for Arizona. You'll have to spare me that, okay?"

"Fair enough." Logan let the question-and-answer stand. He resisted addressing the question of not leaving in the fall. Or having her come to Arizona. He hadn't decided what he wanted to do.

Logan returned to the office after taking Lacey to the airport and found Ms. Rodriguez waiting for him. "I'm sorry, hope you haven't been here long. I had to take Ms. Carpenter to the airport."

"Did she lose her license too?"

"No...have you lost your license?"

"Yes!"

They entered the conference room where she plunked down in an accusatory huff. "It's not gonna be easy driving around here with the cops knowing my car and that I lost my license."

"That's the point, Delores Anne, you're not supposed to be driving."

"I know, but if I can't drive, I can't get a job. I can't see my counselor or go to the grocery store. I can't even go see a movie. You wouldn't believe what cabs cost around here. And they cut me off Social Security disability."

"What about your Dr. Ben? Maybe he can help you out a little."

"Nah, he won't take my calls anymore." She was resigned. "Probably 'cause I'm always calling him over and over after I drink."

"You're not supposed to be drinking either."

"Can't help drinking. And when I do, I can't help calling him. You aren't me."

"I'm not going to argue about this, but I am concerned for your situation."

"I'm sorry. So, why did you want to see me?"

"I wanted to make sure you're ready to plead guilty to the DUI charge today. I managed to get the eluding arrest charge dropped, and there won't be any more jail time, but you'll be on probation for five years."

"Do I have to take urine tests?"

"No, not unless your counselor requires it. You'll be back in court if that happens."

"And no more jail?"

"Nope. Will that work for you?"

"I guess so, if it's the best we could do."

"Honestly, it's the best you could ever hope for. The prosecutor wasn't at all happy about the deal you're getting."

"Did Ben call and ask you to have me plead guilty so he doesn't have to pay for a trial?"

"Hell, no. And that'd be highly unethical on my part."

"Nice to know your ethics aren't limited to sex," Delores Anne shot back. Logan ignored her snippy comment. He was startled and amazed at her proficiency in toggling from super sweet to super bitch in nanoseconds. *Wonder how that diagnosis would read?* he idly wondered. "Let's get to the courthouse before the prosecutor changes her mind."

As they walked to the front door, he noticed Pam and Katie in the office, their heads bent down and eyes averted to paper shuffling and reinforcing the illusion of disinterest. *Yep...there'd be a report to Lacey.*

CHAPTER
47

E VERYTHING WENT ACCORDING to Hoyle and the judge gave her twelve months to pay the $1,500 fine. They took custody of the sentencing order and hustled out the courthouse doors before anyone could change their minds.

Delores Anne was smiling and animated. Her spike heels clicked loudly on the sidewalk. She graciously thanked Logan and ended, "It was easier than I thought." They returned to the office and said goodbye in the parking lot. Delores Anne tread carefully across the gravel, then started down the street toward her apartment. Logan felt stymied. Courtesy and kindness dictated he drive Delores Anne home, but that was juxtaposed with triggering further scrutiny by Pam and Katie.

Logan provided a morning rundown while Katie gazed over her shoulder, out the window. "Is that her walking down the street?"

"Yeah. She lost her license and took a cab here," Logan explained. "She's walking home to save money."

"Good grief! A three-thousand-dollar retainer should cover a ride home," Pam grumbled in utter disgust.

Logan threw up his hands. "You two make me paranoid! You issue bulletins to Lacey about everything I do. So, I was afraid to offer *a client* a ride home!"

"Get outta here and give the woman a ride home," Katie ordered.

"And take her to breakfast if she's hungry," Pam added. "That's just being civil. And Logan, our lips are sealed if that makes you feel better."

"Unbelievable!" Logan grumbled to himself. He continued to shake his head as he walked out to the parking lot, climbed into the Bug, and turned the key in one fluid motion. It was raining when he reached the East End Road. He soon spotted Ms. Rodriguez peering out at the street from under the awning of the Cosmic Kitchen.

Logan pulled up beside her and rolled down his window. "Delores Anne, get in and I'll take you home."

"Thanks," she declined, "but I only have a mile or so to go."

"I know where you live. I drove you home once."

"Really? I don't remember that."

"Yeah. You live across from the Homestead Restaurant." Mindful of Pam's suggestion, Logan asked, "Would you like to stop there first and have some breakfast with me?"

"Gosh, I would. I applied there for work, but I haven't heard anything."

"They'd be lucky to have you. I'll put in a good word for you today."

"Geez, thanks so much," she said as they walked in the front door of the log building.

"I'm happy to do it. It's a great place to eat—the Kachemak Glacier in the background and the beautiful Native American art on the walls. Too bad they close every year at the end of September."

"I love the place too."

"Good morning," said the hostess. "Oh, Lola, good morning. It took me a moment to recognize you. You're all dressed up."

"It doesn't happen very often these days, Sue."

"Well, you look very nice."

"Sue, this is Logan Finch. He works at Lacey Carpenter's office."

"Sure," Sue acknowledged. "I recognize you."

"I was in with friends a few weeks ago for dinner. We really enjoyed it," Logan said.

"I have a nice window seat for the two of you." She checked out Logan's ring finger and her smile grew wider as she seated them.

"Not to talk business, but the owners are getting ready to call you with a job offer," Sue whispered.

Lola couldn't contain her happiness. "Wow, thanks! I'll be watching my phone until I get a call."

"I'll tell them you had lunch here today with a guest. They'll be pleased."

"Again, thanks so much."

"What can I get you two to drink?"

Logan deferred to Lola. "What would you like?"

"I'd like an iced tea, if you have it."

"Make it two ice teas, please," Logan requested.

"Coming right up." Sue quickly returned with their drinks and took their orders for eggs Benedict.

"So, Mr. Attorney, what cases are you doing besides mine?"

"Just one. The state charged my best friend with murder."

"Murder? Really? Can you talk about it?"

"Well, I can give you my opening statement. You can tell me if it's confusing."

Delores Anne was genuinely flattered. "Really? I'd love to."

They ate breakfast while Logan summarized the case. "So, what do you think?"

"I think you have it all wrong."

"You do, do you?" Logan smirked.

"Not to hurt your feelings, but I think you want the jurors to decide Mrs. Hamlin killed her husband."

"Exactly."

"It's obvious she didn't kill him."

"How so?"

"You talked about their expensive vacations and her trailer crammed with stuff from all over the world. Where," Delores Anne shrugged, "did they get the money? His cabinet business was going down the drain. Sounds like they were blackmailing the church. Seems to me the pastor guy and his Guidance Panel buddies got tired of paying. So, they snuffed Mr. Hamlin, then threatened Mrs. Hamlin if she didn't get outta town. After his bones were found, the church realized they had a fall guy. They knew that would solve their little disposal problem. The idiot prosecutor sealed the deal by blaming the murder on your friend."

"Oh, God, it's obvious. Why didn't I see it?"

"You're probably too close to the case. He's your best friend. And I'll bet your clients are suffering from PTSD just like me. They're probably not much help either."

"You're exactly right."

"Great. So, now can you come to my place and have a drink with me?"

"Uh, what?"

She smiled at him, and her leg seductively brushed his. For a split second, he was tempted. *What a beautiful afternoon it would be.* Then he envisioned the fallout if Lacey found out. The beautiful imaginings evaporated like fog. He realized that whether Lacey found out, or not, wasn't the issue. "Delores Anne, I can't."

"What do you mean? My case is over, so you don't have a conflict of interest or whatever you called it."

"No. But worse, I'd have a conflict of conscience."

"What are you talking about?"

"I have a serious girlfriend and, even though she's out of town, I have to say no to your very tempting suggestion."

"Wait a minute. I've had a lot of boyfriends too, but you don't see a ring on my finger, and I don't see a ring on yours. You're not engaged, are you?"

"I'm not. But I wouldn't feel right about it. I can't say anything more."

"How 'bout I buy you a badge to wear around town that says you're just one great guy."

"No badge, Delores Anne. But I really appreciate your analysis of my buddy's case."

They said goodbye at the car. The rain had stopped so Ms. Rodriguez walked the short distance to her apartment. Logan leaned against his car door and watched her deftly avoid the potholes, her dress clinging to every curve. He momentarily contemplated what he was missing when he turned the key in the Bug's ignition. *So...this is what it feels like to be the good guy.*

Logan wanted to shout *hallelujah* to every passerby and share Delores Anne's explanation of the case. When he reached the dock, Mike and Sasha were sitting on their aft-deck railing. The scene was incomplete without Toby. It was Logan's first encounter with them since the heartbreak on the Fourth of July.

"Morning, strangers, how are you guys doing?"

"It's been tough. We miss Toby. More every day, I think." Mike's arm protectively encircled Sasha's shoulders. "And we've been watching for those guys to come back and try to finish the job."

"Jesus, Mike, I hadn't realized you'd be worried about that. They don't want you; I'm the one they'd be hunting."

Sasha dispiritedly gazed across the bay. "Well, like Toby, you're a part of us." The pain of loss resonated in her voice and shrouded her beautiful face. She continued, "So, we're watching out for *us*. That's just the way it is." There was a reflective silence. Sasha continued, "We treated Joe a little bit rough. Almost drowned him before we sent him packing down the dock."

Mike frowned. "We didn't call the police. We were afraid we'd be charged with attempted murder or something like that. So, Sasha and I have been mulling over the church's options. They might report us to the police, or they might double down with threats to sink our boats or kill the three of us. Just their way of 'encouraging' you to drop Pete's case. Or they could decide to do nothing, which is what they've done so far."

Logan frowned slightly. "Well, I'm not calling the police unless you want me to, and it's been ten days and there's been nothing. Right? If they report the Joe incident, it puts a spotlight on the attack on my boat, the bomb threats, me being chased in Anchorage, and Toby being shot. They won't want that. I think they're stuck with doing nothing."

"You're probably right." Mike slammed his fist into his palm. "But I'd love it if they sent a couple more thugs down here."

"I hear ya, Mike. Be great to give that asshole a dose of retribution." Logan wistfully continued, "I miss Toby more than I can say. It's just never going to be the same for me around here. Toby endeared himself to everybody. How are you explaining his disappearance?"

Sasha shrugged. "We're struggling with that. I don't want people to decide we put Toby to sleep, or that he fell overboard. Those things would never, ever happen."

Mike chimed in, "Everyone knows he'd never run away or get hit by a car." Mike and Logan smiled, remembering Toby's exuberance. "The dude was pretty much invincible."

"What about the truth?" Logan quietly suggested. "Somebody killed Toby when he barked at them, and you buried your beloved boat dog at sea."

Mike exhaled dejectedly. "You're right. Sometimes the truth is not only the best explanation but also the only explanation."

"Thanks, Logan," Sasha agreed.

Logan stood, placing his hand on Mike's shoulder. "I'd like to stay, but I've got to excuse myself. I should do some more research on Pete's case. I think we've figured out who the murderer is. Or was, I should say."

"Who?" asked Sasha.

"Can't say anything yet, sorry."

"No problem, we get it." Sasha held her hand across her mouth. "Nobody will hear a thing from us."

"It turned out to be a very productive breakfast," Logan told Pam the next morning.

"Okay." Pam laughed. "I'll bite, do tell."

Logan enthusiastically launched into the Delores Anne–inspired theory. "She thinks the Hamlins were blackmailing the church, or at least the pastor, for five years. When the church members got tired of paying for their silence, Hamlin was knocked off and his wife was sent packing."

"Do you have any evidence to support her theory?"

"Only pieces of Barbara Hamlin's story. After she and Bill provided the alibi, she said the church gifted them with travel vacations and Bill never worked again."

"Huh...amazing," Pam slowly offered. It makes more sense than Mrs. Hamlin killing her husband."

"Don't y'think? I don't know how I missed it all this time."

"I hope you bought her a good breakfast."

"I did. And no drinks!"

"You're a good guy, Logan."

"Thanks, but don't tell anybody! Now, if you'll excuse me, I'm going to rewrite Lacey's opening statement and my closing argument."

"Sounds good."

Logan next took a few phone calls for Lacey, went through the mail, sent a fax to the assisted-living facility asking about his dad, and then called Pete. "Hey, buddy, finally, some good news. Do you guys want to hear about it in person? I'll come your direction, Pete, and meet you at the Salty Dawg at four o'clock."

"Perfect. See you soon."

Erika wearily propped herself against the headboard. The bedside lamp dimly illuminated a waifish shell of his beautiful wife. "So, what did he want?"

"He wants to meet us at four o'clock. He said he has good news and asked if you could be there too."

"Pete, sweetheart, I'm so sorry, I just can't. There is no good news for me. I keep imagining how terrified Emma must have been, and I miss her so much it's almost impossible to breathe, because..." Erika began to sob uncontrollably. "Because Emma will never breathe again. Just hearing that man's name repeatedly, Pete, I'm strangling with hate. I hate Bill Hamlin. I hate his wife. I hate Jansen. I hate the police. They didn't lock him up! They could have saved her!" She lifted her face, swollen and awash in tears. "Will somebody tell me why? Why that happened? Why us? Why her?" Pete sat next to her on the bed, rocking her in his arms. He gently kissed the top of her head, two souls clinging to one another in a grief no words of comfort could touch.

Pete and a frosty margarita greeted Logan when he walked into the bar. "*Hola, amigo, buenos dias!*" Logan said as he sat across the table from Pete.

"Okay, fish on...the good news is that you've signed up for Spanish classes at Homer High?"

"Okay, the accent's a little off," Logan said, undeterred. "But Pete, you're not going to believe this." He quickly trotted out the new theory, ending with a flourish, holding up his margarita in a toast. "So, what d'ya think?"

Logan set his drink on the table, his face registering shock and disappointment as Pete proceeded to critically peck apart the theory. *This was most definitely not the reaction I expected.* Logan's empathy and enthusiasm unraveled at Pete's negativity and inexplicable resignation to a jail sentence. He couldn't refrain from venting aloud.

"I don't care if you like it or not. It's the theory we're going with. Run it by Erika if you want. If she even cares. I'll run it by Lacey if she calls. Let's think it over tonight; we'll talk again in the morning."

Pete's face reddened. "I'm sorry, Logan, you've been working tirelessly on my defense. Erika and I are truly grateful to you and Lacey for your support, but it's just...I'm struggling for any optimism right now. Erika hasn't been sleeping. It's been hard for both of us."

For a few moments, they silently sipped their margaritas. Finally, Logan offered an olive branch to lighten the mood. "So, how 'bout those Cubbies?" Pete had to laugh.

When Lacey called, Logan ran the new scenario by her. He chose not to dilute its feasibility by mentioning Delores Anne's input. Lacey agreed it sounded plausible and asked Logan to rewrite the opening and closing. "I'll look them over when I get back to Anchorage."

"I've already redrafted both documents."

"You know, for a guy with the possibility of getting his client acquitted, you sound kind of down tonight. What's going on?"

"I know, sorry. I'm going fishing tomorrow. I think I need a break. Fishing will get my mind off it all. I'm going to draft Pete into going with me."

"Okay, then." Lacey sounded relieved and changed the subject. "So, what are you wearing?"

"Aww, y'got me there. Aren't I supposed to be the one asking what you're wearing?"

Lacey giggled. "Well...since you asked, it's an oversized gray sweatshirt, stylishly draped to the knees of my blue flannel pajamas, which are, at this very moment, tucked into wool socks and chukka boots. Are you getting hot?"

"Jesus, Lace." Logan laughed for the first time during their call. "That might make the George Clooneys of the world go limp. But I'm a burly rugged outdoor guy. You just bring it on, baby—chukka boots, wool socks, and all."

"I could, just possibly, leave the chukka boots on the boat."

"And, my little fashion plate, if you knew how much I'm missing you, we would not be discussing wardrobe right now."

Lacey giggled again. "I'll call you again Sunday...Meantime, you dream of me, okay?"

"You got it, my sweet fisherwoman!" The night's happy vibe was complete when Pete enthusiastically agreed to go fishing the next morning once he heard that the boat had new deep-cycle marine batteries. *Our winning fish is still out there.*

They stood inside the cabin of *The Coral Dawn* and warmed their hands around steaming coffee mugs as they waited for the engines to warm up. As they surveyed the sun's rays stretching across the bay, Logan broached the elephant in the room. "So, what did Erika think of the new approach?"

"Truthfully, she barely woke up to listen. Sorry, Logan. Whatever you want to do is fine."

"Lacey was in favor of it."

"Great, let's go with it, then." Pete nodded.

Logan shook off the annoyance momentarily drowning his spirits. *Drop it, not gonna allow it to ruin the day.* They trolled for salmon around the end of the spit, then crossed the bay to fish Halibut Cove before cruising in for a bite of lunch. A ferry followed them into the harbor. "It's starting to get a little rough out there. Let's spend the night on this side."

"Fine with me." Pete zipped his jacket, pulling the collar up around his neck.

Their Saturday night was largely uneventful, but not so across the bay.

THE NEXT MORNING WAS good fishing weather, but Logan decided to return to Homer. His patience over Pete and Erika's lack of involvement in his defense and strategy was officially extinct. *What the hell are they thinking? They won't engage. Hell, maybe Pete is guilty...*

The sun warmed their backs as they cleaned yesterday's catch in an awkward, uncomfortable silence. Pete read between the lines when Logan said he had to go to the office to work on some other cases, but he was beyond participating or faking interest. *Logan doesn't have any urgent legal matter taking us back early to Homer. He's frustrated and angry at me. But I can't do it. I can't keep faking interest.* Pete felt despair and, despite Logan's support, he felt alone.

As they crossed the bay, Logan contemplated their theories, none of which eased his worries. *The trial is just a week away.*

"I'm sorry, Mr. Finch. It's Lola, and I'm very sorry for what I've done. I'm sorry for wasting your time on my case, and I'm sorry for...everything. But I've been rejected and abandoned. There's nothing to look forward to, nothing left for me. And it's not your fault, but I just want to say goodbye and thank you."

What? He wasn't sure what to make of Delores Anne's recorded telephone message. There was no point in trying to concentrate on the trial preparation; her words continued to nag at him until he listened to her message one more time. As her final "thank you" trailed off, an ambulance screamed past the office and down the East End Road. He returned her call but got no answer. He had a sinking *oh shit* feeling and abruptly decided to stop by the Homestead Restaurant. He'd grab a bite to eat and see if Lola got that job. Hopefully she did and was working.

As he approached the restaurant, he noticed that the ambulance, red lights flashing, had pulled outside Delores Anne's apartment building. He parked at the restaurant and walked across the street. As he looked up the wooden stairwell, paramedics were wheeling a gurney out of Delores Anne's apartment. Stunned, he watched them maneuver the stretcher down the steps to the ambulance. The lifeless body of his former client had a resuscitator tube in its mouth.

"Excuse me. I'm this woman's attorney. She called me and left a message."

"She won't be calling you for a few days now," the medic grimly replied. "If ever. She was nearly dead when we arrived."

"What happened?"

"Looks like a drug overdose coupled with a lot of alcohol. There were pain pills on her nightstand."

Logan heard police sirens in the distance. He ran up the stairwell and into the open door of her apartment. There was no one inside so he checked her bedroom. There was a bottle of prescription pills and an empty bottle of vodka on the floor beside the bed. He also saw a sealed envelope on the bureau with *Ben* scribbled on it. He stuffed it in his coat pocket, briskly left her apartment, and reached the bottom of the steps as the police cruiser pulled into the parking lot. He strolled across the street and into the Homestead Restaurant.

"Hi, again," Sue said, concern clouding her face. "You look like you've just seen a ghost."

"Good read. EMTs just removed Delores from her apartment on a gurney."

"Oh my God, you're kidding. What happened?"

Logan, ever mindful of the small-town grapevine, was intentionally vague. "I was just coming here to eat when I saw the ambulance, so I'm not sure. I thought maybe she'd be working today."

"Wow. You know, she worked Friday night for her training. But the bartender caught her drinking vodka out of a bottle from behind the bar. The owners had to let her go that same day. We all felt bad. She's a nice lady."

"That's very kind of you. She's a genuinely good person."

"Can I get you something to eat?"

"You know what, I don't think so. I guess I've lost my appetite."

"I understand. I hope she's okay."

Thankfully, Pam and Katie didn't work Sundays and the office was empty when Logan returned. He reached for the bottle of Chivas stashed in his bottom desk drawer. He half-filled his coffee mug, then swiveled his chair around and propped his shoes on the windowsill. For the next two hours, he watched out the window as people casually ducked into Café Cups across the street and went about their lives.

CHAPTER
49

A S LOGAN HUNKERED DOWN in the war room, he chose not to call
Lacey about Delores Anne Rodriguez's incident the night before. It
was ten o'clock, and Katie still hadn't arrived. *Odd, Katie always called if
she was going to be even a minute late.*

When Logan sauntered out to Pam's desk, there stood Katie, tearful
and shaking. "I'm so sorry," she whispered. "I couldn't come in. I don't
know if I can work here anymore."

Logan instinctively hugged Katie. "What happened?"

"You know how crazy busy we've been, so Saturday night I decided to
get dressed up and go dancing. I went to Alice's."

Logan was intimately familiar with Alice's Champagne Palace. The
iconic Homer bar opened in 1946 on East Pioneer Avenue and featured
live bands. He knew it was a favorite hangout of Katie's.

"I was having so much fun dancing. You know how it is, guys buying
you drinks and practically standing in line to dance."

Logan recalled buying a lot of young women drinks in that bar over
the years.

"So, after a few hours of dancing, I decided I'd had enough fun. Jack-
son was bartending and I asked him to call me a cab. Within five minutes,
the taxi pulled up, and when I walked out, two humongous guys just...it
was like they materialized from the shadows. The one guy, without a
beard, opened the passenger door for me, and I remember this distinctly,
he said, 'God bless you,' when I thanked him."

"You're kidding." The comment seemed odd to Pam. "What guy at a
bar in the middle of the night talks like that?"

"I know, right? With the calls we've been getting, it should have
clicked that something was off, but I was focused on getting home." She
paused, regretting her lapse in judgment all over again. "George, the cabbie, dropped me off and left as the same two guys pulled up in a pickup."

Katie then recalled the chilling events in a monotone as though it had happened to someone else, and a long time ago. "Before I could unlock my front door, they were on me. They grabbed my arms, and my feet didn't touch the floor as they walked into the living room. Little Jinxy Cat's eyes were so wide and scared, he yowled and ran to the kitchen.

"The bearded guy held my arms behind me while the God-bless-you pervert yanked down my jeans and ripped off my blouse. I don't remember screaming, but I must have because my own panties were nearly shoved down my throat. Beard Man told me to shut the fuck up or they'd have to hurt me bad.

"Then Mister God-bless-you asshole started to suck my breast. I leaned forward and bit down on his ear until blood was spurting out over both of us. It didn't stop him, though. He slugged me in the stomach so hard he knocked the wind out of me.

"The bearded guy told him to knock it off, but he warned me, 'Evidently your boss isn't getting the point, lady. You tell him if he doesn't drop the Foster case, we'll be back. And if you call the cops, even the nine lives your little kitty has will be over.'

"I have a big knot on the back of my head. So, they must have knocked me out before they left because I don't remember them leaving. I woke up to Jinxy licking my face at three in the morning."

Pam, looking shocked and afraid, said, "Should we call the police?"

"I'm too afraid to call the police. They said they'd come back and get me, and I believe them. They're not from Homer...never seen them before, so who knows where they are now." Now looking at Logan, she said, "But I don't want you to drop the case."

Pam tried not to show her fear. "This is so far outside my wheelhouse, Katie. I don't know what to say."

Logan chimed in, "My gut tells me you and little Jinxy should probably leave Alaska for a while. You'd at least be safe."

"I could...but what about you two, and Lacey and Erika and Pete?"

"We'll be okay. Lacey won't be back in Homer until after the trial. Erika and Pete are together, staying in a hotel, so they're probably safe until they leave for Anchorage later this week. And I agree that I don't think calling the police will get us anywhere. In fact, I'd be more scared of possible retaliation. These guys, whoever they are, are determined. I guess we'll have to fend for ourselves and be extra vigilant."

Pam added, "You know I can't tell my husband about this or he'd put me on the next plane to Hawaii."

Katie frowned. "But I live alone, and they know where. I think I have to leave town for a while."

Logan said, "Good idea. Have you told anyone else about this?"

"No, just you two."

Then Katie said thoughtfully, "Those two cowards came after me because they decided I'm a weak link. I bet they'd never confront you or Pete. Now, I worry most about you."

"Well," Logan replied, "they attacked me in Anchorage a few days ago, but I managed to beat them off with a baseball bat. I'm sure it was the same two guys who attacked you."

Pam said firmly, "We'll be all right, but you go home and pack, okay? I'll make you some plane and hotel reservations for Honolulu and take care of Jinxy while you're away. I'll take you to the airport in the morning."

"All expenses paid, compliments of Pete and me," Logan added.

CHAPTER
50

KATIE DISAPPEARED OUT THE DOOR as Pam took the documents over to the fax machine.

"Are you going to feel okay continuing to work here?" Logan asked Pam.

"Heck, yeah. I have my gun and husband. By the way, did you hear about poor Ms. Rodriguez?"

"Damn, news travels fast in this town. Yeah, I was there when they wheeled her out of her apartment."

"You were? Why?"

"There's a message on the answering machine. I listened to it yesterday when I came in to do some work."

Pam punched the play button and listened to the forlorn drawl. "So, did you go see her after hearing this?"

"Not exactly. I wasn't sure what to do," Logan admitted. "I never thought she'd try to kill herself. Who would do that?"

Pam ticked off the list on her fingers: "Alcoholics, convicted criminals, the jobless, people suffering from PTSD, people without family or friends close by, people with a history of having been molested as a child. And the homeless. So, how many categories does she fit?"

"I'd say all but one. She still has an apartment. For now."

"Tragic...I wonder if the love of her life, Dr. Ben, knows."

"How do you know about Dr. Ben?"

Pam winked at him. "Hey, I know how to read attorney notes."

"You're a snoop." Logan grinned.

"Hey...it's what I do."

"To answer your question, I'm sure he knows. He works at the hospital. I'm going over there to deliver what I assume is her suicide note. I took an envelope made out to *Ben* that she'd left on her bureau."

"You did what? Shouldn't you give it to the cops. What if they investigated this matter as an attempted murder or the result of some foul play?"

"Not a chance. I saw the empty bottle of vodka and the prescription bottle. I also listened to the call and found out she was fired from her new job at the restaurant on the first night. Attempted suicide is the only explanation. I didn't want her private note bandied about this gossipy little town. If she survives, she's entitled to keep some dignity and privacy."

"You're right."

You know, sometimes I think the damage and emotional pain inflicted on children by a child molester is as devastating as the acts of a serial killer." His face flushed, and his eyes watered a bit. Pam nodded.

Logan was directed to the second floor, room 24. As he entered, Delores Anne looked up with an aloof, distant smile. "What a nice surprise."

"It's good to find you awake. And alive. That was quite a scare."

"I know, and I'm sorry. I guess the pain of living was finally worse than my fear of dying. There's a song about suicide being painless. They're right. How did you find out I was in the hospital?"

"First, you called and left a message on my office phone. Then I watched them wheel you out of your apartment."

"I don't remember much. I just felt like all my secrets were on display to you and Zimmerman. You were exposing me to myself. It's like peeling an onion. For the first time, I couldn't block my childhood memories. Drinking and drugs used to let me drift into a safe haze. Then...well, they didn't."

"I guess I understand. But, Delores Anne, if you give yourself some time to peel the onion, you won't have to hide so many secrets from yourself."

"Easier said than done." Then she smiled bravely. "But I'm gonna try."

"Just believe in yourself, you're stronger than you know." Logan kissed her on the forehead before he left. "I'll check on you again later."

While walking out of the hospital, he passed a scruffy janitor pushing a trash can down the hall. He pulled the *Ben* envelope from his pocket, ripped it several times, and deposited it in the garbage can as he passed.

There's nothing in the letter she couldn't say to Dr. Ben in person. She just needs love and time. And a stronger fear of death!

CHAPTER
51

"Hello," SHE SAID IN A HUSHED TONE.
"Mrs. Hamlin, it's Logan Finch. Do you remember me?"
"I certainly do." She laughed in a gravelly voice. "Are you surprised I'm still alive?"

Wow, death is on everyone's mind these days. "I know this is difficult for you, and I am genuinely glad you're okay."

"Why? I could be the one they use to convict your client."

Her cruel snicker gave him a premonition of just how careful his handling of her had to be, now and come trial time. "I sure hope not. But it is why I'd like to see you for a half hour tomorrow. Would that work for you?"

"Well, let's see...I'll be exercisin' at the yacht club tomorrow. Then that facial followed by my hair appointment for the charity dinner with the guv'nr. But Wednesday...I think I can fit you in."

Even drunk, she's a sharp old crone. "Then Wednesday it is." Logan laughed. "How does eleven o'clock sound?"

"Good, see you then."

Checking *Call Mrs. Hamlin* off his to-do list, Logan then phoned Pete and Erika. "What'cha up to?"

Pete's voice was completely flat. "Just sittin' around."

Logan waited a moment, but no details were supplied. "Um, okay, here's the plan. I'm flying up to Anchorage Wednesday morning to meet with Barbara Hamlin and McQuigg again. On Thursday, I hope to meet with our PI, J.D. Cline, and review his report on the state's expert witnesses. So, will you and Erika drive to Anchorage on Friday?"

"You bet. Are we taking the blue Bug or Lacey's ride?"

"Better use Lacey's. I'll probably go down to Arizona after the trial, and Lacey will need to haul her clothes home. You and Erika will be leaving too, so pack your things and check out of the hotel."

"Guess under any scenario I won't need clothes in Homer anymore."

"Right, 'cause you'll be hauling it all back to Seattle."

"Got it. So, you're taking your gear and Lacey's stuff?"

"Lacey's suitcase is in her car for you to take."

"So, who's packing for you?"

"Guess I'm stuck doing it myself. Packing could be tougher than the trial itself!"

"All right. Get us a room and we'll see you Friday."

"Will do. See you then."

Logan scrolled through his checklist to make sure he had all the documents he needed for trial.

Logan arrived in Anchorage at noon, and the prosecutor, Chris Branson, alerted Logan that Officer Albright was scratched from the witness list. He was "out of state with a medical problem." It was a struggle for Logan to refrain from asking if Albright's problem was related to a mental health condition.

The next day, Logan retraced his drive to Eagle River to meet Mrs. Hamlin. Glancing in the rearview mirror, he was relieved to see no white pickup nor anyone else following him. *Maybe Joe's fate kept them away*, Logan thought. *But it was more likely because no one in the prosecutor's office knew about the meeting.*

Pulling into the driveway, Logan scanned Mrs. Hamlin's home and storage shed. *Looks like she hasn't been working her fingers to the bone on any upkeep since my last visit.* The grass straggled into the gravel walkway leading up to the trailer. Logan's eyes moved toward the trailer door as it opened to reveal Barbara Hamlin. She wore the same clothes she'd worn during their last visit. *Cigarette's new*, Logan wryly observed. He politely greeted the cadaverous figure huddled in the doorway. "Git in here, it's fucking cold outside."

Stepping over the threshold, Mrs. Hamlin waved Logan toward an old footstool, indicating the seating arrangements for their visit. Logan noticed Mrs. Hamlin had swept the stool clear of magazines. Nearby was a blanket encrusted with cat hair and urine.

Logan gingerly placed his feet between the overflowing ashtray and empty bottle of Jack Daniels, then carefully eased down onto the stool. A lit cigarette jutted from the corner of Mrs. Hamlin's mouth. Not a drop splashed out of her drink as she landed with a practiced thud onto her worn-out easy chair. Although he wouldn't have guessed it at the time, he realized she had been on her best behavior during their first visit. While trying to acclimate to the stench, Logan began, "I have just a few more questions."

"Well," she interrupted, "there are some things I fergot to mention. It's about the money Jansen was giving ta the church. The Jansens were rich. His little bakery was the only one in town, and the town was growin' by leaps and bounds whilst Jansen was murdering them girls. I don't think he paid taxes neither. He always had cash. And that wife a his traveled all over the country—without his lying ass going with her and their kids. That's how he could murder so many girls and rape them in his own house!"

"No, I don't believe you did tell me that...although you mentioned you and Mr. Hamlin did your fair share of traveling too." Logan glanced at the dust-covered tchotchkes covering the surrounding shelves. "You also said neither of you was employed then. Can you tell me how that happened?"

"Fuck you, it's none of your goddamn business." Frowning, Mrs. Hamlin stood to return to her kitchen for another whiskey pour.

Logan calculated the situation and plunged in. "Barbara, I have a little theory about who killed your husband. I think the church had him done away with."

Her glass filled, she shuffled back into the living room. "Exactly what I been sayin' all along, for Chrissake. I swear t'God, they're coming after me next. I can't believe they ain't done it yet." She downed the fresh shot.

"Maybe because you aren't blackmailing them anymore."

With surprising agility, Mrs. Hamlin threw her shot glass at him, catching his right shoulder. Grabbing a broom from the corner, she charged in his direction, screaming, "You son of a bitch! Get the fuck outta my house. You son of a bitch, I'll see you in court. You just try and prove we was blackmailing the church." She screamed a last parting shot as Logan fled out the door and down the steps to the rental car. "Good luck with that, you fucker!"

He now knew the Hamlins were bribed for their silence, but he couldn't prove anything unless she cooperated. *I probably went too far with her this morning. If she worked with him, she'd probably sign her own death warrant. But in her mind, it might be a relief not to live looking over her shoulder.*

The sun shined bright in the vast Alaskan sky as Logan walked the four blocks from his hotel to J.D. Cline's office across from the Hilton Hotel. He was greeted by a cute and affable secretary as he entered the office. "Good morning, Mr. Finch. J.D.'s expecting you. Can I get you some coffee?"

"No, no thanks. I'm all coffee'd out."

"Then follow me, please."

As they reached the door, a handsome, middle-aged man opened it and thrust his hand in Logan's direction. "Hi. I'm J.D. Very glad to meet you, Mr. Finch."

"Very good to meet you as well. You can call me Logan."

"Very well. Let's sit down and we'll review my short report and I'll answer any questions." As they sat down, Logan noticed the multiple golf trophies and plaques surrounding the desk. Then both men glanced out the large picture window to the bus in front of the Hilton where a dozen flight attendants were disembarking for their overnight stays.

"Great view," Logan said.

"Beats Denali anytime," J.D. said as he handed Logan a file. "You can review the two-page report as I summarize it for you."

"That works."

"Simply stated, everyone's written reports matched their statements to me. The only noteworthy information was the courthouse security guard, Al Stacks, recalling the punch Pete landed on Hamlin's jaw. He said it was the 'most violent thing' he'd ever seen outside using a lethal weapon. And he's a former Marine."

"So, that guy's not going to help."

"Oh, and the prosecutor called and told me that Officer Albright was scratched from the witness list. He was 'out of state with a medical problem.'"

Logan smiled. "I think his problem is related to a mental health condition."

"Ya don't say. Are you ready for what the newspapers are calling the murder trial of the decade here in Anchorage?"

"I hope so. It's gonna be a tough one."

Logan walked back to his hotel, satisfied that J.D. had done his job and saved him a lot of time. He wouldn't be needed at the trial.

CHAPTER
52

Pete and Erika arrived in Anchorage late Friday afternoon without fanfare. They ate with Logan at Fletcher's. As usual, they were subdued throughout the dinner. Logan didn't mention the meeting with Mrs. Hamlin and was relieved when they didn't ask and left early for bed.

Lacey arrived by cab Saturday afternoon. Logan eagerly met her in the hotel lobby and was disappointed when she gave him only the briefest of hugs. They joined Pete and Erika for dinner at Simon & Seafort's Saloon & Grill. Logan led things off with a toast to Lacey's safe return. His toast included comments on her strength and courage, but Lacey barely acknowledged his homage. Later, when he placed his hand over hers, she pulled away. She camouflaged the withdrawal by picking up her glass of wine. "So, tell me what I've missed and where we are in the trial preparation."

Logan recalled his meeting with J.D. Cline and gave only sparse information about the Barbara Hamlin meeting. Erika was surprised Barbara Hamlin had met with him. "So, where does she live? What's it like?"

"It defies description. The woman's a hoarder. She lives alone in a crumbling trailer supported by a lean-to shed filled to the gunnels with God knows what."

Lacey was pleased with the report, but she too had no idea how to prove the bribery piece without Mrs. Hamlin's cooperation, which was highly questionable at this point. She then excused herself after dinner, claiming she was exhausted and needed to sleep.

Sunday morning, Lacey and Logan met with McQuigg at his house on the Park Strip. Tim had little to add but was pleasantly surprised about the possible bribery defense. "It makes perfect sense if you can get it before the jury. You have the foundation for bringing it up in your opening. But if Mrs. Hamlin denies it, you'll look like a fool."

When they returned to the hotel, Lacey again excused herself—this time to work on the opening statement and her cross-examination questions. She continued to be distant. The trial was just hours away, yet Pete, Erika, and Lacey weren't interested in discussing the case with him.

Logan presented his oral argument to the judge over the pending motions Monday morning. He glanced at Lacey, who gave him...nothing. Pete sat grim-faced and pale, as if a guilty verdict had been entered. The last thing Pete had done before the trial began was call his wife. The judge had excluded Erika from attending the proceedings because she was going to be a witness. So, at the end of the trial day, she promised to meet Pete outside the courtroom.

At least Logan had McQuigg. Over Branson's objections, McQuigg sat at the defense table with him, Lacey, and Pete while they picked the jury. Once the clerk distributed the jurors' answers to the court's initial written questions, McQuigg pored over his copy like he was in search of the Holy Grail.

Judge Sumner resolved all pretrial matters by 10:30 a.m. and fifty prospective jurors entered the courtroom. All morning they had been sitting around, and they looked bored and slightly irritated at the long wait. They knew they were potential jurors for the Hamlin murder trial, and most were jittery at the possibility of deciding the fate of a man's life. Logan did his best to make as much eye contact with the prospective jurors as possible.

After the judge thanked everyone for their participation, Branson launched into his inquisition. He emphasized the legal right for the prosecution and the jury to convict a person based only on circumstantial evidence. "The state doesn't need eyewitnesses, forensic evidence, fingerprints, or confessions to gain a conviction."

Branson, Logan knew, deliberately failed to mention the burden of proof. He would demonstrate motive and opportunity. He would use logic to drive the jurors into concluding Pete had committed the murder.

Logan's approach was distinctly different as well as somewhat unusual. He would explain *burden of proof* without mentioning *beyond a reasonable doubt*. He opened his questioning of potential jurors by asking, "Is it part of your responsibility to render a verdict that answers: Who committed the murder?"

More than half the jury pool agreed this was part of their obligation. McQuigg noted those jurors on the Excel spreadsheet on his laptop. *Not the best defense jurors.* It was Law School 101: educate jurors who incorrectly believe the jury was to find the murderer. Logan knew better at this stage of his career. *It's a complete waste of time. Jurors can't help themselves. They want a neat, tidy ending where someone is fingered for the crime.*

Logan moved on to address the presumption of innocence. He asked the potential jurors if they understood that a defendant was innocent until proven guilty. Yes, they all confidently nodded. "Can you," Logan asked, "start the trial knowing the defendant was innocent?" Everyone raised their hand.

Logan then asked questions about their jobs, children, and other seemingly irrelevant information. The queries were designed to warm up the panel to the defendant and his legal team. In doing so, Logan discovered he was relaxing, his words and actions becoming more fluid, more confident. As he loosened up, his confidence rose. Logan liked these people. He knew them. He was one of them. They were mostly Alaskans at heart and would like Pete and despise the Hamlins, he was certain. Logan's temperament improved as the morning progressed.

After more trivial questions, Logan casually asked, "If you were asked to vote right now, would you say the defendant was innocent?" Only half of the hands went up. Again, McQuigg documented every raised hand.

"Juror number 10, could you tell me why you did not raise your hand?"

Juror number 10 was a white woman with a cardigan draped over her tank top. "Because I would need to hear the evidence before I could decide if the defendant is innocent or guilty," she said confidently.

"How many people agree? Please raise your hand." Once again, at least 50 percent of the prospective jurors raised their hands.

"Okay, juror number 4, you did raise your hand. Why?"

Juror number 4, an older gentleman of indeterminate racial background wearing a 'Gone Fishing' T-shirt, looked startled. "Umm, because you asked what I would vote right now, and because I haven't heard any evidence, I would have to decide the defendant was innocent. He's presumed innocent."

"Exactly," Logan said. "And the judge will instruct you that that is, in fact, the law." The juror smiled sheepishly.

There were more questions asked by the prosecutor, Logan, and the judge. After all the preemptions and excused jurors for bias were utilized, and with McQuigg's input, there remained fourteen jurors, including two alternates. They had three mothers with daughters, six relative newcomers to the state, a retired cop, a fireman, and maybe a religious zealot. Logan and McQuigg were pleased.

They broke for lunch at twelve thirty. Pete immediately called Erika. When she didn't answer, he became agitated and called again. No answer. After exchanging glances with Logan, Lacey calmly suggested, "Erika probably is grabbing something to eat, which is what we should do."

Pete took a deep breath, "Of course, you're right."

The team crossed the street to Elevation 92. They weren't given a table with a view of the inlet, but scenery was the last thing on their minds. There was much to discuss. "I think we have a pretty good jury for this type of case," Logan stated. "All of the jurors have children and three have grandchildren. We even have a retired cop."

"Yeah, but they don't all have daughters," Pete cautioned.

"What do you think, Tim?" Lacey asked.

"I think this is a tough case, and it's all going to depend on Mrs. Hamlin. Unfortunately, Pete's testimony can't save him."

"So, you think Pete should not testify?" Logan asked.

"I've been thinking long and hard about that one," Tim said. "And I still don't know. I'm afraid Erika isn't believable, so Pete may have to help establish his alibi. I think you make that call when it becomes necessary."

Pete looked down at the tablecloth, his mouth pinched and tight. Logan had come to the proverbial end of his rope with Pete's moping around. He refused to be defeated before they even began. If Pete wasn't willing to fight for himself, then, dammit, Logan would do it for him. That's what trial attorneys do, come hell or high water, as his dad liked to say.

"Okay, then!" Logan slapped the table, startling Lacey who almost jumped out of her seat. "Let's do this!"

Tim smiled. "Reminds me of John Belushi in *Animal House*. I love the enthusiasm. I'll hang around for a while, if you don't mind. I'm officially off the clock."

Logan signaled the waitress and ordered another beer for Tim. "Man, you deserve this. Your assistance has been invaluable, my friend. Just as Lacey promised."

"Yes," Pete added. "Thank you very much."

When the waitress put the pint on the table, Tim raised the glass in a toast, tipping it toward Pete. "Best of luck, friend." Pete smiled wanly but didn't return the toast. Logan did, however. *And we need all the luck we can get.*

CHAPTER 53

WHILE WALKING BACK TO THE COURTHOUSE, Pete called Erika again. No answer. "I'm worried. This whole experience has been grueling, and now that it's showtime—I don't know."

Logan thought about Delores Anne's suicide attempt. *Could Erika be clinically depressed? Before, it would have been unthinkable, but if Pete ends up going away for life...*

Lacey intervened. "Pete, it's a beautiful summer day. She's probably out enjoying it. Right now, let's focus on getting you through today's proceedings, and then she'll be outside the courtroom to meet you as planned, okay?"

When they returned to the courtroom, Logan and Lacey were surprised to see over thirty people attending the opening statement phase of the trial. They recognized reporters from the *Anchorage Daily News* and the *Homer Tribune* sitting on the defense side. Cameras were barred from the courtroom, but a guy with sketching materials sat in the front row next to Logan's favorite leprechaun, Jim Carter, and J.D. Cline. There were also a dozen spectators who'd read about the trial, crowding into the rows of benches to watch. Logan always wondered about the ambulance chasers and gore hounds. *Don't they have better things to do with their lives?*

Behind the prosecutor's table, tiny Ingrid Johansen from the Evangelical Baptist church sat between two unsmiling men in suits and ties. Logan thought, *They must be Ron Tasker and his mini-me son, Terry. The remaining people are probably recruited from the prosecutor's office as a show of strength.*

It was typical for prosecutors to draft their office personnel to sit behind the prosecutor's table during trials. Everyone in the office was expected to attend opening statements and closing arguments. This morning, even the great and powerful Gerald Abbott, whose ample girth obscured his chair, was in attendance. Abbott sat with Chris Branson at the prosecutor's table. This ploy was an effective tool to sway juries in favor of convictions. Jurors were unaware these government employees would be nowhere near the courtroom when the jury rendered its verdict. They'd already done their job and, on a personal level, they didn't care.

"I forgot we'd have an audience," Logan whispered to Lacey, and he nodded as they took their seats at the defense table.

The judge brought the trial to life, and Branson gave the state's opening statement. He walked through the evidence and, with a showman-like flourish, presented the decedent's skull, teeth, bones, and X-rays. The jurors stared in fascination. This was probably the first time they'd seen human bones in real life, or at least this close.

Branson summarized his expert witnesses' expected testimony and swaggered back to the prosecutor's table where he closed with, "All of the admissible evidence in this case points to just one man as the murderer of William Hamlin." His voice raised, he gestured dramatically to Pete. "That man is Peter Foster!" As he returned to his seat, in full view of the jury, he theatrically wiped his lips with a monogramed handkerchief, as if to remove his disgust.

Pete, his hands sedately folded on the tabletop before him, stared steadily at Branson. Logan saw a muscle in Pete's jawline tense. *Subtle, but good. It's about time he stops skulking like a guilty man.*

Now it was Lacey's turn on the courtroom stage. As she stood and hooked the clasp at the waist of the collarless charcoal blazer that she wore over a black sleeveless silk blouse and matching skirt, Logan was momentarily struck by how fragile she appeared. Yet, although at least ten pounds seemed to have melted overnight from her sparse frame, Lacey's demeanor was composed and professional. She and Logan had decided in advance they needed Mrs. Hamlin to point the finger at the church, or a third party, as the judge said. They also decided to invoke Pete's testimony, even though he may not testify.

Lacey's thick hair was caught in a loose chignon at the nape of her neck. As she stepped out from behind the defense table, pushing an auburn tendril behind her left ear, she approached the jury box. She looked at each of them and warmly smiled.

"Your Honor, Mr. Prosecutor, Madame Clerk, ladies and gentlemen of the jury, and the support staff from the prosecuting attorney's office, thank you for taking your valuable time to assist us in this critical matter. I'm Lacey Carpenter, and together with Logan Finch, we represent Mr. Pete Foster. An opening statement is a time for me to summarize the evidence you are about to hear from a myriad of witnesses."

As she glanced at the prosecutor's table, she continued, "Let me first say we have no qualms about what you are going to hear from the state's expert witnesses. A person or persons murdered Mr. Hamlin on September 4, 1988. The state recovered a skull and various bones in 2003. Earlier this year, dental records established the bones were those of Mr. Hamlin.

"And, as the prosecutor correctly pointed out, there are no fingerprints, no eyewitnesses, no confessions, and no forensic evidence tying Pete to the crime scene. The only evidence linking Pete to the murder is the shallow grave where the decedent's bones were located. They were along the property line of the five-acre parcel of land previously owned by Pete and adjacent to the Huffman Dog Park. Although Pete struck Mr. Hamlin at the sentencing hearing for Hamlin's friend, convicted serial killer Jack Jansen, their brief interaction occurred about four years before someone decided to kill Mr. Hamlin."

Turning back to the jury box and stepping even closer, making eye contact with every juror, Lacey continued, "The state's witness, Detective Sorensen, will tell you the Hamlins lied to the police about Jansen's whereabouts on a night when one of his intended murder victims escaped. She fled from him, narrowly avoiding death. But because the Hamlins lied, Jack Jansen went out and murdered at least ten more innocent girls. The Fosters believed, and still believe to this day, one of those girls was their beloved seventeen-year-old daughter, Emma."

Turning away from the jury box, she hesitated and raised her hand to her chin, appearing to be in deep thought before turning back to the jurors. "So, who killed the lying Mr. Hamlin? Mrs. Hamlin will tell you who might be the real killer. She will tell you a third party coerced her and her husband to provide the alibi for Jansen after his arrest. She will tell you how her husband blackmailed this third party while Jansen killed more girls. She will tell you how, after four long years, the third party got tired of paying the Hamlins, and it was around that time Mr. Hamlin disappeared. She will tell you she believes and fears this third party will kill her for testifying to these facts."

Upon hearing this account for the first time, Branson and Abbott appeared stunned.

Lacey anticipated their response and turned to face the prosecutors, directing the jurors' full attention to Branson and Abbott, who were beginning to feel that they were on trial.

"Now, the prosecution has made a big deal out of Mrs. Erika Foster's answer to a Washington State detective's question. As she watched her husband being handcuffed and arrested, the detective asked whether she knew William Hamlin. Erika Foster said she didn't. She will testify and admit she answered incorrectly."

Turning back to the jurors, she quieted her voice into an almost sorrowful whisper. "However, she will also tell you how frightened she was when they arrested her husband in their home—for murder. Imagine how you would feel if, without warning, multiple police officers, in full battle gear, stormed into your sanctuary and invaded your home while executing a search warrant. She was frightened and in shock, as any of you would have been. She wasn't thinking. She was just a woman whose husband answered a doorbell and inadvertently opened the floodgates to troopers who abruptly snatched her husband from their home. You cannot assume that, in those surreal moments, Mrs. Foster had the presence of mind to think of anything other than, no, this can't be happening."

She paused and raised her voice back to normal. "The defendant, if he testifies, and there's no requirement he do so, will tell you that he is not a murderer. After he struck Mr. Hamlin at the courthouse, he knew that hurting Hamlin would not bring back his murdered child. Please imagine losing a child to a heinous murderer because some guy lied to the police. Then imagine that the cops and prosecutors refused to punish that liar. You'd be angry. You'd want revenge."

She turned toward Pete and nodded in his direction. "But why would anyone wait five more years after the courthouse incident to seek revenge against Mr. Hamlin? We all know that pain and anger diminish over time. Even though Pete had numerous opportunities to seek revenge at the neighboring dog park over the years, he would have acted soon after Hamlins' false alibi was discovered. The time for revenge was in 1983 and not 1988. And many other people had the same opportunity for a revenge killing, people whose daughters had also been murdered as a direct result of Mr. Hamlin's lying alibi. But common sense tells us there was no revenge killing related to the death of Mr. Hamlin.

"The evidence will show that every day many people walked their dogs at the dog park adjacent to the Foster home. There was no report Pete ever communicated with Mr. Hamlin at the park. Mrs. Hamlin will testify she and her husband never saw Pete at the park and, further, her husband had never told her he'd seen Pete at the park when he went alone. If Pete had revenge on his mind, it's logical there would be evidence of communication or confrontation. There is none."

Looking now at the judge, she directed, "Right now, as you sit here, the judge will tell you that Pete is innocent of the charge against him. Totally innocent." Turning back to the jurors, she continued. "The prosecution must change your mind and convince you, *beyond a reasonable doubt*, that he is guilty. It's a huge burden because Alaska has decided we want to take all precautions to ensure an innocent man is never sent to prison.

"Ladies and gentlemen, the evidence will demonstrate quite clearly that Pete did not murder Mr. Hamlin. The facts in this case will also reveal who most likely killed Mr. Hamlin and why." Whispers were heard throughout the courtroom. The judge gaveled the room quiet. "Thank you for your time and patience. Mr. Logan Finch will speak with you again at the close of this case."

With that, she took her seat next to Logan. But not without a quick glance to show him that she knew she'd nailed it. And she had. Beautifully.

CHAPTER
54

T HE STATE OPTED TO BEGIN THE EXAMINATION of Mrs. Hamlin rather than take an early recess. She began by describing the 911 call, followed by her meeting with Officer Albright. She then described the visits her husband made on Sunday afternoons to the dog park. She briefly touched on the statements she gave to the police and her two interviews with Mr. Finch.

It was getting late in the afternoon when Logan began his cross-examination. He proceeded cautiously as he stood and smiled at Mrs. Hamlin. "Good afternoon, Mrs. Hamlin. Do you remember me?"

"Of course I do. You're the guy who harassed me at my house in Eagle River."

Logan knew it was essential to appear professional and stay above the fray. He showed no emotion other than a tolerant smile like a kind adult might make in the face of an obstinate child. "Well, ma'am, I assure you I did not mean to harass you in any manner whatsoever. Can we begin your testimony by proceeding from a clean slate?"

"I don't know, can we?"

The jurors frowned, and Logan knew he was winning this tug-of-war. The more she baited him, and the less he showed annoyance, the better it looked for Pete. "Of course we can. Now, I don't mean to pry, and I know how painful this is for you, but I wonder why you failed to mention anything about your husband's affair to the jury during your direct examination?"

Mrs. Hamlin's fingers twitched; a gesture Logan had seen before among heavy smokers. She craved a cigarette. "I just didn't think it was important."

Logan turned partially away from her so both she and the jury could see the perplexed crinkle of his eyebrows. He noticed a few jurors following suit, mimicking his concern.

Gerald Abbott jumped to his feet, his face reddened, "Neither does the state, Your Honor.

It's irrelevant."

Judge Sumner waved the litigator back down in his seat. "Although I appreciate the objection, Mr. Abbott, you know only one attorney can participate in the testimony of a witness. Mr. Branson examined this witness, and now it is up to him, and only him, to address this court with objections."

Logan, wanting to show his deference to the court (at least for now, since it was on his side), addressed the judge directly. "Thank you, Your Honor. I'll need a bit of the court's patience while I lay the foundation for relevance." Then, in a real sign of cooperation, he added,

"We can do this with or without the jury's presence."

The judge responded, "You may proceed, but if we get too far astray from the issues in this case, I will excuse the jury and allow you to protect your record on appeal."

"Thank you." Logan knew he had just passed the first test of the judge's openness regarding the introduction of evidence. "Now, Mrs. Hamlin, when your husband disappeared in September of 1988, he was in the middle of an affair, true?"

"Not that it's any of your business, but yeah, I thought he was having an affair back then."

"And when your husband disappeared, you thought he had left the state or was about to leave the state with his lover?"

As expected, Mrs. Hamlin couldn't let the comment go, and Logan anxiously awaited her response. *She's probably wishing she had another shot glass to throw at me.* "Lover! You call a tramp like that his lover? My husband was a married man! Only a slimy slut would ever date a married man!" She glared at the jury panel, daring them to contradict her. "Everyone knows that."

Logan had hit the soft spot. She was getting rattled and defensive. *Perfect.* Between hints of infidelity and Mrs. Hamlin's feisty responses, the jurors gave one another furtive glances as they sat at the edge of their seats in rapt attention. "Yes, ma'am, they do. And what was or is this person's name?"

"I already told you, I don't know the name. Never did. But Dr. Ron Tasker and those asinine followers of his knew."

"But Ron Tasker implied to you it was a man, true? Not a woman?"

Mrs. Hamlin rose from the witness stand and shouted, "Are you saying my husband was a goddamn queer?"

Judge Sumner intervened. "Mrs. Hamlin, please, sit down. The jury will disregard the last question and answer. "Mr. Finch, you know better than that. If it happens again, there will be sanctions."

Logan expected an objection and motion to strike the testimony...but nothing came. *Bingo. Now, third party, you're about to be given an identity.*

"You mentioned followers." Logan's voice was intentionally neutral. "Who were his followers?" The legs of Gerald Abbott's chair scraped over the hardwood floor as he lurched toward Branson to prod him to object. To Logan's surprise, Branson ignored him.

Mrs. Hamlin was visibly frustrated. "Back in eighty-eight, there was my husband. He was a follower," she said, and then looked pointedly at the gallery where Ingrid sat with the two men in suits and nodded, "of Tasker and his kid." Then she stared at the prosecutor's table. "And that guy."

"I'm sorry, Mrs. Hamlin, are you referring to my client?" Logan asked with contrived ignorance.

"No. That guy," she answered, pointing. "The lawyer guy, Abbott."

Abbott's face flushed to the color of a fine merlot as he forcefully nudged Branson to object. Branson continued to ignore him, triggering Abbott to eject himself explosively from between the arms of his chair and to his feet. Logan camouflaged his elation with a look of complete surprise. He glanced at the jury and shrugged his shoulders, as if to confirm Abbott's actions were highly unusual. Apoplectic, Abbott stuttered, "Your Honor. Your Honor, I object as to relevance. This testimony is defamatory, and you must stop it immediately!"

The judge picked up his gavel this time, pointing the handle at Abbott as he spoke. "Mr. Abbott, for the second and last time, you are out of order. There will be sanctions if it happens again, and those sanctions will require you to leave the courtroom and pay an uncomfortable fine. Do you understand, sir?" Abbott's eyes darted wildly from the jury to the judge to Mrs. Hamlin and back again. "Do. You. Understand. Sir?" the judge repeated.

When Abbott nodded and collapsed, wedging back into his chair, the judge directed Logan to proceed. "Yes, Your Honor. Thank you.

Mrs. Hamlin, did you ask Mr. Tasker or any of his followers for the name of the person with whom your husband had his torrid love affair?" Branson finally objected.

"Sustained," the judge said.

But before Logan could tack, Mrs. Hamlin's gravelly voice, sharp with bitterness and anger, spat derisively, "Torrid? My husband was about as *torrid* in bed as a limp noodle!"

Judge Sumner put a curt halt to the jury's snickering. "Mrs. Hamlin, I sustained the objection. That means you don't answer. The jurors are not to consider the last answer." The jury nodded their understanding but were irresistibly fascinated by what Mrs. Hamlin had to say. Officially, the answer was off the record, but for better or worse, it left an indelible print on the minds of the jurors.

"Please proceed, Mr. Finch," Judge Sumner directed with a slight smirk on his face.

Logan walked back to the defense table for a quick look at his notes. He avoided eye contact with Lacey, Pete, and even Tim. He needed to stay focused. He felt as though he was on the deck of *The Coral Dawn*, reeling in a prize-winning halibut. Even though he could see it thrashing just a few feet from the bow, that didn't mean it was in the boat. Like the halibut, bringing it aboard would be a dangerous task.

"Mrs. Hamlin, isn't it true your husband saw his lover every weekend while you were working at the church?"

"Real fine God-fearin' guy, right?" The lines in her face deepened with sorrow as she recalled that part of her life. "Yep...I worked, thinking he was taking our little dog to the park." She looked at the jury again. "Then I found out that he was leaving our Layla in the car while he was slinking around. When he started coming home later every Sunday, I got suspicious, so I checked inside his SUV. Then I knew. I'll never forget the smell of cheap cologne."

"It's been a long time ago, but if you remember, did you work at the church on Monday, September 4, 1988?"

"If it was Labor Day, yeah, I was workin'."

"And that was the day your husband disappeared, was it not?"

"It was. And y'all know it."

Some of the jurors cringed. Logan didn't make a staged response. He didn't need to any longer. "Now, Mrs. Hamlin, in June of 1983, you and your husband were asked by Dr. Ron Tasker to provide an alibi for the serial killer Jack Jansen. True?"

"God help me, yes. Tasker calls us in the middle of the night, says to tell the police Jansen was at our home playing cards most th'night. But that's got nuthin' to do with who killed my husband four years later."

"Are you sure, ma'am?"

Following years of seething resentment, she speculated, "I guess anybody coulda killed him. Maybe it was his *lover*, as you call it. It coulda even been some of the followers of the great Dr. Tasker!"

Branson didn't need nudging. "Objection, Your Honor. The question calls for gross speculation and..."

"Sustained," the judge said. "The jury will disregard the last answer given by the witness."

Can't un-ring a bell. The jury heard that testimony and it'll stick like Gorilla Glue. Things are going even better than I expected. Logan quietly inhaled, feeling like a weightlifter before the next set. "Between the time you lied to the police in 1983 and the disappearance of your husband in 1988, did you ever see Mr. Foster at the dog park?"

"Never."

"Between the time you lied to the police in 1983 and the disappearance of your husband in 1988, did you ever work?"

"Damn right, I worked. Ev'r Sunday we was in Alaska, I worked my ass off at th'church."

"And during that same time, did your husband work?"

"Objection," Branson said. "Relevance."

Logan acquiesced to the prior objections, but he fought this one, knowing he had the jury's sympathies and their curiosity. "Your Honor, the relevance will become clear after just a couple of more questions."

"Objection overruled, but you're teetering on the tightrope of my patience, Mr. Finch."

The judge looked at Mrs. Hamlin, and Logan could see even his professionally impartial eyes found her attitude repellent. "The witness will answer the question."

"Already told you that too," she snapped. "Our cabinet business went cold in the mid-eighties, so my husband was mostly unemployed till he disappeared."

A career spanning years spent in a courtroom had honed his trial persona to that of a skilled actor. His follow-up question was deceptively conversational. "And you used a lot of your free time to travel, didn't you?"

"Bill traveled a lot more than me. He always told me he was going with the followers, or them guys that called themselves the Guidance Panel. But nobody can tell me different. I know who he was really going on those trips with."

"But isn't it fair to say you and Bill visited every continent on Earth between the day you lied to the police in 1983 and the day of your husband's disappearance?"

"Hell, I don't know...never really thought about it."

"Ever been to Europe?"

"Yeah. But just a few times."

"Southeast Asia?"

"Yeah."

"Australia? Brazil? South Africa?"

"Yeah. So what? Lotsa people go to those places."

"Not when they're unemployed."

"Objection," Branson said. "Mr. Finch is testifying."

"Sustained," the judge said. "The jury will disregard the testimony of Mr. Finch, and he will refrain from testifying further in this case unless he wishes to withdraw his representation of Mr. Foster and take the witness stand. You can save your arguments for closing, Counselor."

Logan knew he had pushed this as far as he could and raised his hands in supplication.

"No, Your Honor, and I apologize for the misstep."

Only Logan and Mrs. Hamlin heard the judge murmur, "Misstep, my ass."

"Mrs. Hamlin, do you know where the money came from to pay for all your trips?"

"Not really. Bill handled all that stuff. I only know that after we talked to the police, the church or Dr. Tasker paid for our first trip to Hawaii. We stayed in the Halekulani right on the beach. It was gorgeous, and the church paid for everything."

"Were you ever charged with any crimes for lying to the police or providing the false alibi?"

"No. And the statute of limitations has run on that one, so you're barking up a dead tree there, Mr. Attorney."

The look of amazement on Logan's face was effortless as he immediately fired off the next question. "You don't think I have the power to bring criminal charges against you for that, do you? Wouldn't that be Mr. Abbott over there?"

Barbara Hamlin's smug countenance wavered. "I don't know." Abbott aggressively elbowed Branson, who didn't budge from his seat. Judge Sumner glanced at the prosecutor's table, anticipating an objection. When none was forthcoming, he turned back to the jury. The judge knew why there was no objection.

"Between the time you lied to the police in 1983 and the disappearance of your husband in 1988, did you ever see Pete Foster at the dog park next to his home on Huffman Road?"

"No. Never."

Logan had gone as far as he could. The halibut was in the boat. He could only hope he'd sown enough doubt in the jurors' minds about Tasker, Abbott, and the Guidance Panel to lead to an acquittal. "I have no further questions of this witness, Your Honor."

As he returned to his seat, his eyes locked with Branson's for a quick moment. The lawyer seemed almost pleased. *Maybe Branson understood the depth of Abbott's conflict of interest that led to more horrifying deaths,* Logan speculated, *which is why he hadn't been more aggressive in his objections.*

"Ladies and gentlemen," the judge said. "I believe this is an excellent time to adjourn for the day. We'll return here tomorrow morning at eight thirty and continue with the testimony at nine. Please do not discuss this case with anyone on or off the jury, including family members, and please refrain from doing any independent research, reading news accounts, or watching the news on television. Thank you. We'll see you in the morning."

The judge exited the courtroom and Logan immediately approached the bailiff, the clerk, and court reporter and thanked them for their efforts. He had done this throughout his career. He genuinely appreciated their skill and professionalism. Many staff members were former legal secretaries for the judges they now worked for at the courthouse. He understood the powerful influence these individuals had with the judge hearing a case and his approach to that case. Staff dined with the judge and took every break, throughout the day and year, with him or her. The judge not only valued their opinion but recognized the importance of hearing from them and respecting their views; in doing so, he or she maintained a competent, dependable staff throughout the trial and the ensuing years.

The media, including all three local television stations, confronted the defense team when they entered the hallway. "If your client didn't commit the murder, who did?" shouted one reporter.

"We think we know who committed this crime, but it's up to the government to find the murderer, not my client," Logan replied.

"How long do you think the trial will last?" shouted another.

"I think about six days or so. We'll see you all tomorrow. In a couple of days, I should be able to estimate the day for closing arguments."

As they exited the courthouse, Lacey placed a hand on Logan's back. "Nicely done, partner," she said. But when he thanked her, she didn't meet his eyes, and her hand returned to her side.

Pete seemed relieved, though shell-shocked. "I wanted to applaud when she exploded at having to answer questions about her husband's philandering, but I knew I had to be a statue the whole time. The scrutiny is a lot harder than I expected."

"Keep it up and maybe, just maybe, you won't have to take the stand."

"God, wouldn't that be great? It's embarrassing enough sitting at the table. I sure don't want to be answering Branson's questions up there on the hot seat."

As they walked out of the courtroom, Pete checked his phone and was relieved to get the message from Erika. "Hey, honey. Sorry I'm not there, but rather than standing around the courthouse all day, I decided to treat myself, so I'm at the spa. Call me when you get out, okay? Let me know where you all end up at, and I'll meet you there."

They walked across the street to the Whale's Tail, and once they were seated Pete called Erika and put her on speakerphone. "Hey, sweetie, you're on speaker. We're all at the Captain Cook. Come on over!"

"Hi, everybody." Erika sounded relaxed and like her old self. "I apologize, but I'll have to beg out. After spending the afternoon at the spa, I came back to our room and ordered room service and a little wine. How did it go?" Pete took her off the speaker to give her the day's highlights as their drinks arrived.

McQuigg joined them for dinner. "Brilliant examination," Tim said, "but if the church did kill Bill Hamlin, Mrs. Hamlin's next."

"Right. If Barbara disappeared tonight, it would help the case, but, Jesus, let's hope nothing violent happens to her," Logan said.

"A gruesome possibility...I like it," Tim kidded with a wink. They nervously chuckled at the gallows humor. By the time dinner arrived, the defense team was all talked out. They ate while Logan silently mulled over strategies for the following day.

CHAPTER

55

THAT NIGHT, LOGAN REASONED their secondary strategy would be to subliminally persuade the jurors that Hamlin deserved to die for what he did. *It's a long shot, but it might help the jury return with an acquittal.* He talked it over with Lacey. By phone. She still sounded tired and gently declined to spend time with him but agreed with his approach. And depending on how the remaining testimony unraveled, at closing they could add Mrs. Hamlin's name as a suspect. The jury already hated her.

The next morning, the courtroom was near capacity as twenty political science majors from the University of Alaska filled the back of the courtroom. The trial gawkers from yesterday scrambled for the few remaining seats. The jurors were privately disappointed. There would be no more installments of colorful testimony from Mrs. Hamlin. Branson had wisely determined not to call her back to the stand. Logan just hoped she was still alive. Branson's next witness was Detective Crystal Sorensen. Her testimony benefitted the defense as she intentionally introduced her experience to include her investigation of the Jansen murders on Branson's direct examination. That opened the door for Logan to inquire about the false alibi the Hamlins gave her.

After Branson questioned Sorensen about her part in the murder investigation, it was Logan's turn. "Good morning, Detective Sorensen."

"Good morning, Mr. Finch."

"If my recollection serves me correctly, you were one of two officers assigned to visit the Hamlin home in June of 1983?"

"I was."

"And what was the purpose of your visit?"

"To confirm with the Hamlins the alibi Jansen gave Anchorage PD earlier that morning."

"And what was Mr. Jansen's alibi regarding his whereabouts on that night?"

"He said he'd been playing cards at the Hamlin home the entire evening and didn't go home until about 1:00 a.m."

Branson objected. "Hearsay."

"Sustained, unless the statement is in your report and was introduced on direct."

Logan stepped to the defense table, and Lacey handed him the report. "It was, Your Honor."

"The objection is overruled. Proceed, Mr. Finch."

"How long had you been working for the APD when you interviewed the Hamlins?"

"Not long. I was a rookie cop."

"Did you ask the Hamlins any other questions about Jansen's card-playing presence at their home?"

"No. But I sure wish I would have."

There being no objection, Logan pounced on her comment. "Did you later find out the Hamlins lied to you about Jansen's presence in their home on June 13?"

"Yes. Shortly after Jansen's arrest in October, he admitted he'd never been to the Hamlin home that night. Then he said he'd murdered at least ten more girls after the Hamlins lied for him."

"After you found out their alibi was false, did you do any further investigation or prepare any supplemental reports?"

"Once we found out their alibi was false, I prepared another report strongly urging the prosecutor to charge the Hamlins with serious crimes, including aiding and abetting first-degree murder."

"Who did you send the supplemental report to?"

"Gerald Abbott." She nodded in Abbott's direction for the jury.

Logan handed the report to Sorensen. "Is this a true and correct copy of your supplemental report?"

"It is." Abbott flinched and shifted uncomfortably in his seat. A ripple of recognition passed through the jury.

"The defense asks the court to admit this report as an exhibit."

Judge Sumner responded, "The court, hearing no objection, admits the report as Defense Exhibit A."

"Did you ever talk to Mr. Abbott about this report?"

"Yes."

"And what was his response to your recommendations?"

"He fired me."

Branson jumped up. "Objection, Your Honor. Irrelevant and immaterial."

"I must say, Mr. Finch, your line of questioning seems to be going far afield."

"I can assure the court the relevance will become apparent in short order."

"I will allow you some leeway based on that assurance. Objection overruled."

"Thank you, Your Honor. Ms. Sorensen, he fired you, and what did you do then?"

"I applied for a job with the Alaska State Troopers."

"Did you ever revisit the Jansen and Hamlin cases?"

"Absolutely. Over the next four years, I worked my way up to homicide detective with the state. When they found the skeletal remains of Mr. Hamlin in South Anchorage, I was assigned to investigate the case."

"Did your investigation include any thoughts about other possible suspects than the defendant, Pete Foster?"

"My report indicated that there were any number of suspects who had motive and opportunity to kill Mr. Hamlin."

"Who were those other suspects?"

"My report in November last year concluded that before any formal charges are brought, more investigation was necessary. At least four other individuals were parties of interest, namely, Mrs. Hamlin, Mr. Hamlin's love interest, the parents of other missing girls, and unknown members of the Hamlins' church."

Jackpot. Another witness named the third party. *Now, the wrap-up.* "To the best of your knowledge, were further investigations done as to any of those parties of interest?"

"None that I'm aware of. The investigation primarily belonged to the Anchorage Police Department. I was called in to assist in the initial investigation, but there wasn't enough time to complete it. I was really surprised when Pete Foster was charged with the murder so soon after my report."

"Objection," Branson said. "Gross speculation."

"Sustained," the judge said. "The jury will disregard the last answer."

Great answer. Logan was almost giddy with delight. *This woman knows how to testify.* "Who did you believe to be the primary suspect after your brief investigation?"

"Mrs. Hamlin was a prime suspect, especially because of the affair she thought her husband was having, and the fact that she received one hundred thousand dollars in life insurance proceeds." Branson and Abbott bowed their heads and wished they had never called this witness to the stand.

"Who made the final decision to charge Mr. Foster?"

"Those decisions are always made by the state attorney general's office. So, I'd have to assume it was Mr. Abbott who made it, as he now works for the state."

"Objection. Calls for speculation." Branson sounded defeated.

"Sustained, and the jury will disregard the answer."

Logan sensed that the jury's attention, along with their suspicions, were now directed at Abbott. "Thank you. I have no further questions." The judge asked Branson if he had any redirect.

"The state has no further questions of this witness."

Logan was delighted with the testimony. *Would it be enough?* He had his doubts but wasn't ready to rely on Pete to make the case. Emotionally, Pete was floundering. It was just the second day of the trial and his eyes were gaunt and hollow; he looked haunted.

Branson then called Al Stacks and John Callow, whose testimony matched their reports. Logan thought Callow's statement regarding Erika's denial she knew the Hamlins was particularly damaging. Then Branson announced they had just four witnesses left for the following day's testimony. It was 4:10 p.m. when the judge excused the jury.

CHAPTER
56

TODAY, TO PETE'S RELIEF, Erika met them outside the courtroom. They exited through the massive light oak courthouse doors. Logan suggested meeting at the Elevation 92 restaurant for dinner. "Wish we were ninety-two feet above this nightmare," he said, referring to the restaurant's near-sea-level location. They ordered before Erika commented on the beautiful weather. Conversation then evolved into—what else?—Alaska's favorite pastime, halibut fishing. "This trial's going to be over soon," Logan said confidently as he toasted Pete. "Then, buddy, there's a fishing expedition calling our names. If we snag an award-winning halibut, it'll be worth a helluva lot more than the five thousand bucks you won at the derby years ago!"

"Yeah. That's a do-over I wouldn't mind," Pete said. "How many years ago was that anyway?"

"Wasn't it in the late eighties?" Erika prompted. "Now that I'm thinking about it, I remember you two took the whole weekend to fish in the derby that year."

"Those were great days," Pete reminisced.

Logan grabbed his stomach and excused himself from the table. He mumbled, and they heard the word "bathroom" as he walked briskly out of the dining area.

"I hope he's okay," Lacey said.

"Probably just nerves. But he seemed pleased with how the trial is going," Pete added.

Logan didn't go to the bathroom. He walked outside and called The Homer Tribune. He asked for the news editor.

"May I help you?"

Logan explained what he needed, and she told him it would take at least a week to retrieve that issue from the newspaper's archives. Damn, too long to wait. Pete could be in prison for life by then. "Thanks, but that won't work."

The editor then suggested going to the Homer Library where the newspaper might be

preserved on microfiche, but it was closing in a few minutes and wouldn't be open again until Thursday.

Logan hurriedly returned to the table and announced that he was feeling sick and had to go back to his hotel room. He insisted everyone enjoy dinner and he would see them in the morning.

He then sprinted from the restaurant, grabbed a cab to the airport and caught the 6:55 flight to Homer."

CHAPTER
57

LOGAN PUSHED HIS TITANIUM-REENFORCED LEGS into an awkward run across the tarmac of the Homer airport, jumped into the blue Bug, fastened his seat belt, and was hurtling to the office within seconds. Focused on finding the newspaper, he threw the front door open and bolted up the stairs. He shrugged off an OMG pause as he confronted the mountainous stacks of boxes. Like a man on a life-or-death mission, he frantically sifted through the teetering heaps of boxes until he spotted a box with "1988" emblazoned across the side in black marker. Typically irreverent, Logan nevertheless closed his eyes momentarily, fervently imploring, Please, please, please, before ripping off the taped lid.

Unbelievably, incredibly—there it was. The newspaper had been left as an afterthought on top of the manila file folders. The front page, dated September 8, 1988, featured the picture of Pete standing beside his 305-pound halibut, holding his trophy and the $5,000 check. "Winner of the Second Annual Homer Halibut Derby on September 4," the headline read. The article confirmed the deadline for the catch was at 4:00 p.m., and the photo was taken at the boat harbor at sunset, probably closer to 9:00 p.m.

Logan sat on the dusty floor for a minute, stunned by his luck and absorbing the significance of what he'd found. He stiffly stood up, rolled the newspaper and carefully slipped it into the dusty brown leather briefcase situated on the top of a box. With a flip of the light switch, he hurried down the stairwell so caught up with excitement that it took a moment for the sound of footsteps to register. He'd rushed in so quickly from the airport, he hadn't turned on the office lights, but there in the twilight, he saw a large man—he couldn't tell who—running out the front door.

"Stop!" Logan yelled. "What the hell are you doing in here? Hey!"

Just as he reached the front door, he felt a rumbling before an explosion blasted him off the porch and he flew over the steps, across the lawn, and landed in the street. His ears rang so loud, they ached. Then every-thing went black.

When he woke the next morning, he was in a hospital bed. Pete and Lacey hovered. He mumbled, "Was there an earthquake?"

Pete smiled. "It's okay, buddy, no earthquakes."

"What are you guys doing here, what happened?"

Lacey sat on the edge of the bed and gently took his hand. "A bomb exploded in the office. You were found unconscious and bleeding."

Logan tried to sit up. "Wait, where's my briefcase?"

Lacey squeezed his hand. "Shhh, Logan, it's Wednesday morning, July 21st, and you're in the Homer hospital. You were hanging onto your brief-case when the paramedics found you in the street. It's over there in the corner. The trial's been continued until tomorrow. I've been in touch with Branson all day long and he's good with the short continuance. Now, do you mind telling us what the hell you're doing in Homer in the middle of a trial in Anchorage?"

"More research," he mumbled. "How did you know I was here?"

"I was your 'In Case of Emergency' number," Lacey said. "I couldn't believe it. 'No need to come down tonight,' they said, 'he's still uncon-scious.'"

Pete chimed in, "You'll be glad to know the state troopers arrested two guys in a white pickup truck driving back to Anchorage. They found bomb-making materials in the pickup, which led to their partial confes-sions that included, 'God made us do it.' No surprises there, right?"

"I might appreciate that information more if my head didn't hurt so damn bad. It's like there's a ringing every time I say something. What I wouldn't give for a vodka tonic."

Lacey smiled. "Yeah... no vodka tonics. At least not until tomorrow night. In the morning, we'll get you sprung from this joint and back to Anchorage. The judge wants us there at ten. So, quit complaining about your headaches and try not to limp when you go to the bathroom."

"But I don't have to go to the bathroom."

"You better go when the doc gets here and show him that you don't limp," Pete said. "At least the bleeding stopped, I think."

"Bleeding? I was bleeding?"

Pete heartily laughed for the first time in weeks. "Your knees, buddy. You tried to do the Fosbury Flop and failed when you landed on your face in the street."

"The street!" Logan's eyes widened. "What happened to the office?"

"Well, that's the good news . . . we'll never have to clean the upstairs. The fire took care of that." Pete grinned.

Lacey filled in the gaps. "The files in the metal cabinets downstairs are fine. Because of the bomb threats, Katie put all the computer information on storage disks, and they're in the safe. So, outside of some old furniture, we're okay. And I canceled my annual commercial fishing jaunt because of the office situation, and, given the very generous check I just got from Pete and Erika, I'm taking the rest of the summer off!"

"In the meantime, the insurance company will rebuild the office," Pete added. "But, hey, enough of this. We'll come get you at seven in the morning. That'll give us time to catch the eight-thirty commuter plane and get to court by ten."

Logan looked at Pete. "But how will you get to Anchorage?"

"Same way I got here. I'm flying. Figured you shouldn't be the only guy risking life and limb on this case!"

"Wow . . . okay, great. Now, for God's sake, will somebody turn off that fucking overhead light so that I can get some sleep?" Lacey blew Logan a kiss, hit the light switch, and she and Pete left. As Logan slept, his dreams were a kaleidoscope of the events his life had become.

CHAPTER
58

L OGAN WAS PRESENTING evidentiary documents to the court clerk as members of the press entered the courtroom along with Tim McQuigg, the Leprechaun, and an assortment of spectators and attorneys. The case was apparently gaining in popularity. Gerald Abbott absented himself from the festivities. There were no spectators from the Prosecutor's office.

Logan handed copies of the new evidence to Branson and retained two copies for himself. "Defense Exhibit 1," Logan said to Branson and smiled.

As he spoke, the bailiff walked in and announced, "All rise for the Honorable Judge John Sumner."

The judge entered, sat down, and directed everyone in the courtroom to sit. While Branson was pouring over the exhibit, Logan addressed the court. "Your Honor, we have a very reasonable request. I would like to call the defendant to the stand. I know the prosecution has four more witnesses waiting to testify, but I believe their testimony will not be necessary if I can question my client."

The judge looked over to Branson who stood and approached the court clerk. "Your Honor, before responding, may I look at the original exhibit just submitted by the defense?"

"Of course."

After a brief scan, Branson declared, "I have no objection to the witness being called out of order under the circumstances."

The jurors entered and Logan rose and called Mr. Peter Foster to the stand. Pete was in shock as he had not expected to testify. Lacey looked stunned. An audible gasp was heard in the courtroom and McQuigg grabbed Logan's arm, whispering, "That wasn't the plan."

"We're okay," Logan replied.

Pete swore to tell the truth and, clearing his throat nervously, gave his name and address to the court.

Logan began his examination with "Good morning, Mr. Foster. May I call you Pete?"

"Of course."

"I'm going to get straight to the point, Pete. Do you know where you were on Monday afternoon and evening on September 4, 1988?"

"I think so. That was over fifteen years ago... I was probably at home."

"May I approach the witness, Your Honor?"

"You may."

"Pete, I want to show you something that may refresh your recollection as to where you were on September 4, 1988, the day Mr. Hamlin disappeared."

"Okay."

Logan handed Pete a copy of the newspaper article dated September 8, 1988. "Can you identify this exhibit?"

Pete squinted as tears welled up in his eyes. "I can."

"Does this exhibit refresh your recollection as to exactly where you were on September 4, 1988."

"It does."

"Where were you?"

"I was in Homer. I caught the biggest halibut in the Derby and the photo was taken when I was awarded the prize in the late afternoon in Homer."

"And, Pete, who else was there at the time."

"You, of course. We fished the entire three-day weekend together and didn't drive back to Anchorage until Tuesday, the fifth."

"Your Honor, I can take the stand and confirm that the defendant was with me just as he testified."

"Will that be necessary, Mr. Branson?" the judge asked.

"No, Your Honor. In addition to this testimony, an anonymous caller alerted my office yesterday that the possible murder weapon, a Colt .45 caliber revolver, had been seen in the utility shed next to Mrs. Hamlin's trailer. Troopers are currently executing a search warrant on the property. Depending on whether they find the .45, and if ballistics testing on the gun confirms it was the murder weapon, there will be charges brought against Mrs. Hamlin."

"Mr. Branson, do you have a motion to put before the Court?"

"I do, Your Honor. Based on the discovery of exculpatory evidence and the probable arrest of Mrs. Hamlin for the murder of her deceased husband, the State moves to dismiss the first-degree murder charge against Mr. Peter Foster, with prejudice."

"Counsel, I assume there's no objection?"

"No – I mean, yes, Your Honor," Logan replied.

"I would just like to know if there's any good reason why this information could not have been brought to the prosecutor's or the court's attention some months ago, Counsel?" the judge asked.

"No, Your Honor," Logan said, shaking his head. "There was an oversight."

"Hmmm. Motion granted."

The jury was excused from the courtroom and thanked by the judge for their service. "Congratulations, Mr. Foster. It is good to know you're innocent. This court stands in adjournment." The judge gave a nod to Logan, who returned it and smiled at the acknowledgment.

Logan was too sore to be hugged, so Pete just patted his arm. "I can't thank you enough for all you did for us! And I'm sorry about the hospital experience."

"No problem, and I didn't do this for you. I was afraid that if I lost the case, the

Innocence Project attorneys would get the verdict overturned and I'd look bad."

Erika sprang from her seat and hugged Pete. She had her old color back, rosy cheeks, and a sparkle in her eyes.

"Hey there, where's my hug?" Logan moaned.

"Oh, sorry. You get a big hug too. And Lacey too." Erika laughed.

The press rushed Logan and Lacey as the cameras entered the courtroom. Logan stepped back and nodded to Lacey. She smiled and happily took center stage. A *Homer Tribune* reporter tackled the burning question first. "Why did it take so long to recall the story about the halibut fishing derby?"

"It happened a long time ago, and in the aftermath of their daughter's murder, the Fosters tried to move on from their past here in Alaska," Lacey answered.

The *Channel 7 Eyewitness* reporter asked, "So, how do you think Mrs. Hamlin killed her husband?"

"We don't know. Mr. Branson and his people will be handling that matter, and I see him over there preparing to leave the courtroom." The reporters turned and flocked to Branson while Logan and Lacey seized the opportunity to exit.

"Great job, Counselor," Logan said. He went to put an arm around her shoulder, but she
skipped ahead.
"Thanks."

The trial was over, and Logan looked forward to talking about it, but really, once they finished the debriefing, what would he say? *I want to make love one last time before jetting off till next year's fishing season . . . Damn, with dad still in assisted living, it's not like I have a choice. Maybe it's better the relationship cools off this way—easier to leave.*

In the hall, McQuigg suggested they rendezvous at Simon & Seafort's for some postmortem kibitzing about the trial. Once there, they toasted, laughed, and speculated about Barbara Hamlin's future. Everyone was jubilant as they contemplated posttrial life.

When Logan announced his intention to go immediately to Tucson to visit his father in the facility, despite her earlier resolve, Lacey's face fell. It was just no good. Anticipating his departure, she was struggling to emotionally detach. Nothing ever prepared her for when he left. *And he always leaves. And I know that. I knew it this time, and I got involved . . . again. And it hurts . . . again.*

Pete toyed with going back to Homer to catch another derby-winning halibut. "Like hell," Erika protested. She grabbed his ear and teasingly instructed, "You, Mr. Foster, are coming home with me!"

Lacey chauffeured Pete and Erika to the airport while Logan returned the rental car. Pete bought two first-class tickets on Delta, and a third on Alaska. Logan would find a connector flight to Tucson once he arrived in Seattle. They toted their luggage to the ticket counters and, after checking in, Pete and Erika hugged and thanked Logan and Lacey again.

"Told you I was hiring the best attorney in all Alaska," Pete said with a smile. "I owe you more than I can ever repay, but I will be sending you a check."

Pete and Erika walked ahead while Logan stopped to hug Lacey. "I'm gonna miss you. Lots. Maybe I'll be back this fall, or you can come to Arizona to visit."

"Oh." Lacey shook her head. "I don't think so . . . but I'll miss you too." Tears welled up in their eyes.

"Okay . . . I'd better go before this gets too maudlin."

"You go." She looked up at him with a brave, albeit quivering, smile. "Give me a call when you get to Seattle." A single tear trickled down her cheek.

"I promise." As Logan began walking down the corridor, he thought about his mom. *She died in peace as dad held her. There was no loneliness for either of them.*

Lacey returned to her twelfth-floor hotel room and flung herself face down on the bed and cried with abandon. She barely heard or paid attention to the knocking on the door. It persisted. "GO. A. WAY!" she fiercely instructed.

"Room service."

Irritated, she shouted, "I DIDN'T ORDER ROOM SERVICE!"

"No, ma'am. Someone ordered it for you."

She trudged sullenly to the door, smudging the tears and makeup from her face with the back of her hand.

"Sure hopin' there ain't gonna be an earthquake tonight, lil' lady." Sheepishly, Logan added, sans the John Wayne accent, "Or any night in the foreseeable future."

"You're back! You came back!" Lacey shouted and jumped into his arms.

"For good. I don't give a damn about earthquakes anymore." Logan started kissing her from the top of her head and down both sides of her face. He tilted her chin up, seriously adding, "Lace, I want our hearts to grow old together, if you'll have me?"

"Of course—"

"Wait," he interrupted. "Wait, I have something to go along with that question." He

pulled his mother's wedding ring from his pocket and kneeled. Lacey's eyes were shimmering green pools of happiness as he slid it on her finger.

She held her left hand up, twisting it slightly to catch the lights . . . then her beautiful smile faded, and she became serious. "This is good on any floor, right?"

Logan laughed reassuringly. "On any floor, couch, bed, sink, or counter."

"How about all of the above?" she pressed, giggling. "After all, we have time now."

"Yeah. The rest of our lives."

EPILOGUE

"**L**OGAN CALLED," PETE SAID as the cabbie unloaded their suitcases. "Our computers and guns were released, and he said he'd ship them down to us next week." Anticipating Erika's reaction, he offhandedly added, "He wants us to pick his luggage up at the airport. Sounds like he's still in Anchorage."

Erika had a big smile on her face as she held the front door open for Pete, who was struggling in with the last of their luggage. "I just knew he would choose Lacey this time. Smart move on his part." Then, thinking of Lacey, she added, "And it's about time!"

"Yeah, yeah," Pete admitted. He shook his head slowly in feigned resignation...*another happy single guy bites the dust*. After wrestling the last bag up the flight of stairs to their bedroom, he looked down at their yacht gently bobbing against the dock. "I'm going to open the windows on the boat, get the breeze blowing through, and freshen it up. We might take it out tomorrow. May as well bring up those pistols too."

"Pistols?" Erika asked.

"Yeah, the snub-nosed .38 in the galley, and there's the .45 I've always kept next to the bed. I want to get rid of them.

"Oh, right...okay," Erika said as she turned to confront the mounds of laundry.

Pete didn't see her watching him from the bedroom balcony when he checked the lines on the dock. Everything appeared untouched and intact when he climbed aboard and unlocked the salon door. He jiggled open the drawer in the galley and felt behind the silverware tray. Yep, the .38 was right where he'd left it. It felt cold in his hand. Thoughts of slow sunset cruises along the shores of Lake Washington and sipping wine in the Baccarat crystal glasses were foremost on Pete's mind as he rummaged through his false-bottomed nightstand in the aft cabin. *Huh, not here.* Then he checked the drawers in both nightstands, and the drawers in the kitchen and guest stateroom, and both heads. Nope, the gun wasn't on the boat. His head was down as he ambled up the lawn to the house, trying to remember where it might be.

Watching Pete walk up the lawn, Erika's mind replayed that unforgettable September 5 afternoon in 1988...Labor Day. *She was alone at the Huffman Dog Park when Hamlin's black SUV arrived. She stood concealed in the shadows and the fingers on her right hand nervously gripped the .45 hidden in the pocket of her navy trench coat. Seething resentment at Hamlin's obvious joy in his dog's excited antics propelled her forward the moment he bent down to pick up the dog's ball. Shoving the gun in his back, she felt eerily calm when she quietly ordered him to leave the dog in the car and close the door.*

Hamlin felt the gun's pressure and, pushing his dog back, closed the door. "Listen, lady, I haven't seen you. My wallet's in my back pocket; it's yours. I'll get on the ground and cover my face with my jacket. Take whatever time you need to disappear. Just don't shoot me."

"I don't want your money, you idiot. Start walking."

"Ah, damn," he replied. "Please, you don't need to hurt me."

"Move, or I'll drop you right here."

The dog continued to bark wildly as they walked down the trail to a more secluded area where she stopped him. "Take off your clothes."

"Ah, Jesus, you've gotta be kidding."

"This isn't a negotiation."

The second she clicked the hammer back, he started tearing off his clothes. "Okay," he whined with irritation. "Now what?"

Her throat, tight with pent-up anger, strained her voice into a shrill command. "Run. Run for your life."

As he ran terrified and naked down the trail, she brought her right arm up and aimed. The bullet slammed into his back and propelled him forward. She heard the wind whoosh from his lungs before he tripped, falling on his face. She held the gun down at her side as he slowly and painfully rolled over. His eyes were wet with tears, but he hadn't forgotten her face.

"Why? I don't understand."

"No? My daughter didn't either." She pulled the trigger.

Pete knew the gun had been there the last time he was on the boat. He remembered concealing it in the false-bottom drawer. The yacht was locked while they were in Alaska. The false bottom was impossible to detect. Only one other person knew about the drawer...suddenly, comprehension struck him with the intensity of a tsunami as his gaze slowly moved up from the lawn to the balcony of their bedroom. There was Erika, ashen-faced and motionless, looking down at him.

The pieces fell into place as Pete recalled not being able to reach her during Mrs. Hamlin's testimony and how odd it was that she hadn't met him when she said she would, and that she'd failed to join their group for dinner. Mulling over the gun found in Mrs. Hamlin's storage shed, it occurred to him that there would undoubtedly be metal shavings in the garage from the removal of the serial numbers on the .45.

The days and years flashed before Pete when he feared they might lose their minds in grief when Emma disappeared. He recalled the helpless rage felt only by parents upon hearing the graphic and grisly details of their child's horrific murder. They were forced to choke down an all-consuming injustice when the two people who provided the fateful alibi to the murderer who killed their daughter were never charged with aiding, abetting, or assisting in her murder.

From the moment of being hauled off to jail, he'd wrestled with this insidious suspicion and, on the off chance it might be true, he protected Erika. If he revealed too much, he feared Logan would pick up on those suspicions and follow them. Yet, there was no anger or resentment as Pete stepped into the house and laid the .38 on the kitchen counter before walking upstairs to their bedroom.

Erika stood silhouetted at the window, watching a float plane bank left to land at the Kenmore Air Harbor. Her explanation was monotone. "I had to...When you went fishing that weekend, I'd planned to kill myself. Life was unbearable without her. But then, I couldn't do it because we're all that's left of her."

Her voice cracked and she turned around to face Pete. Their eyes met, reflecting the empathy of having endured hell together. Pete closed his eyes as his mind absorbed the truth. He embraced his wife. It was over. They were home, albeit without Emma, but at least they could live now, knowing their beautiful little girl finally had the justice she deserved.